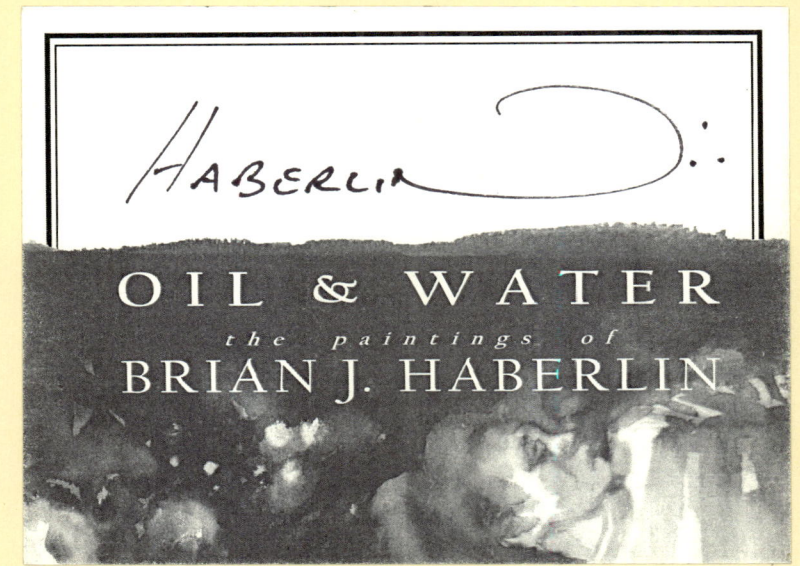

Haberlin

OIL & WATER
the paintings of
BRIAN J. HABERLIN

OIL & WATER

the paintings of

BRIAN J. HABERLIN

...

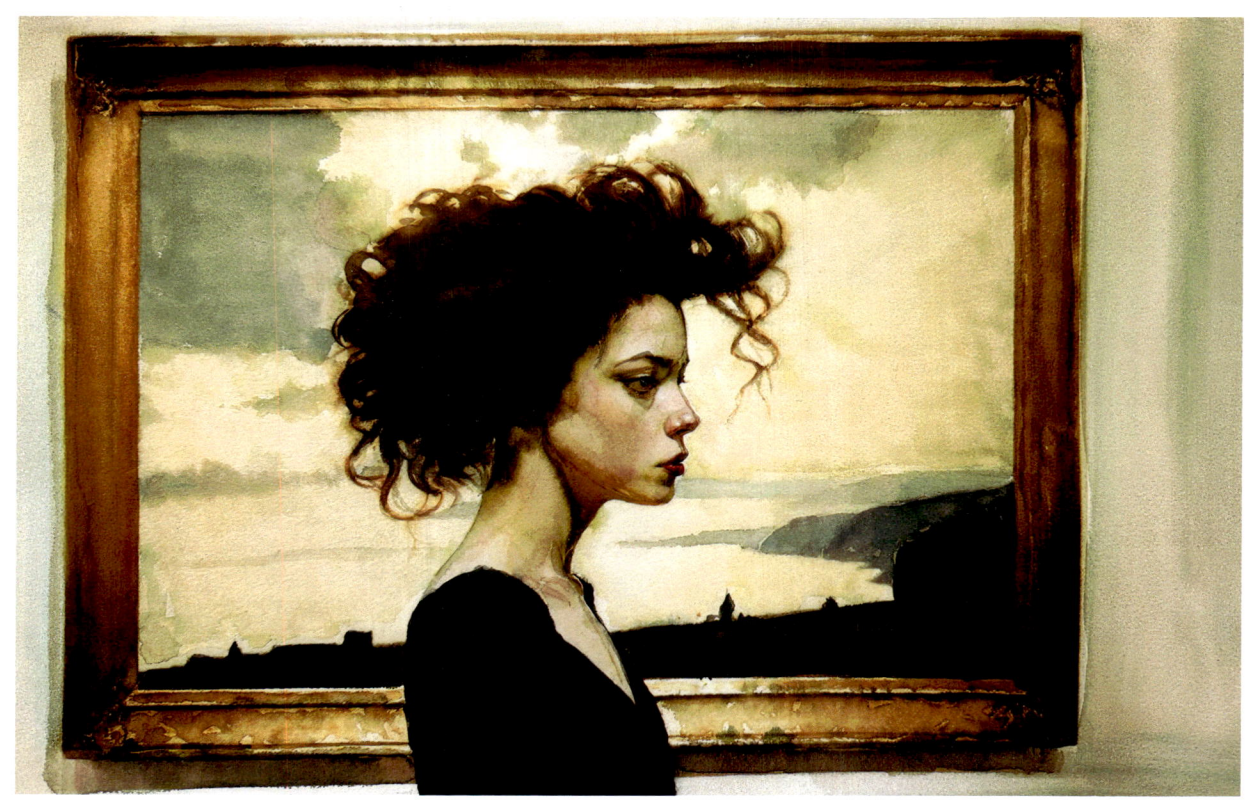

First Edition: October, 2025
Patron Edition ISBN: 978-1-936644-31-5 | Direct Edition ISBN: 978-1-5343-3181-5

above: "Part of the Landscape" | watercolor | 8" x 15"

Something Like an Introduction
foreword by Jim Valentino

Writing an introduction is not as easy as it looks, especially when the book in question is by someone you admire, respect, and consider a friend.

Brian Haberlin is a something of a Renaissance man, multi-talented, multi-versed in any number of disciplines, accomplished in all. He co-created *Witchblade* and was the editor-in-chief of the *Spawn* franchise, lending his writing and drawing talents to the titular character as well as to *Medieval Spawn*. He has written and drawn several series for my own little corner of the Image Universe, including *Hellcop*, *The Marked*, *The Last Barbarians* and *Sonata* among others. Writer, editor, illustrator, painter, sculptor, businessman. By any yardstick, a pretty talented guy despite his singing voice (but we'll let that one go).

Over the last couple of years, he has been increasingly turning his attention to his painting. I've watched his watercolors and oils improve with each progressive brush stroke. So much so that I not only encouraged the publication of this book, but asked him (well, kind of begged him, actually) to let me publish it.

Comics (let's call them what they are rather than the all-too-precious "graphic novels") are an extremely difficult field to break into. The venues are limited, and the competition fierce. Once an artist has broken into the business, they must prove themselves over-and-over again. Every new project is an audition for which one must set ego aside and reinvent oneself.

The world of fine art is even more difficult to gain a foothold in. Gallery showings are nigh unto impossible to get an invitation to. An invitation is granted only after an artist has been "discovered" (no one is quite certain how you do that) and then touted by the anointed few, and even then you're at the mercy of the critics.

Brian seems to have made the transition without breaking a sweat (which may prove that he's also proficient at prestidigitation).

To prove yourself in one difficult to enter field is praiseworthy. To do it in two is nearly impossible. Yet he has managed to do it, and his reputation has grown exponentially with each new showing.

As a publisher, I wanted to collect as many of these works as possible between two covers for my own personal enjoyment as well as for posterity.

While this is the first such collection of Brian's work, I submit that it will not be the last. I look forward to his growth as an artist with each new painting, every new idea. And while I intend to savor and study every painting in this tome, I can't wait to see what he does in Volume Two.

Jim Valentino
Portland, OR
June, 2025

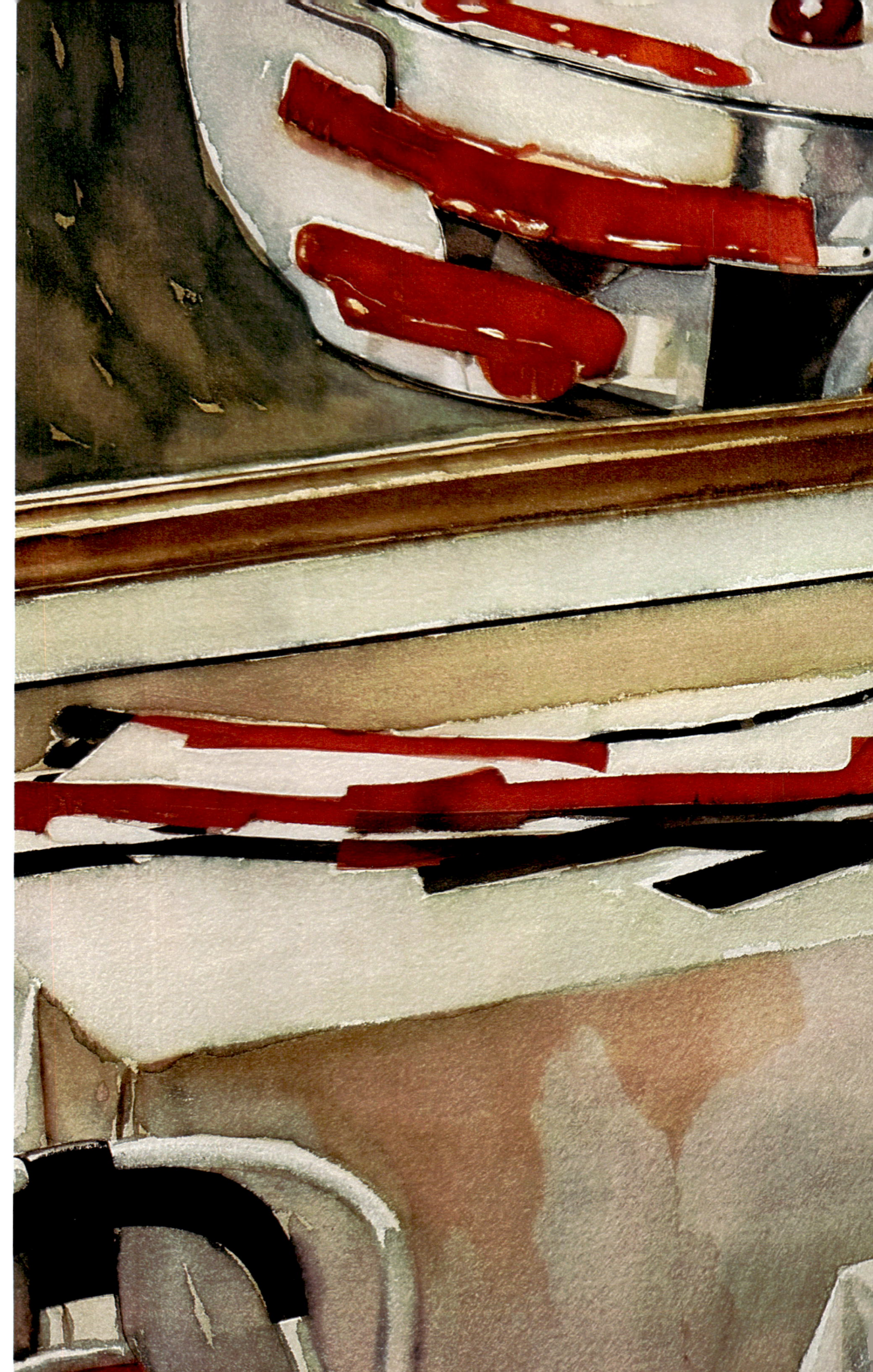

MUSEUMS

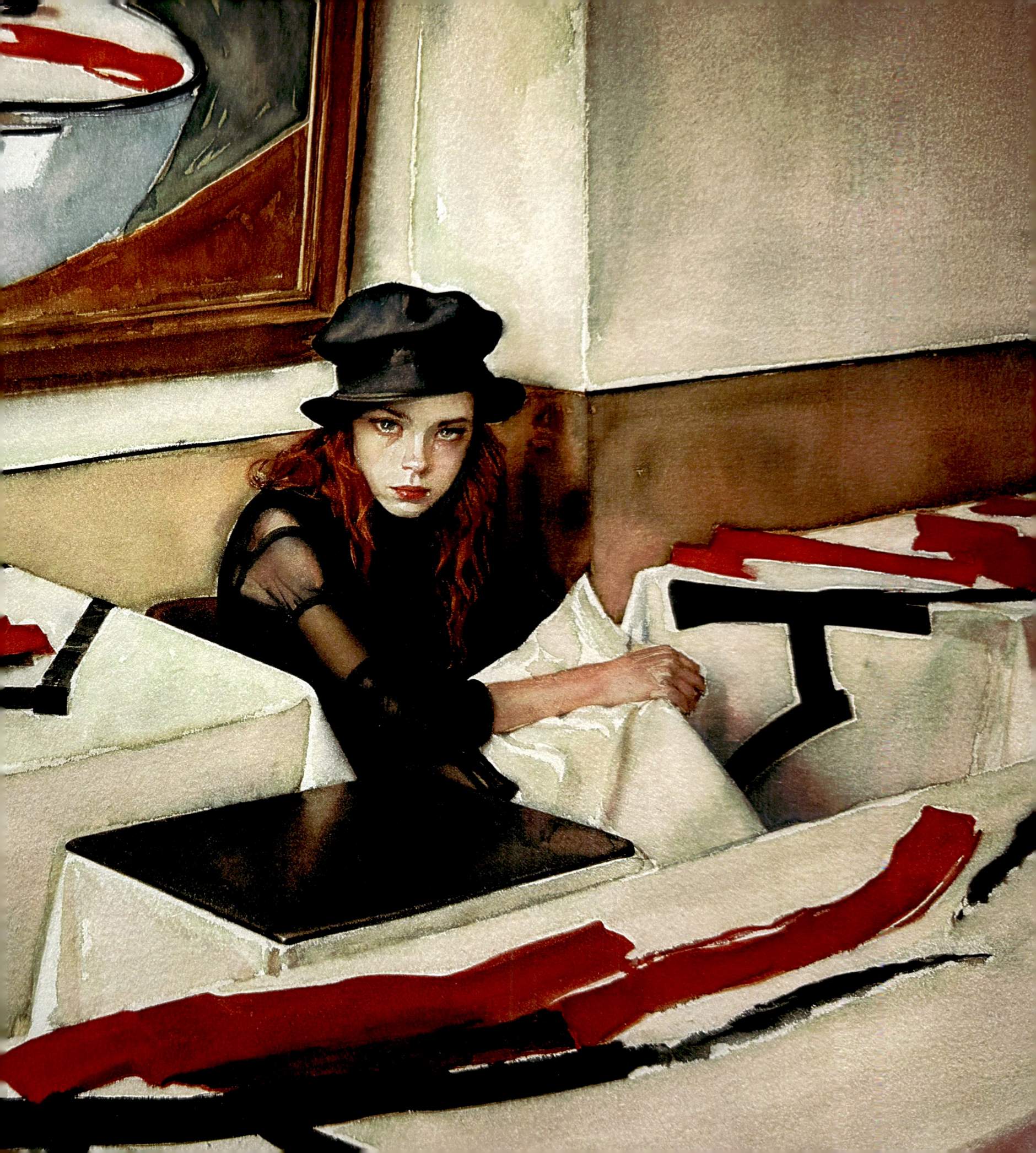

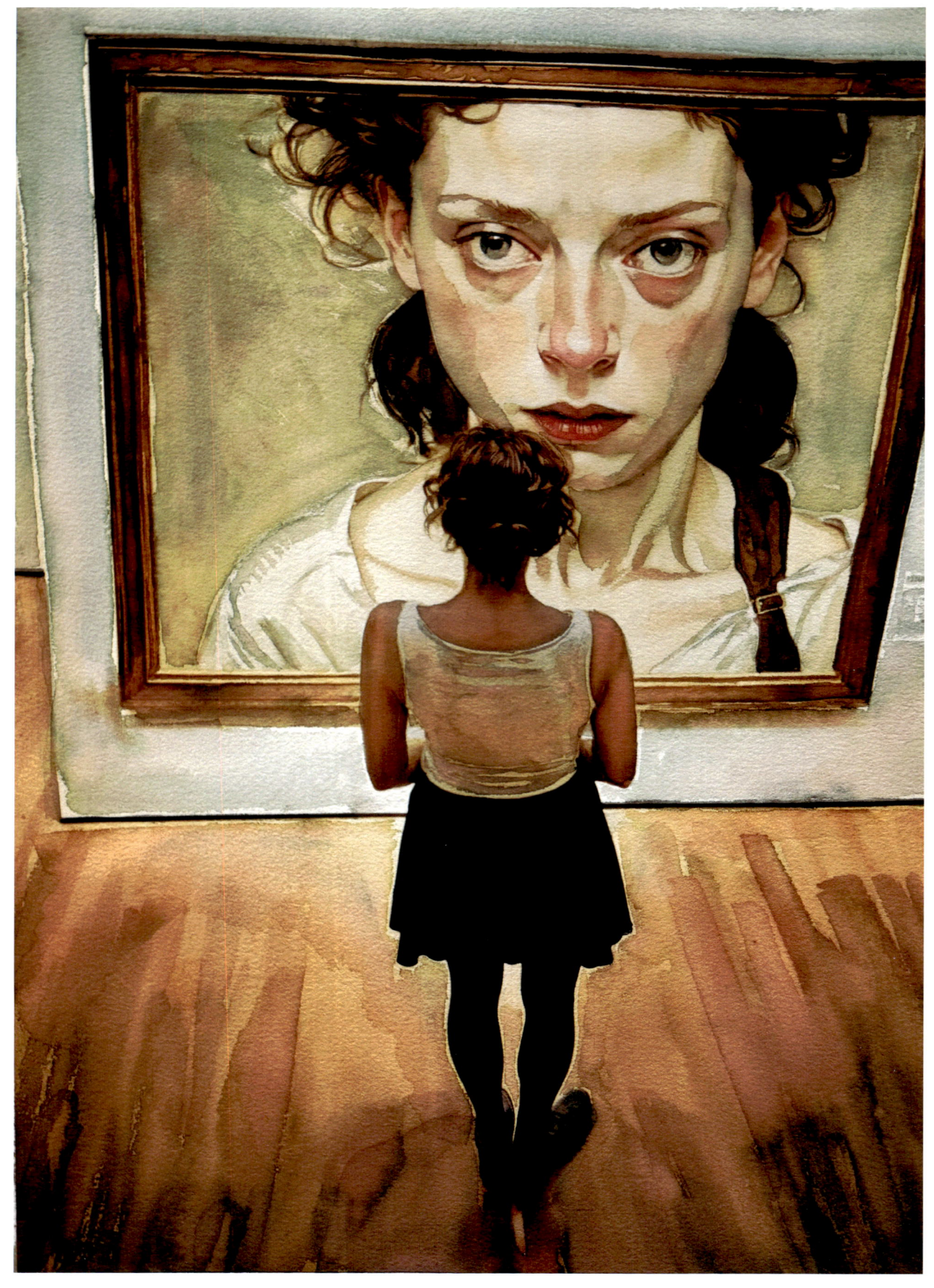

above: "At the Colonnade" | watercolor | 15" x 10" | Private Collection
previous spread: "Athena" | watercolor | 9" x 15" | Private Collection

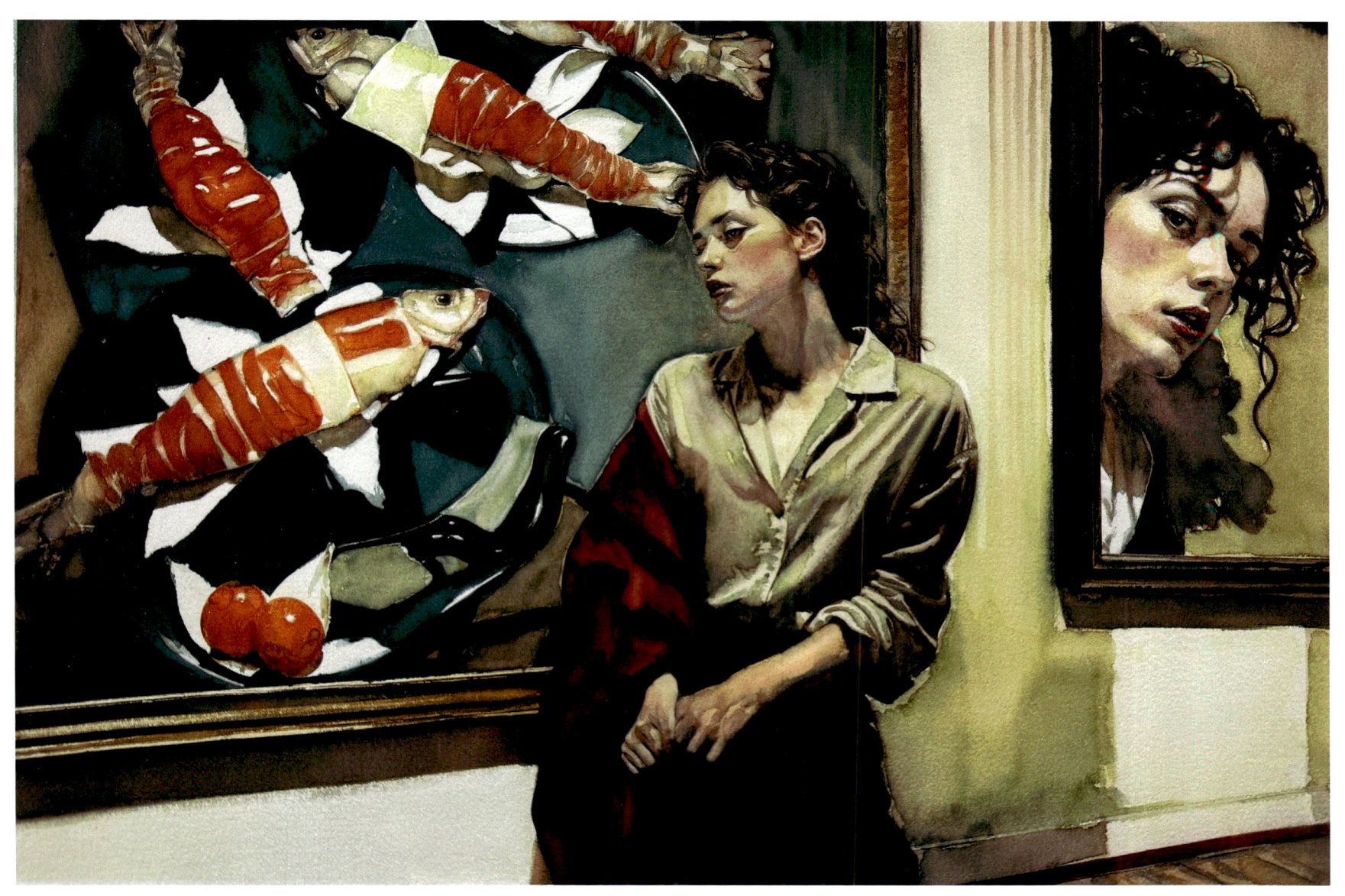

"Koi" | watercolor | 10" x 15" | Private Collection

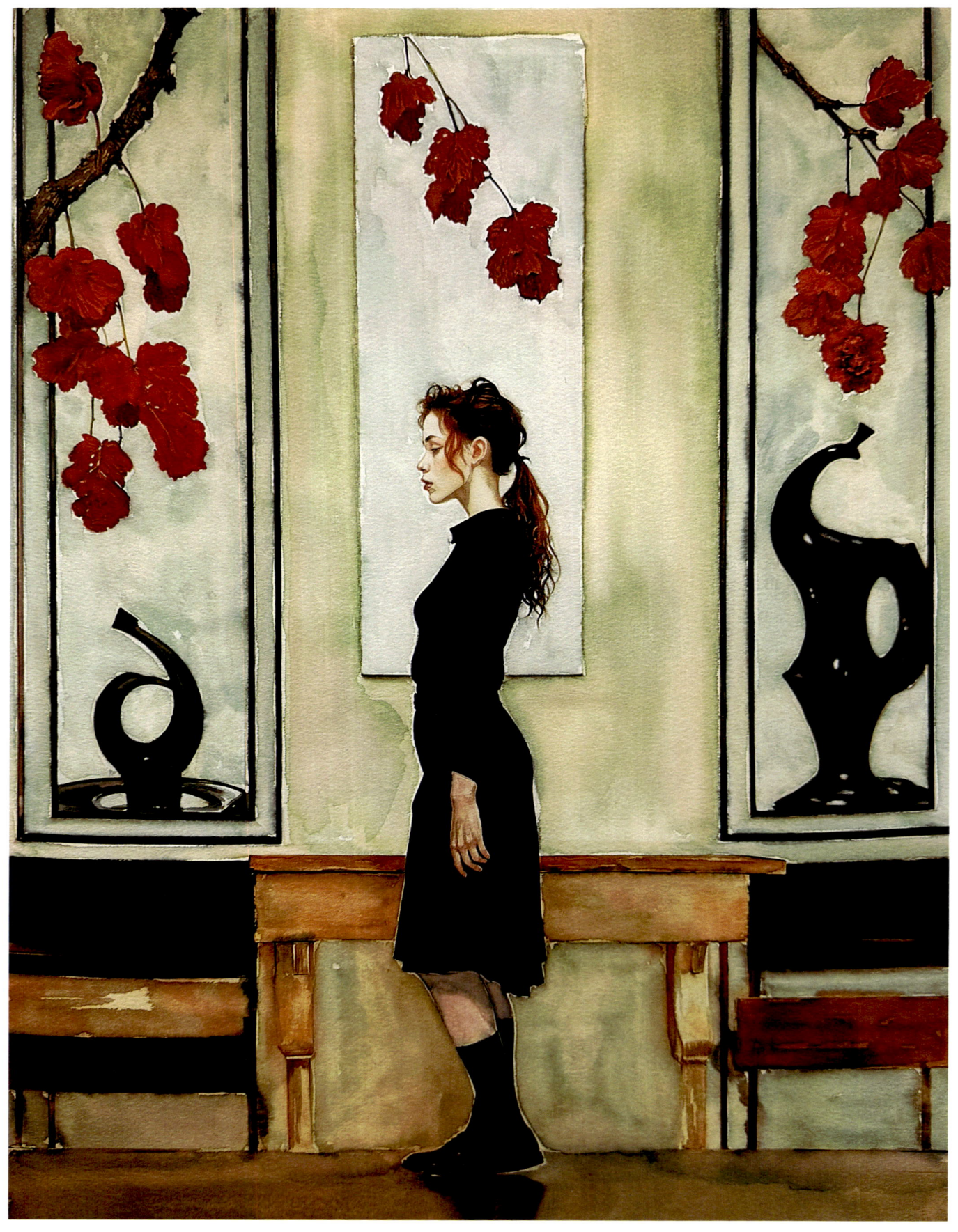

"East Wing" | watercolor | 15" x 10" | Private Collection

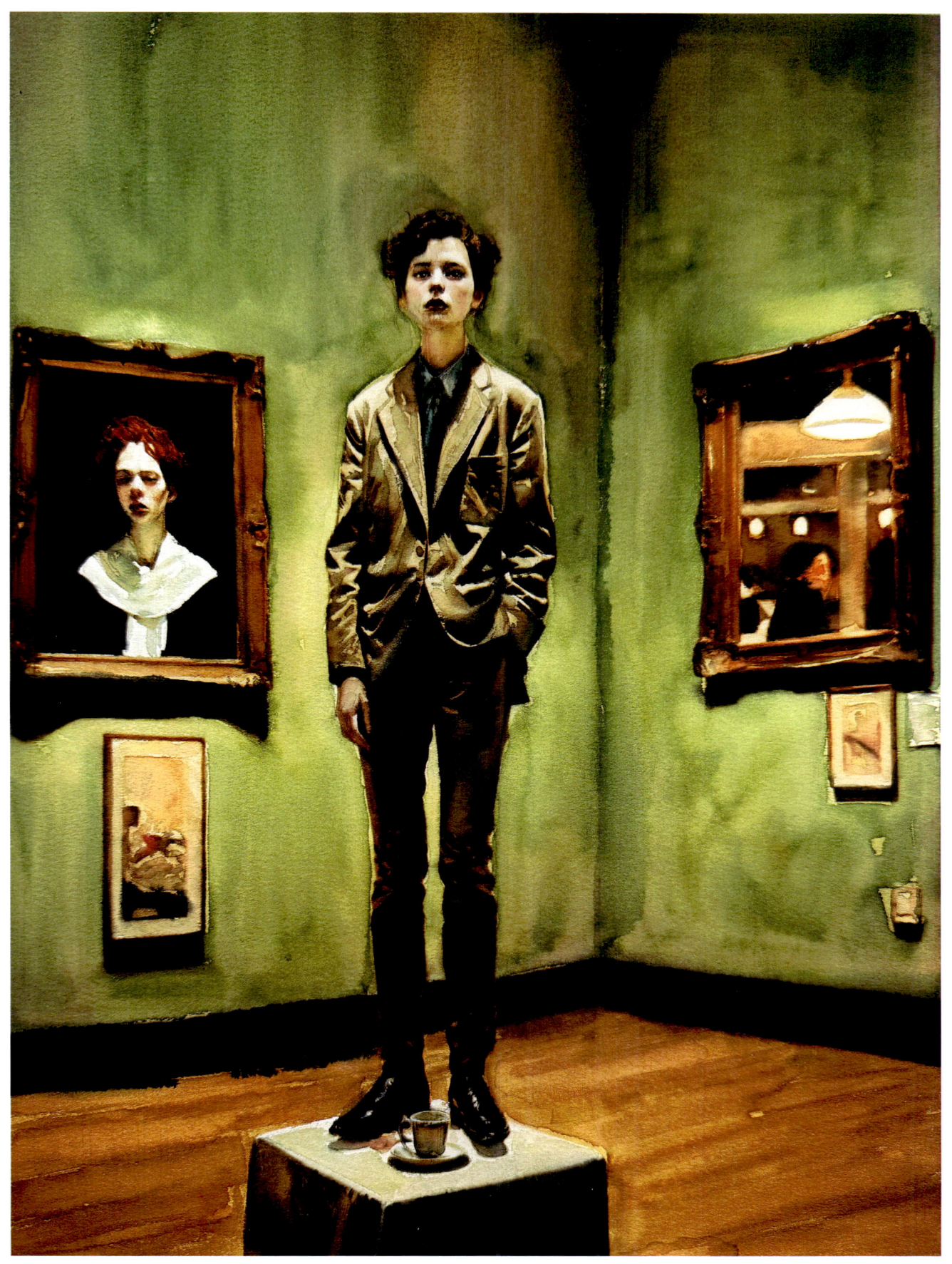

"New Installation" | watercolor | 18" x 14" | Private Collection

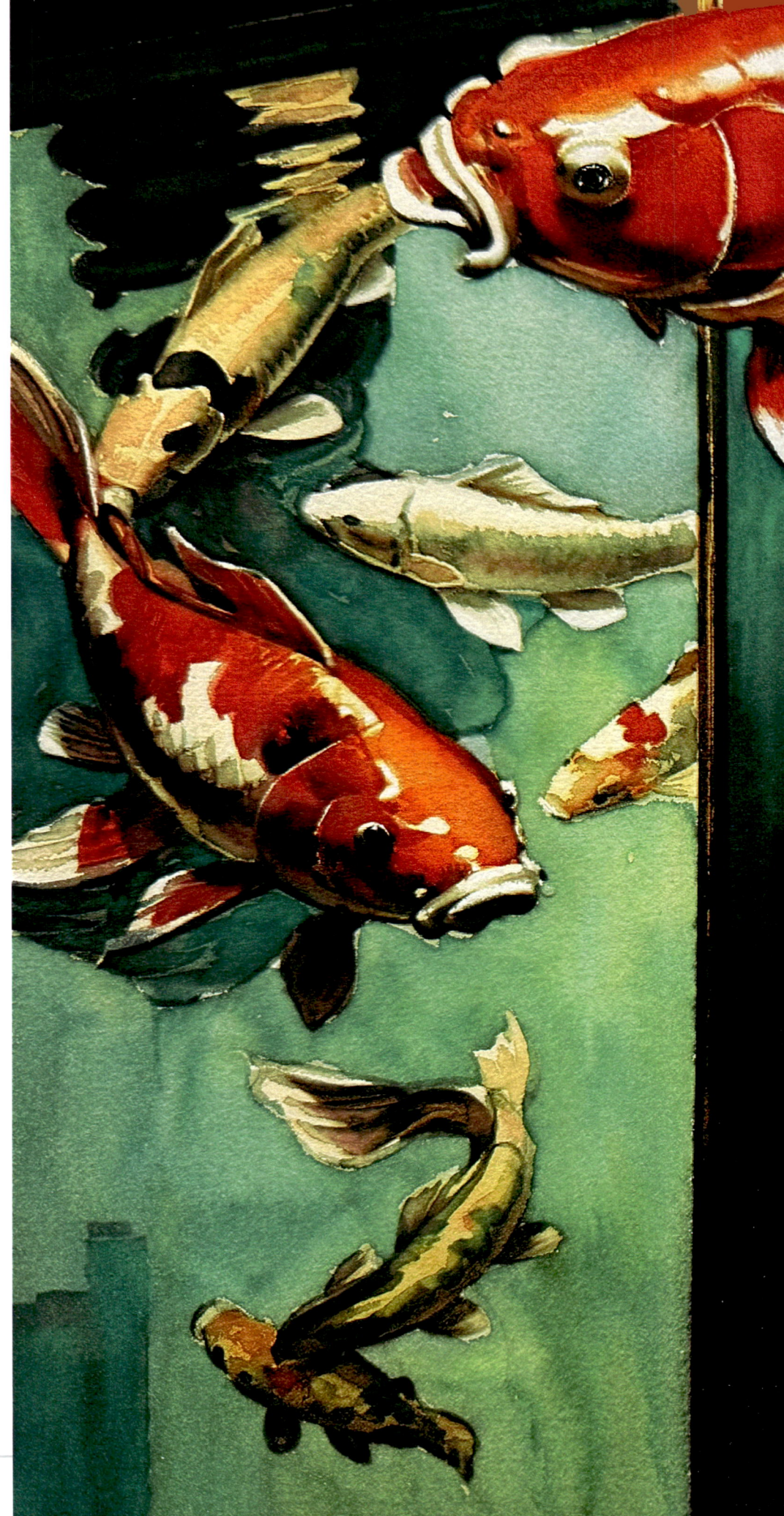

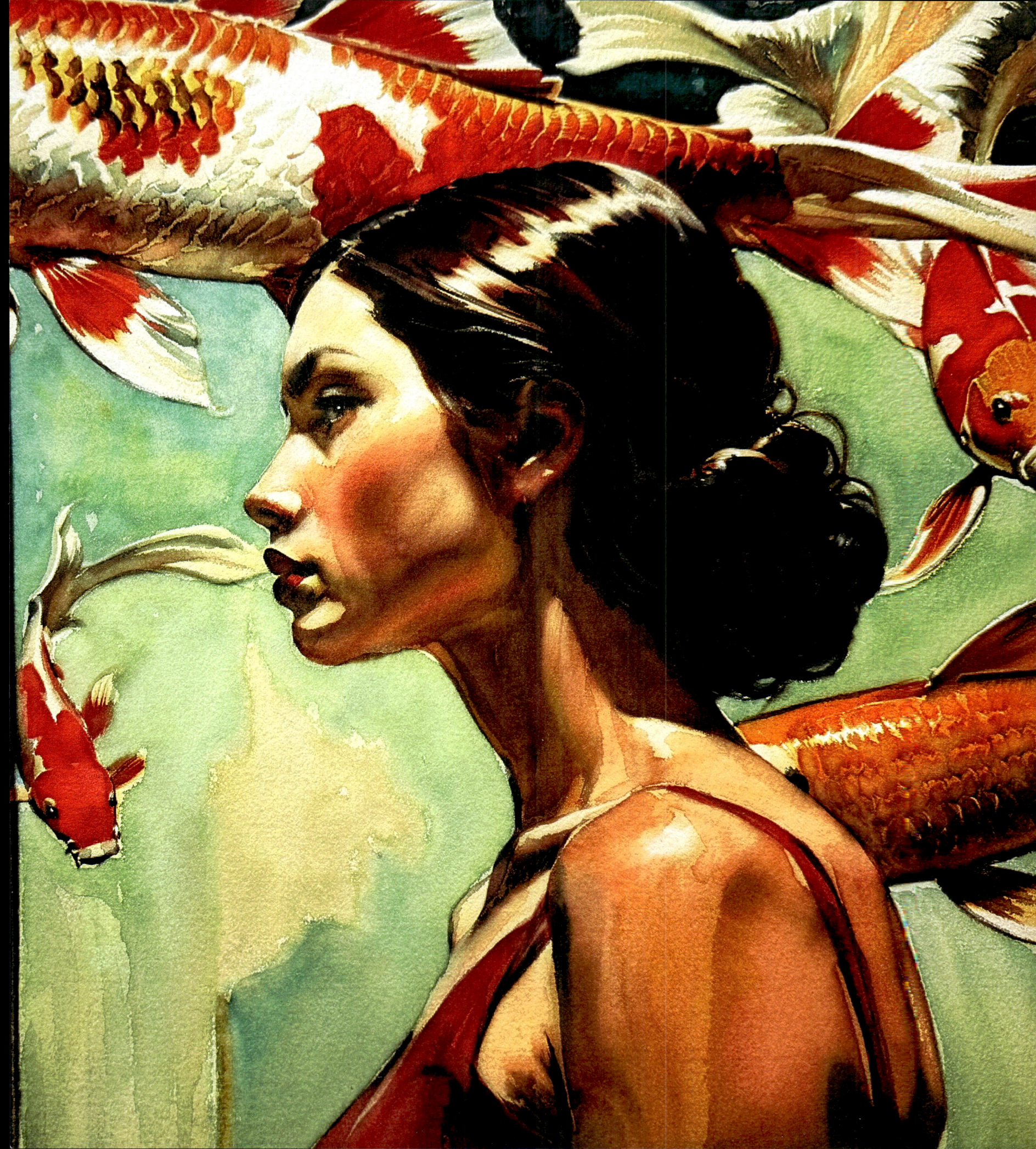

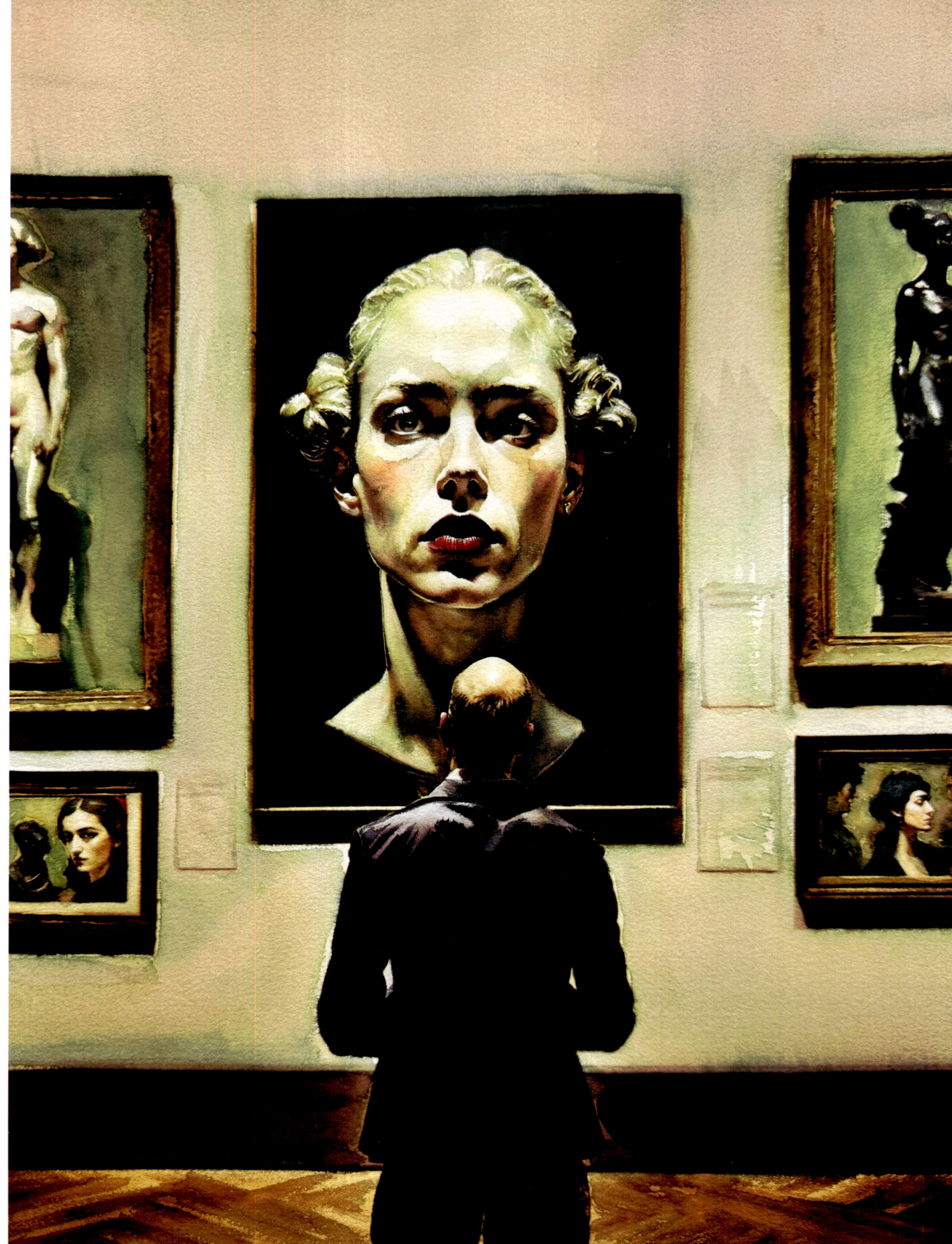

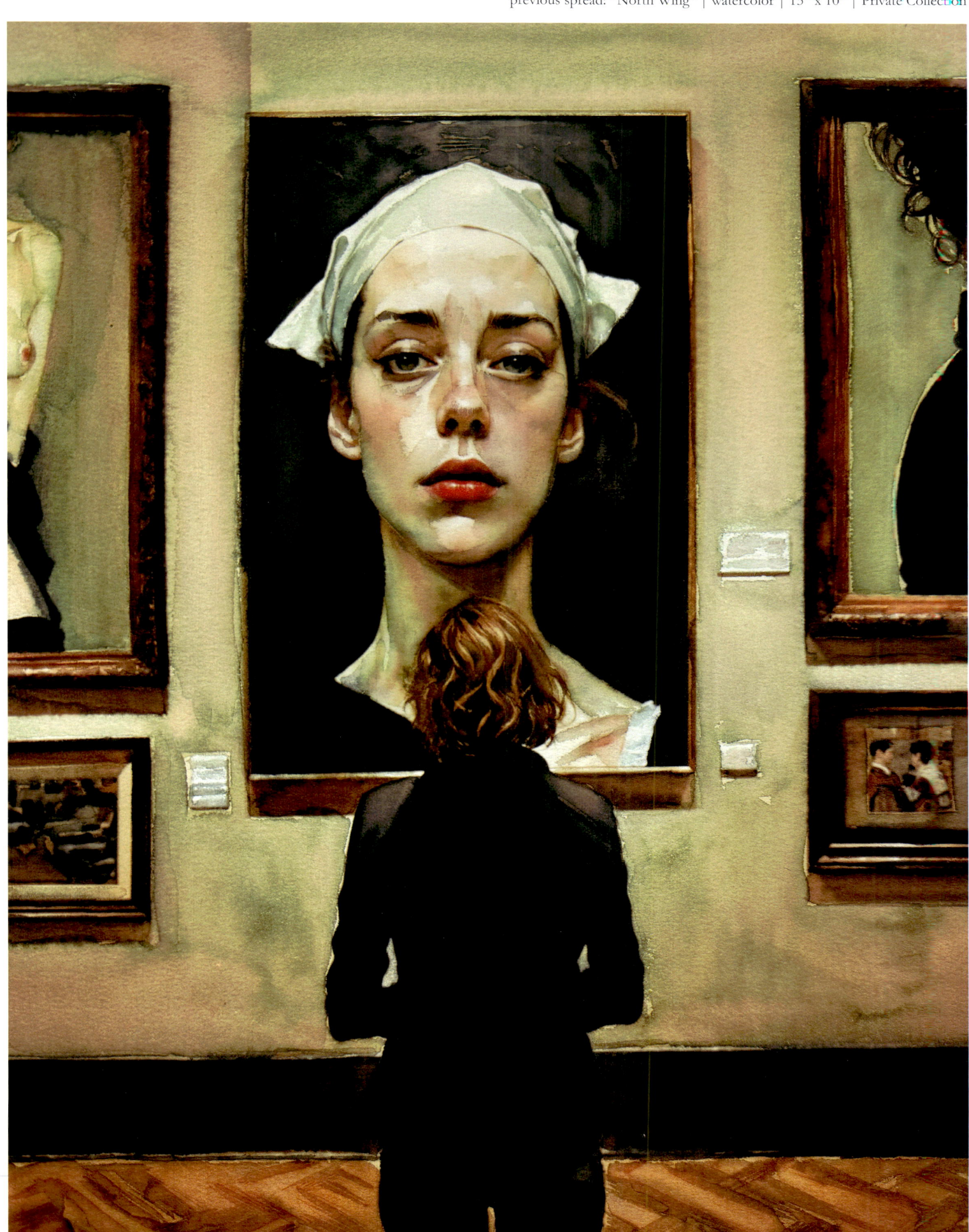

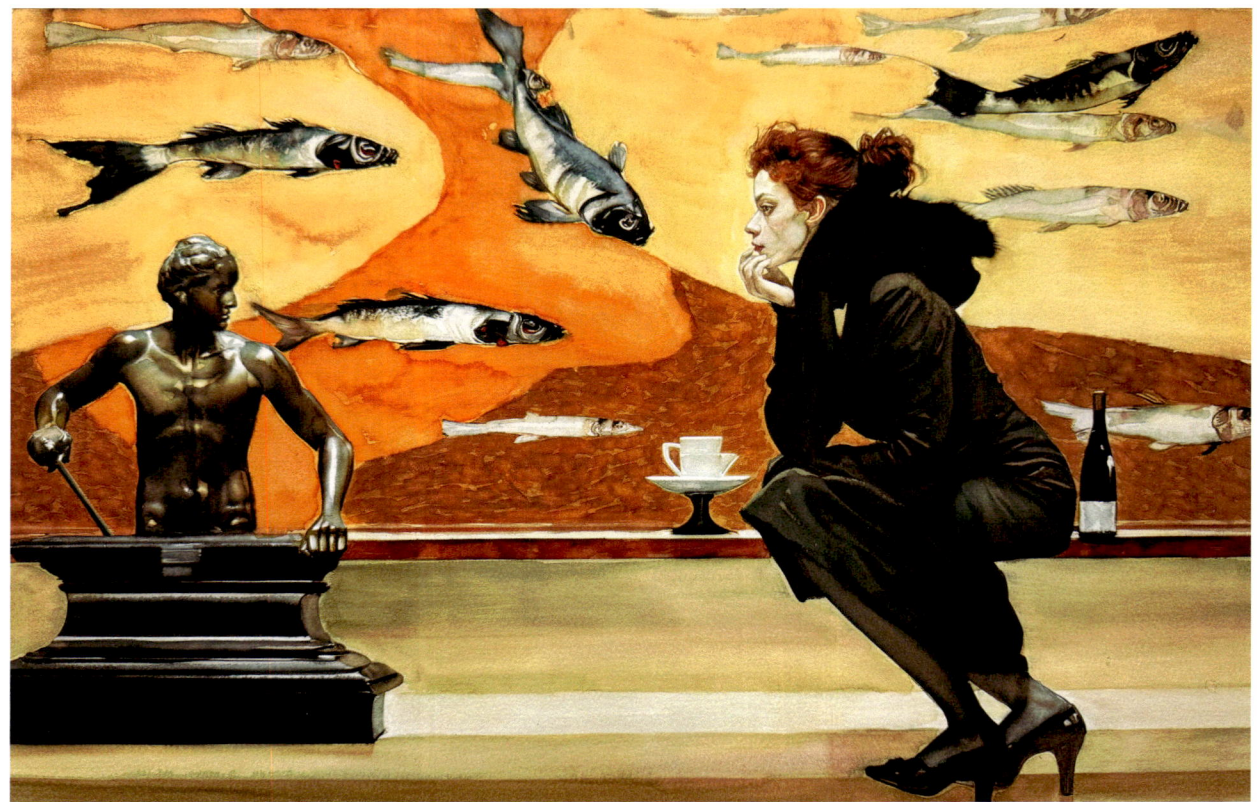

"Robin" | watercolor | 12" x 18" | Private Collection

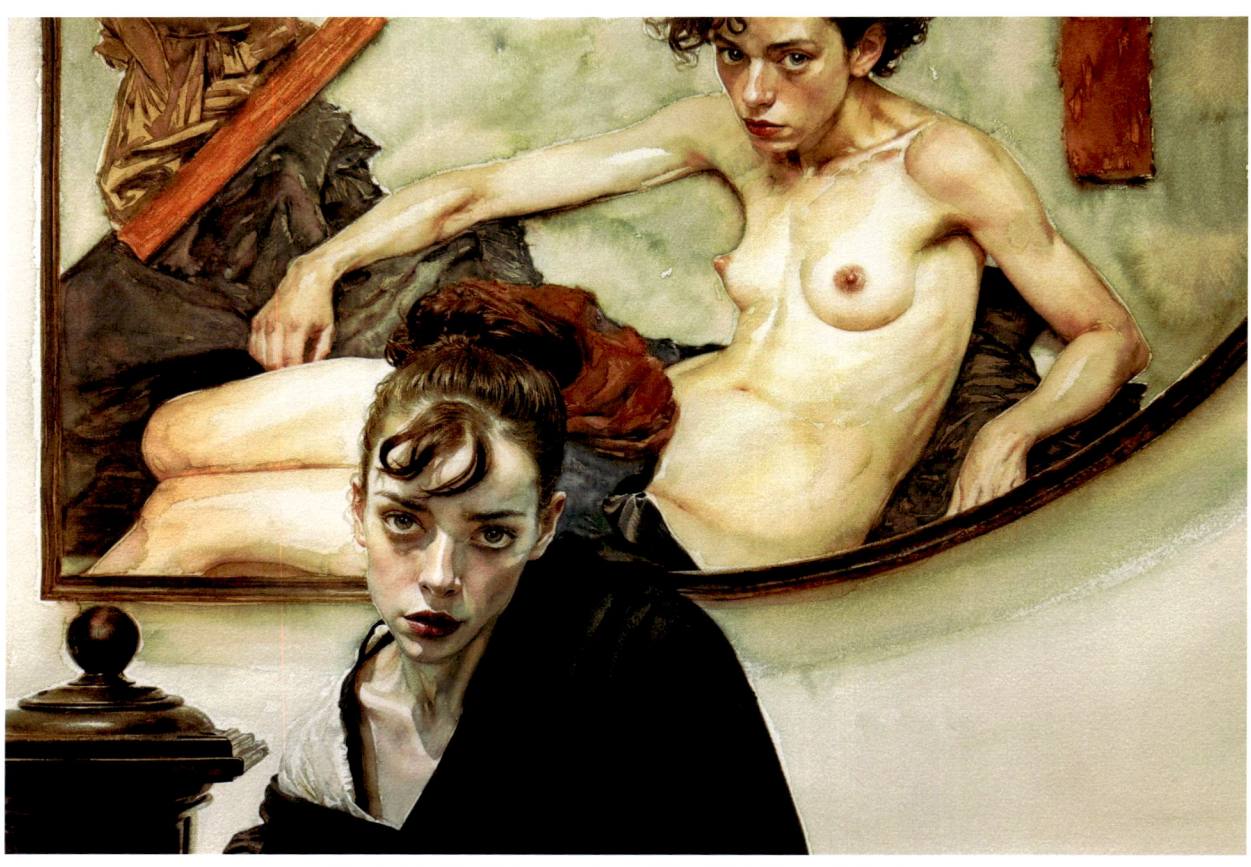

"Can I Help You?" | watercolor | 12" x 15" | Private Collection
opposite: "Beth" | watercolor | 16" x 12" | Private Collection

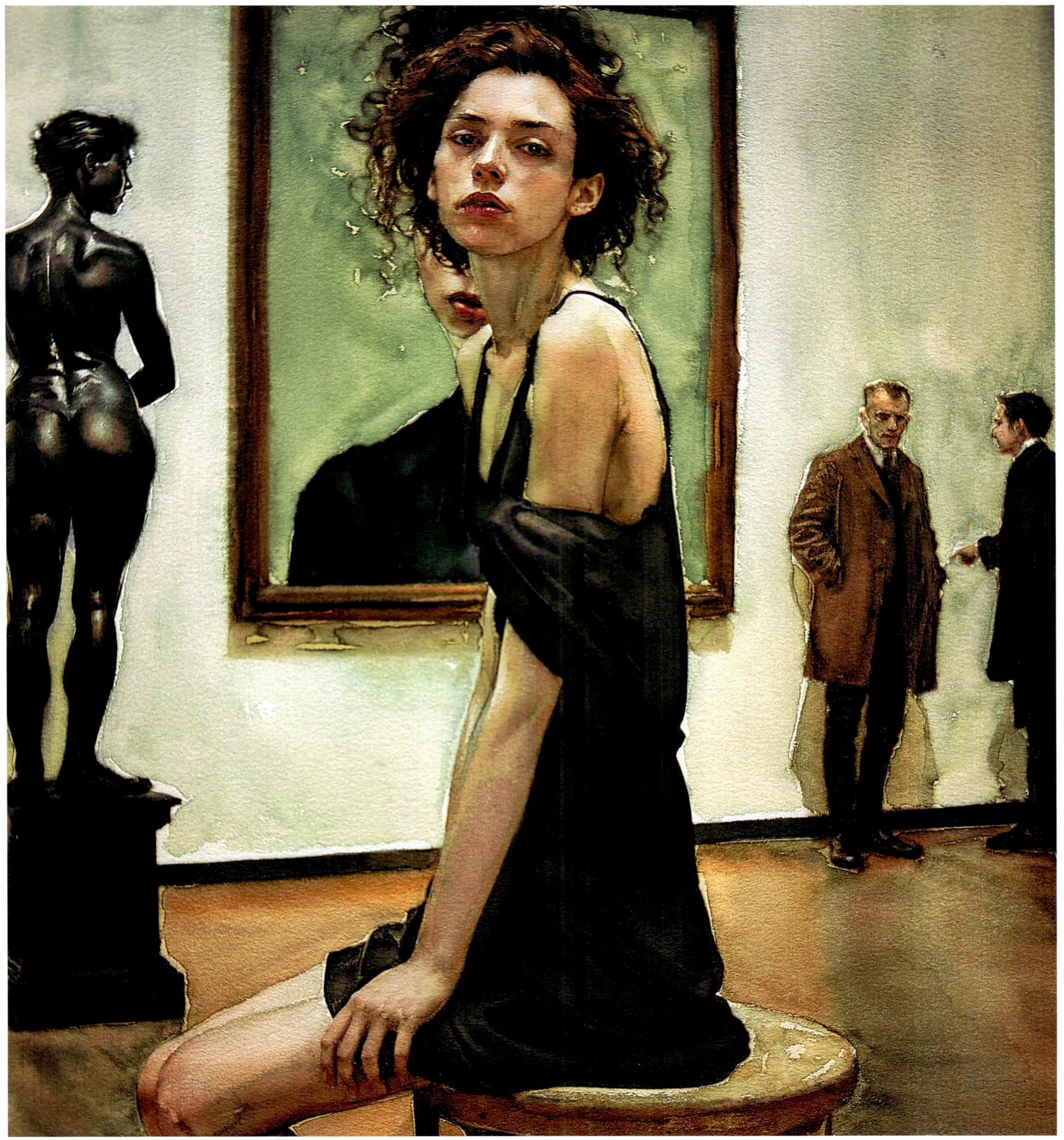

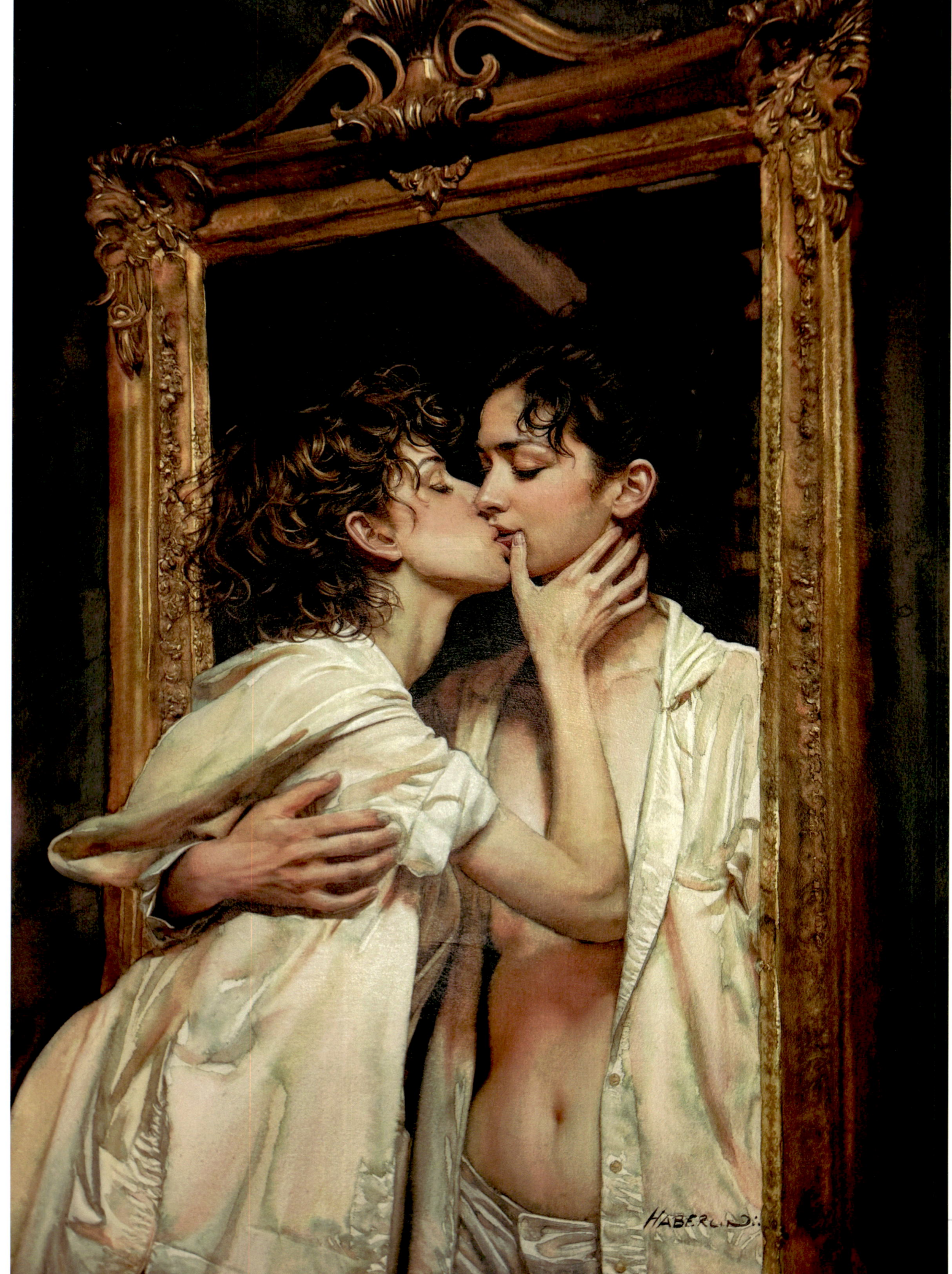

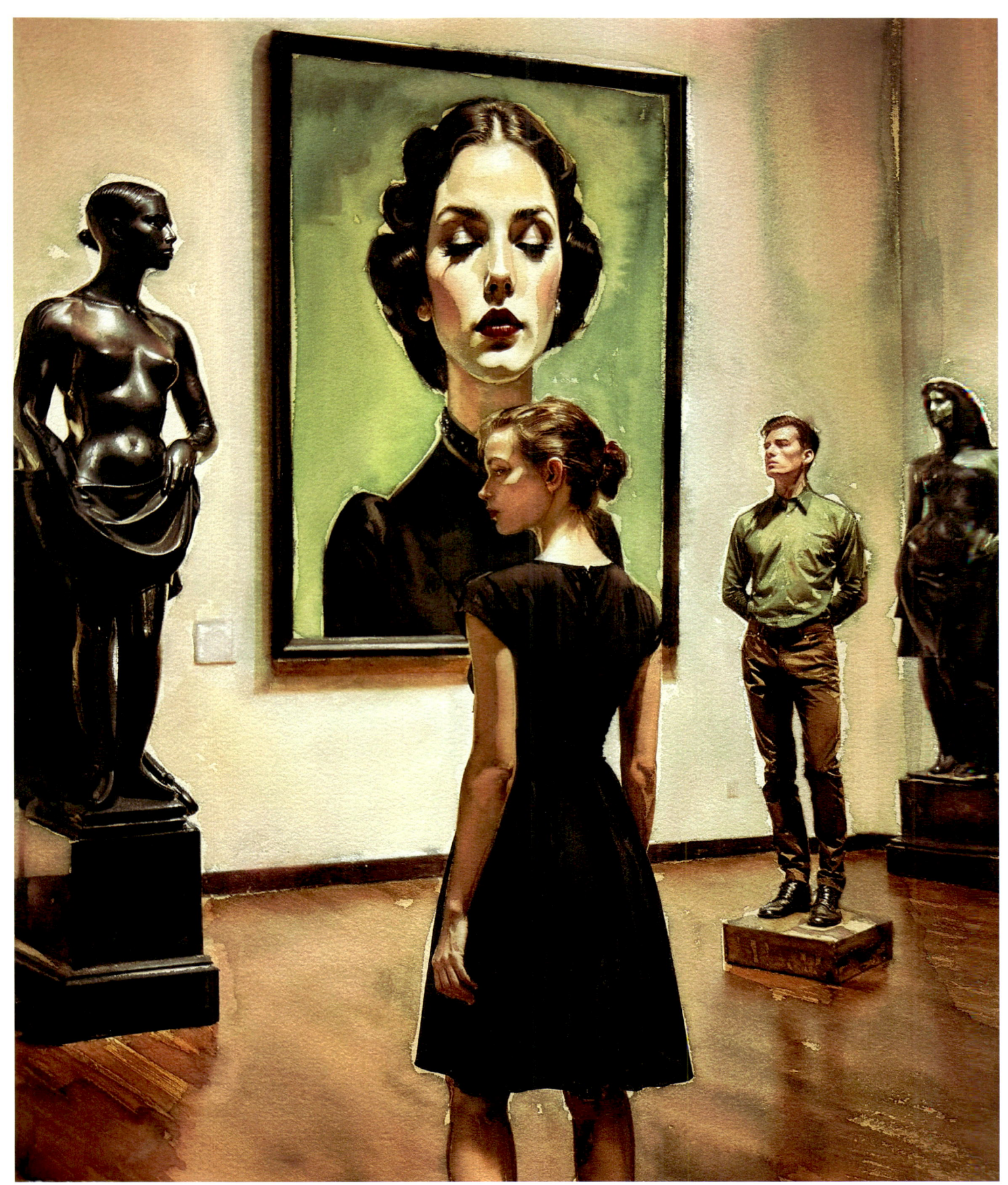

above: "Statues" | watercolor | 15" x 10" | Private Collection
opposite: "Pygmalion" | watercolor | 24" x 17" | Private Collection

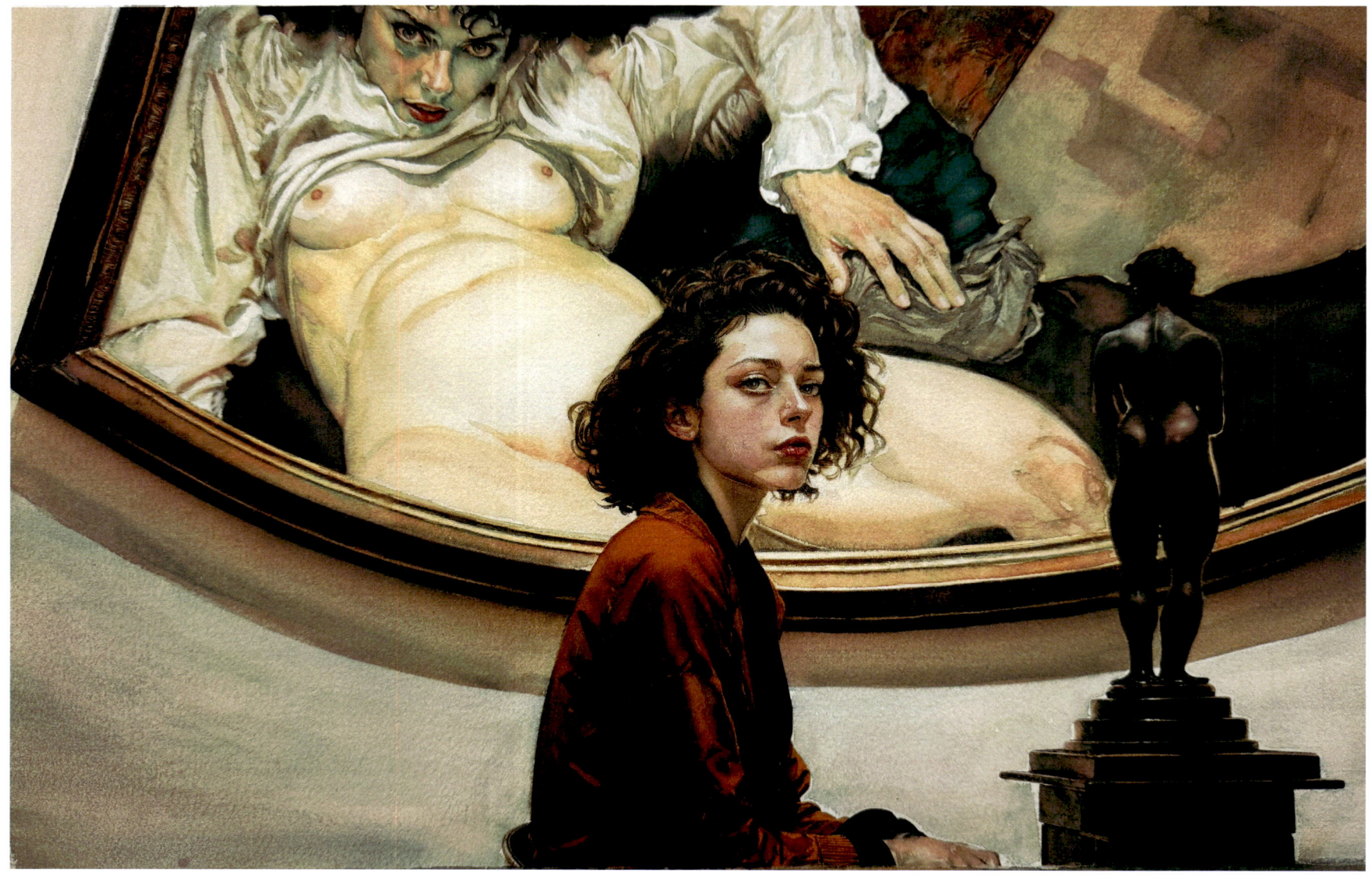

"Shirley" | watercolor | 10" x 15" | Private Collection

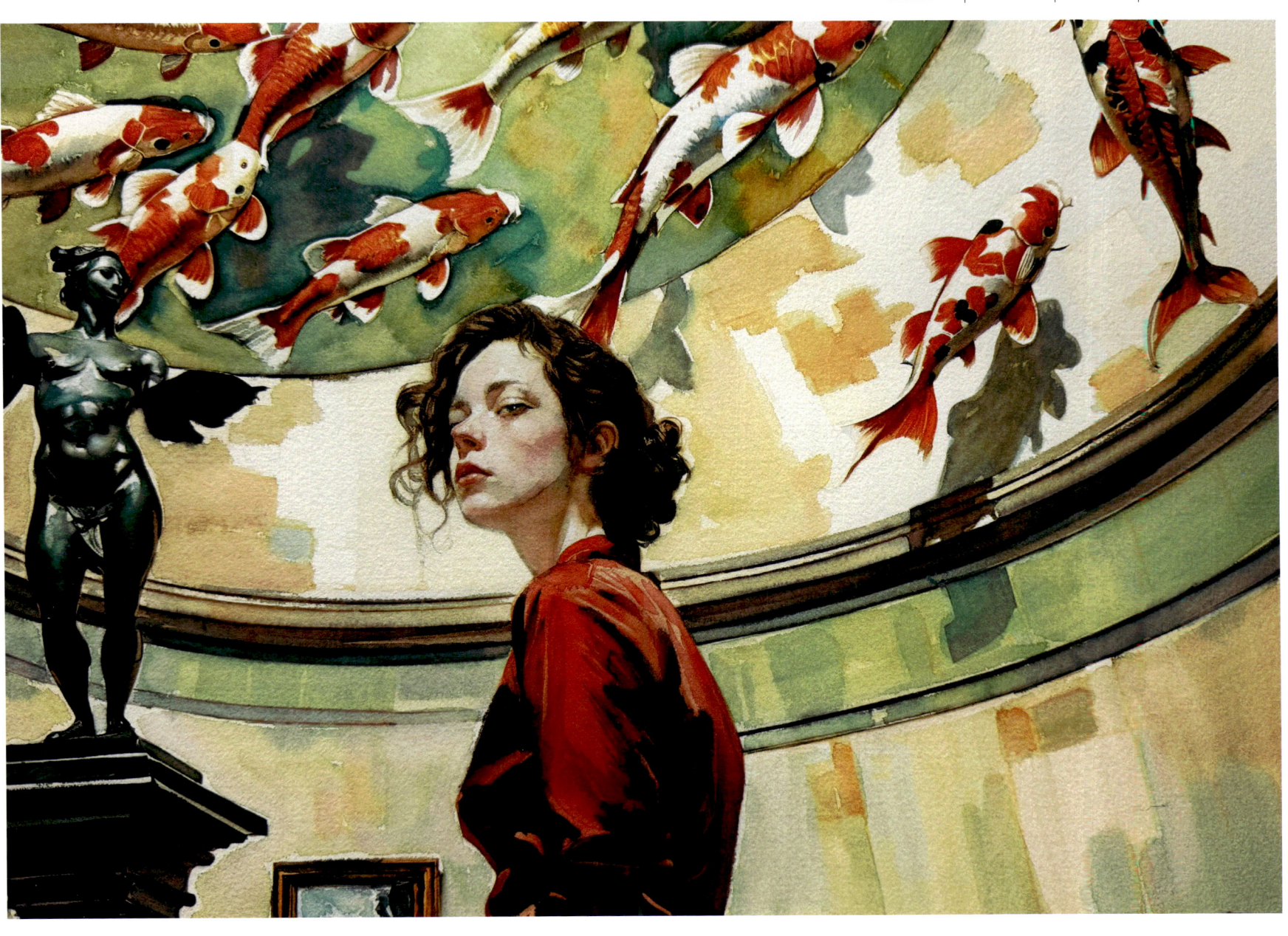

FABRICS

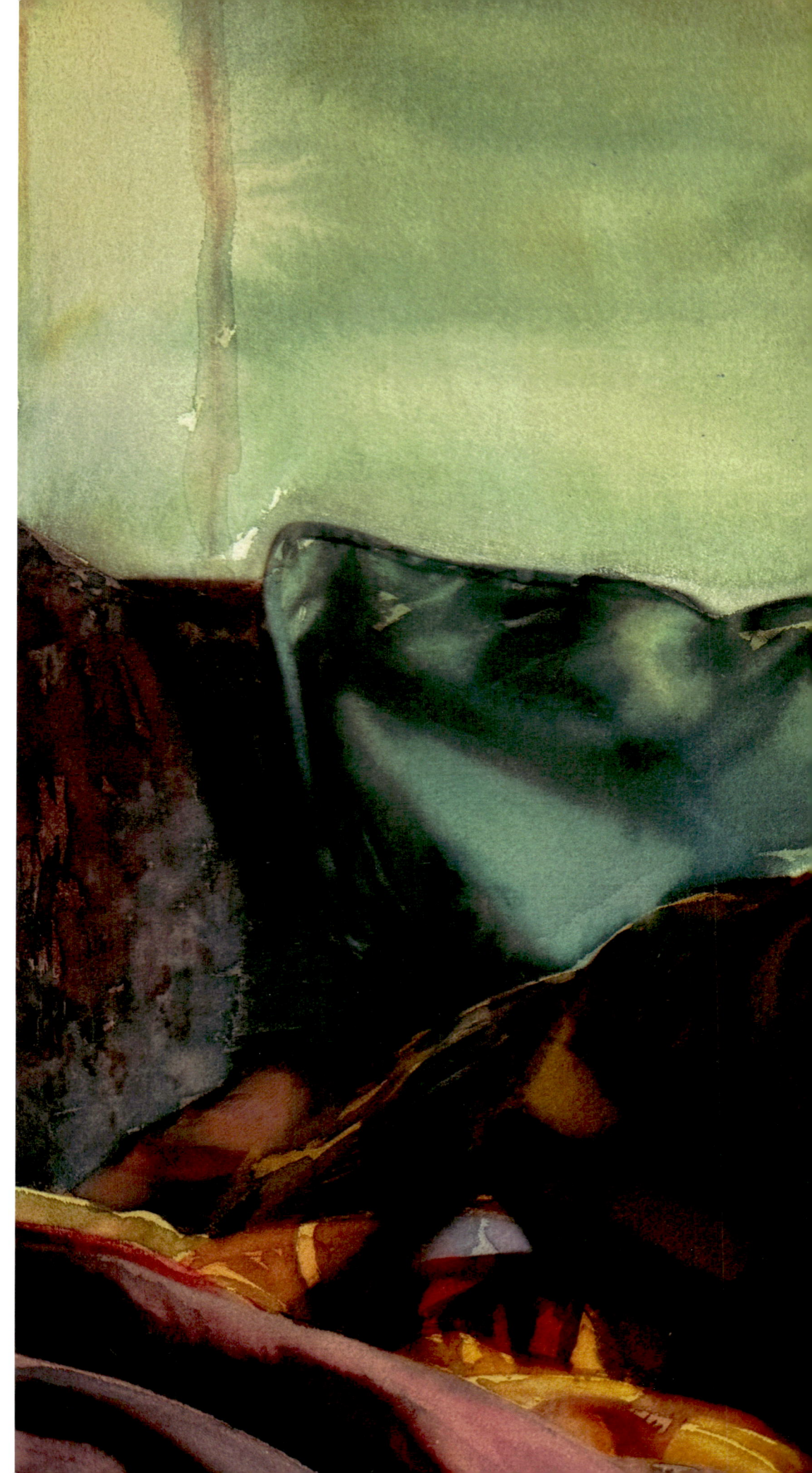

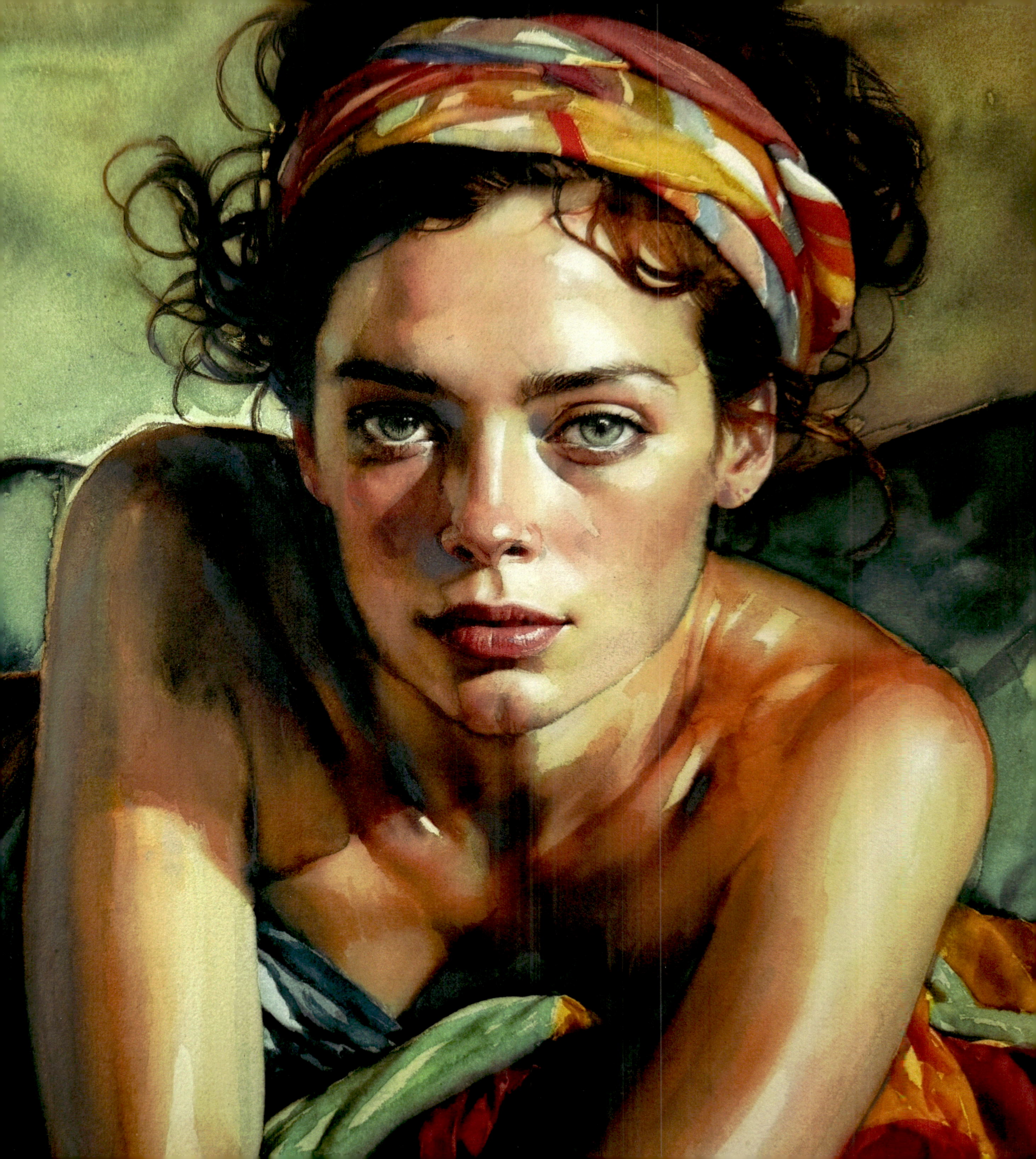

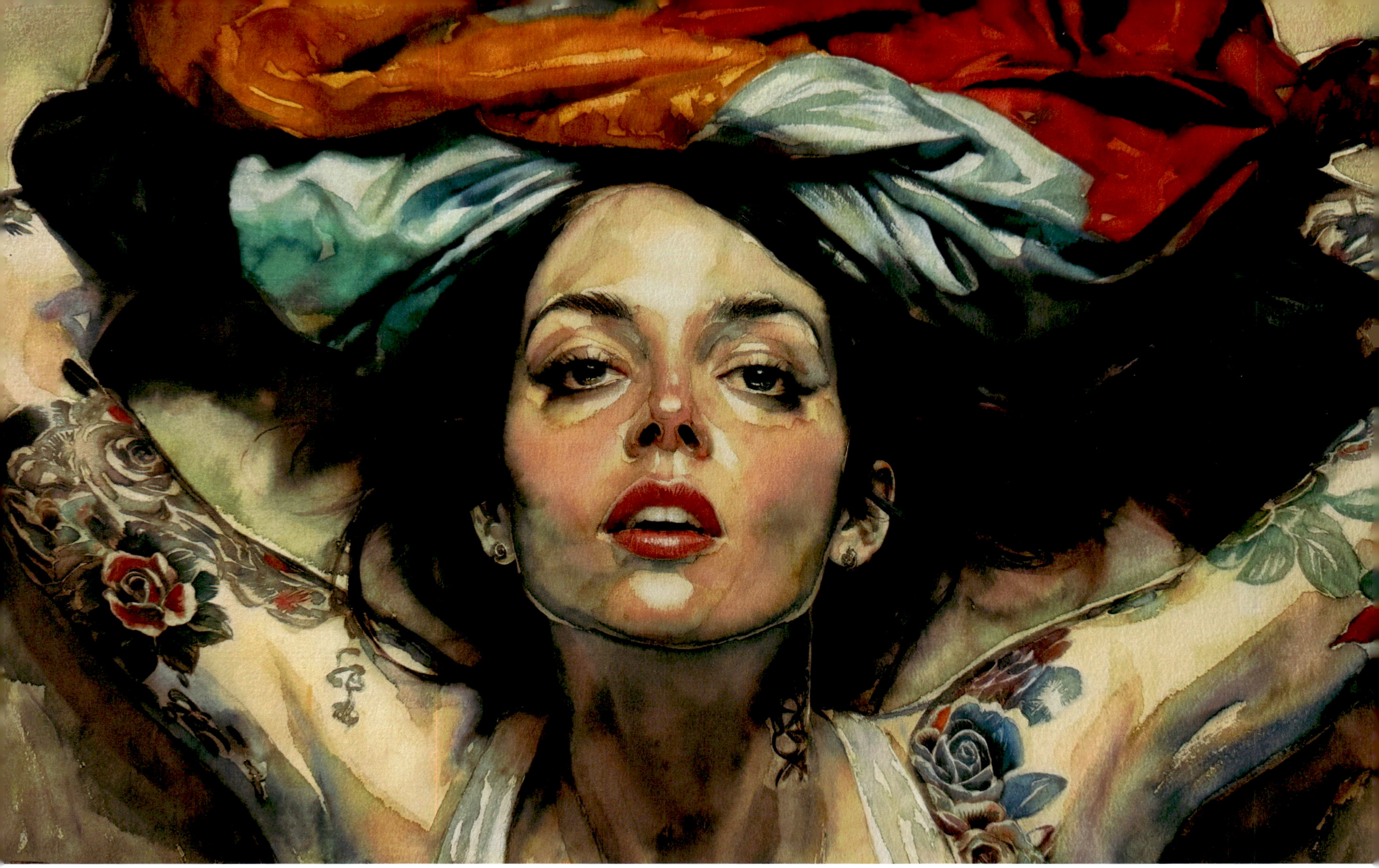

above: "Veronica" | watercolor | 12" x 16" | Private Collection

previous spread:
"Summer Glow" | watercolor | 12" x 16" | Private Collection

"Welcome to the Club" | watercolor | 12" x 15" | Private Collection

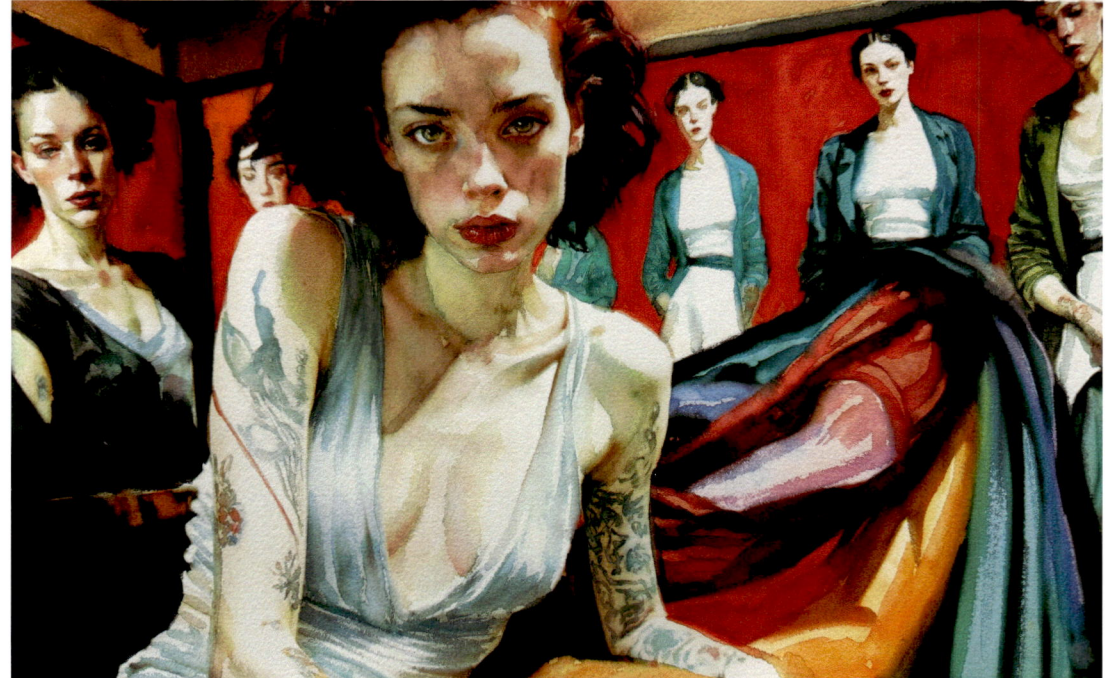

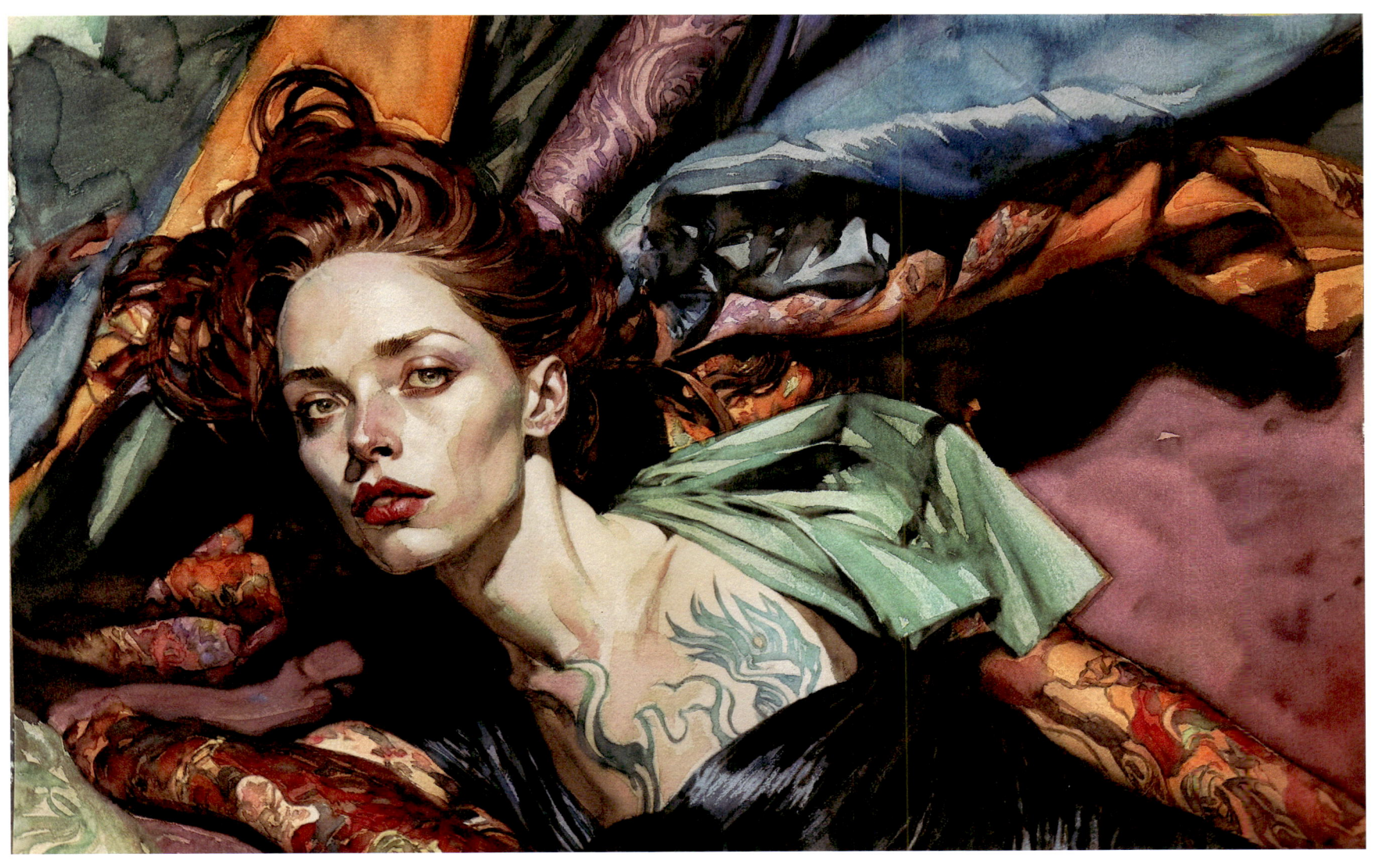

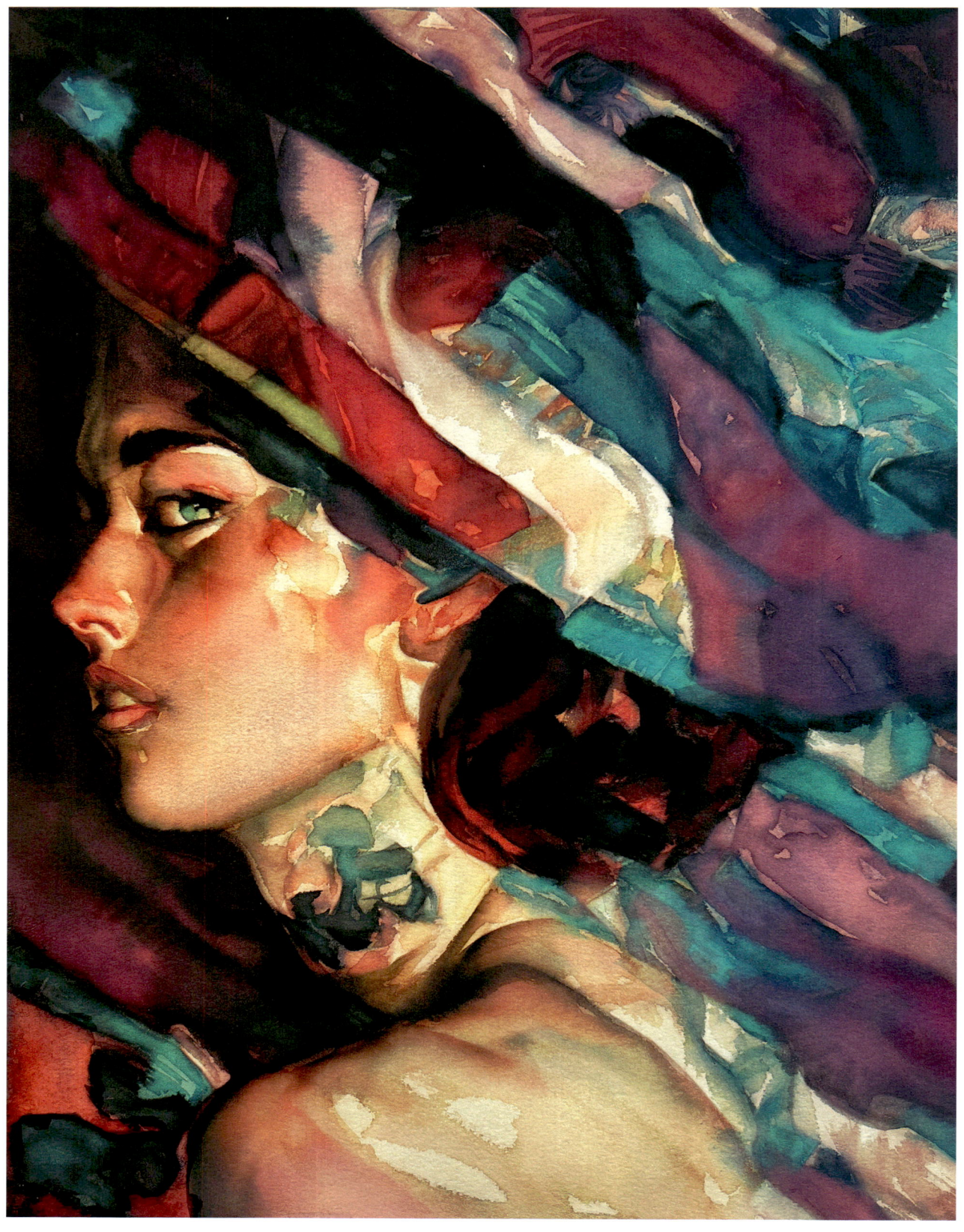

above: "Ribbons" | watercolor | 12" x 8" | Private Collection
opposite: "Frances" | watercolor | 18" x 12" | Private Collection

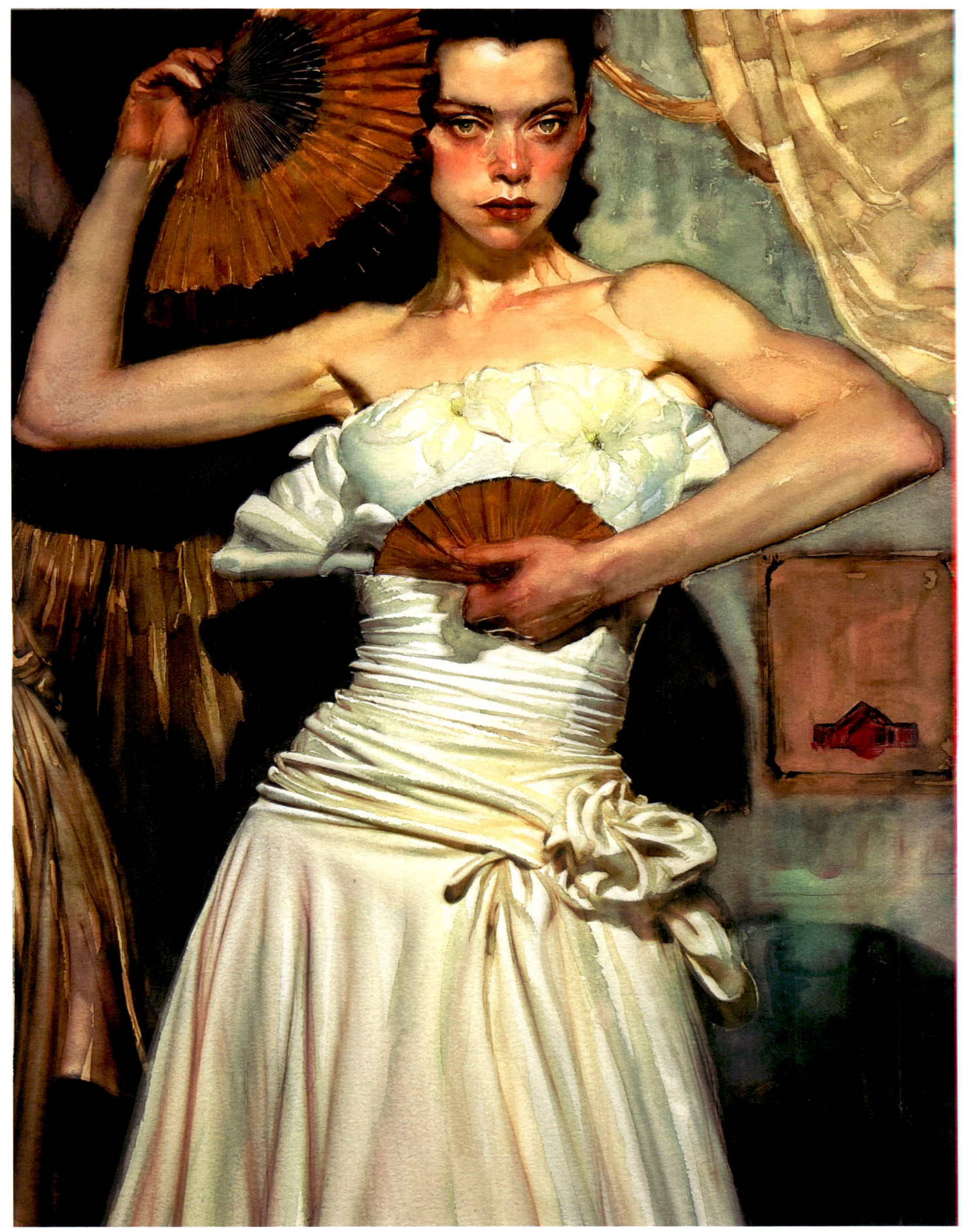

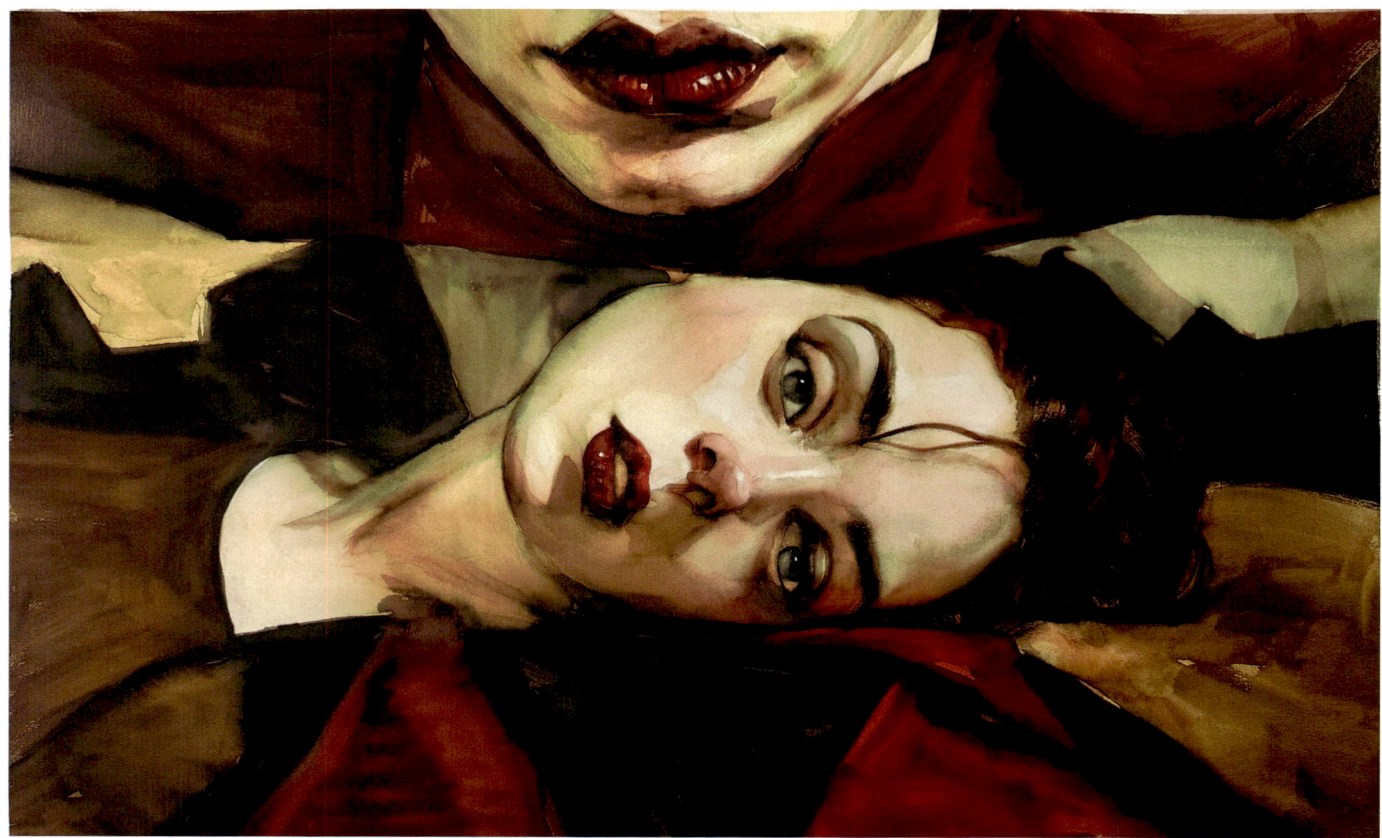

above: "Dream" | watercolor | 20" x 30" | Private Collection
below: "Emmie" | watercolor | 12" x 18" | Private Collection
opposite: "Rose 2" | watercolor | 12" x 8" | Private Collection

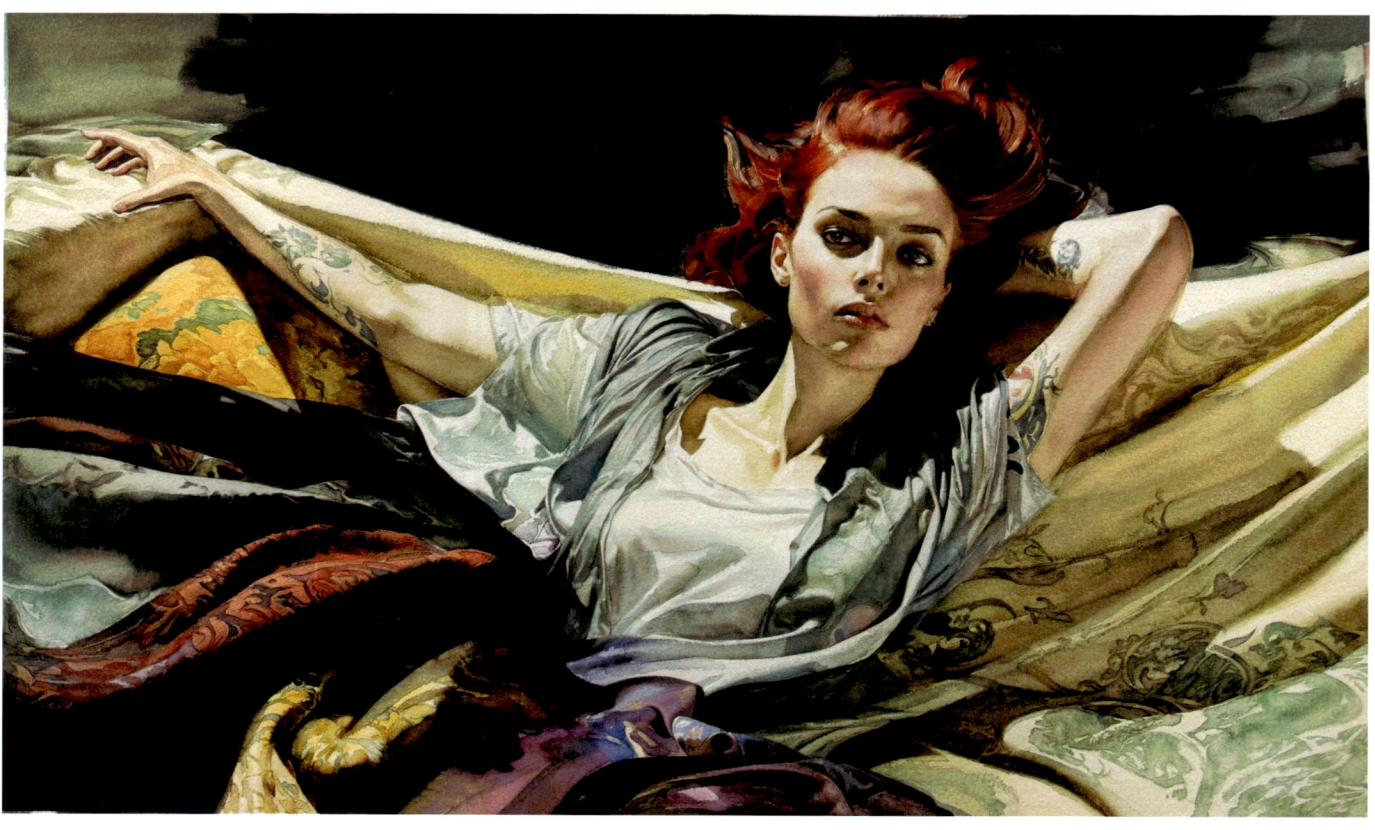

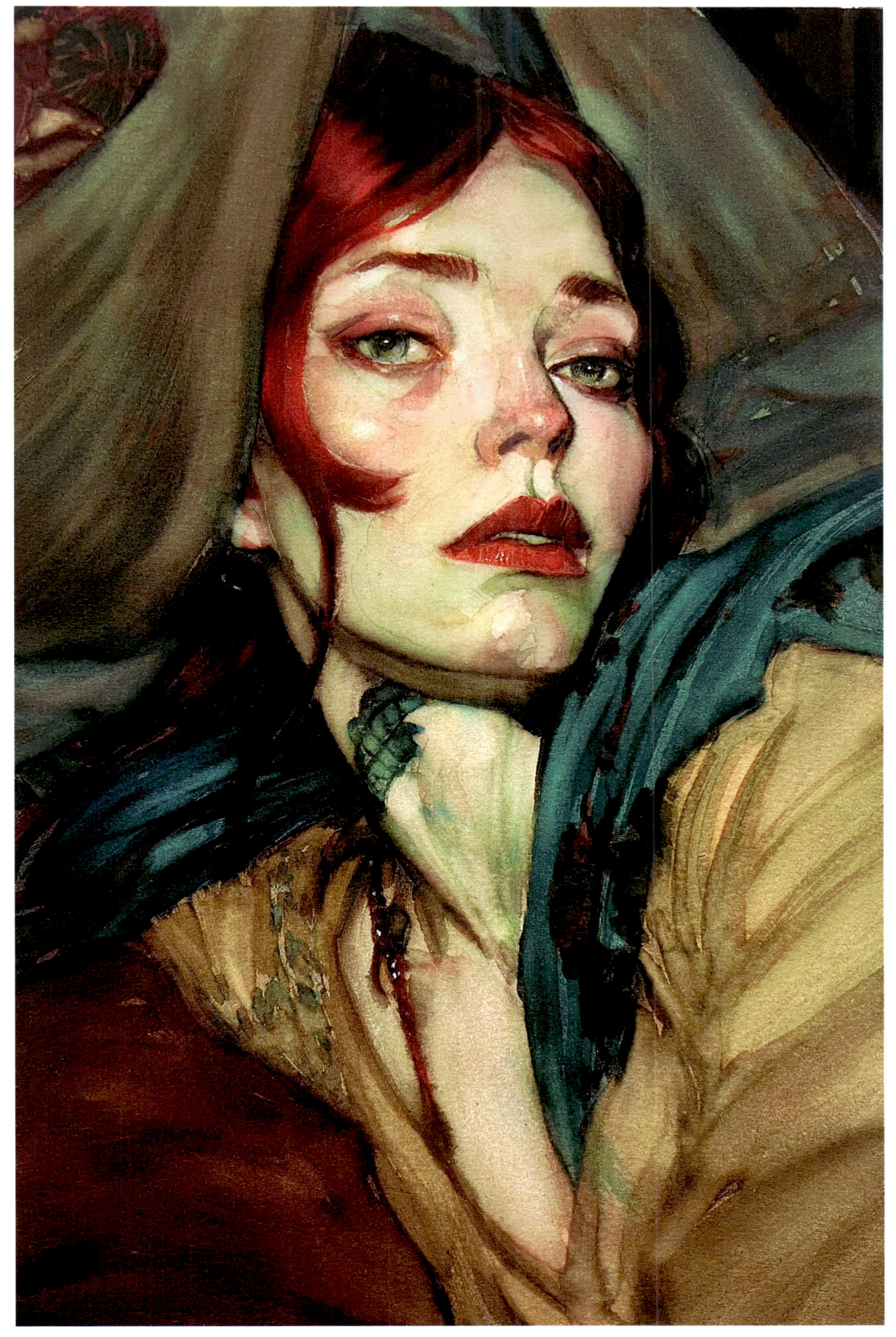

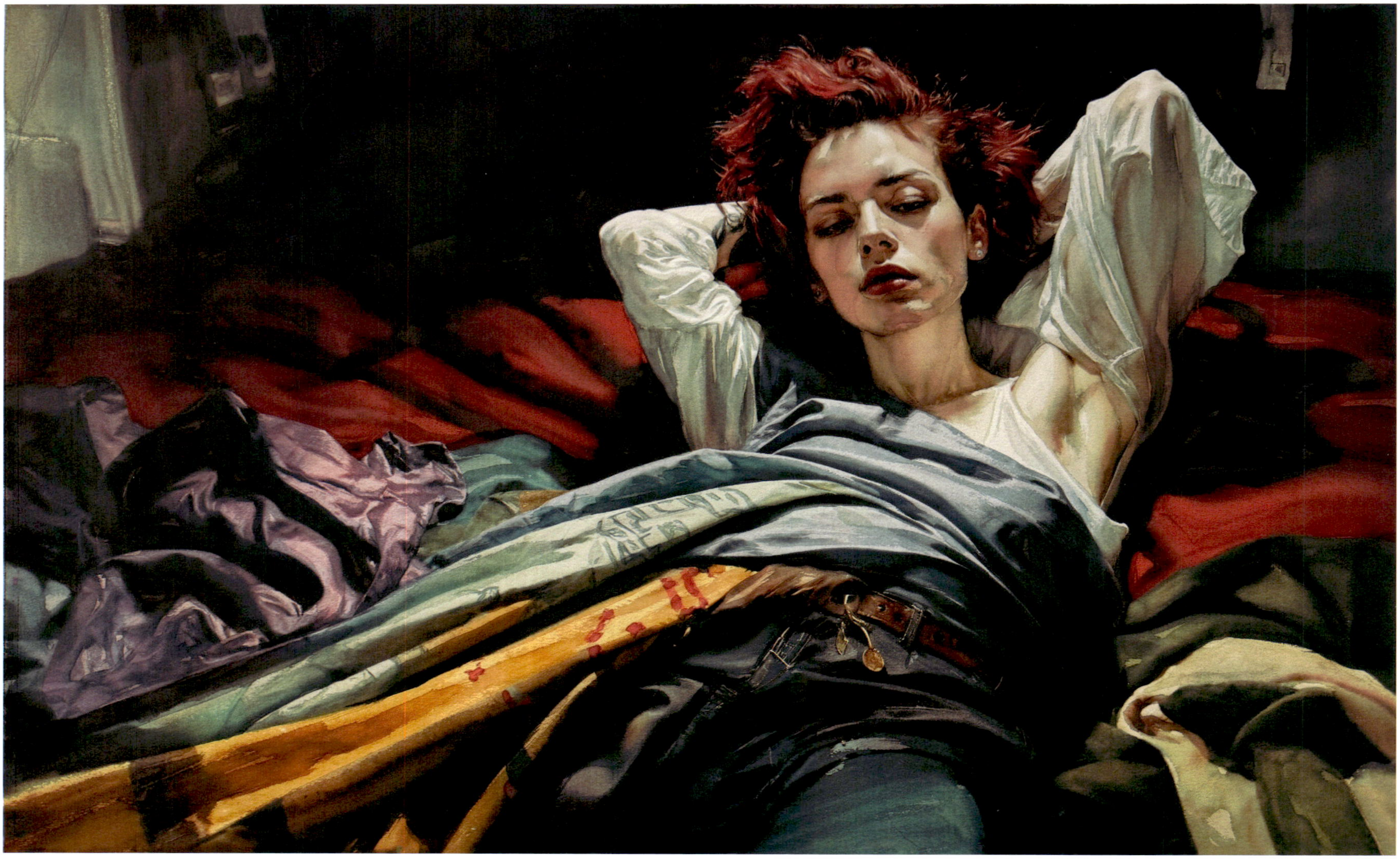

above: "After Thought" | watercolor | 14" x 23"
below: "After Thought" *Study*

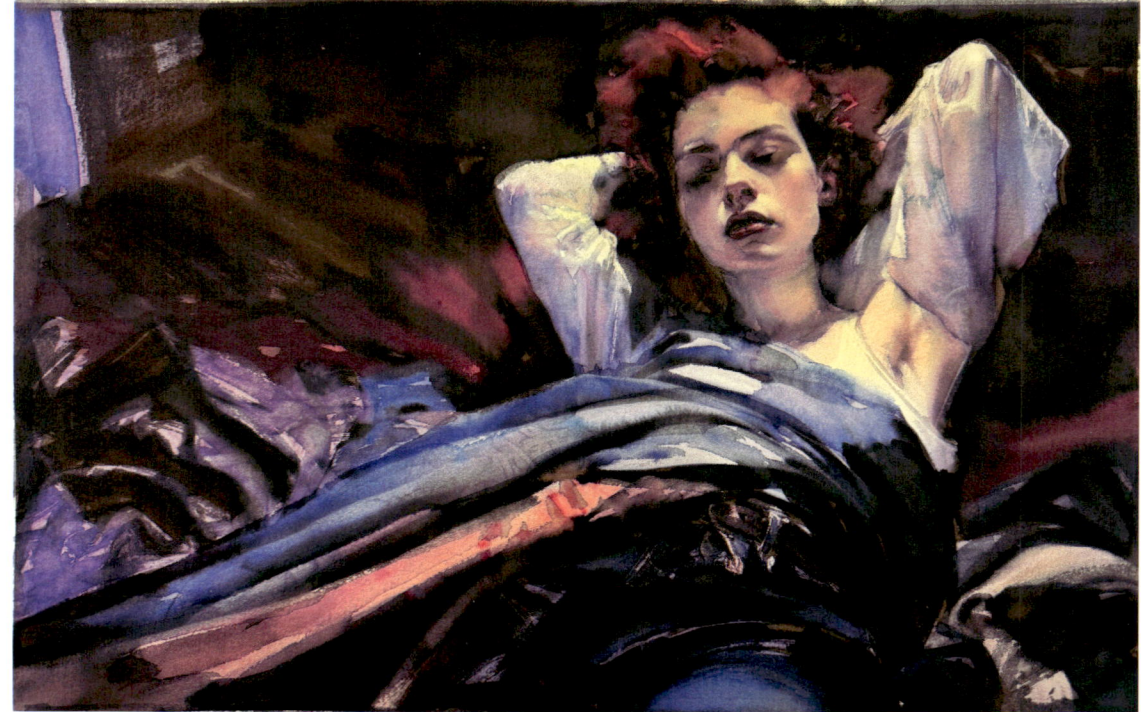

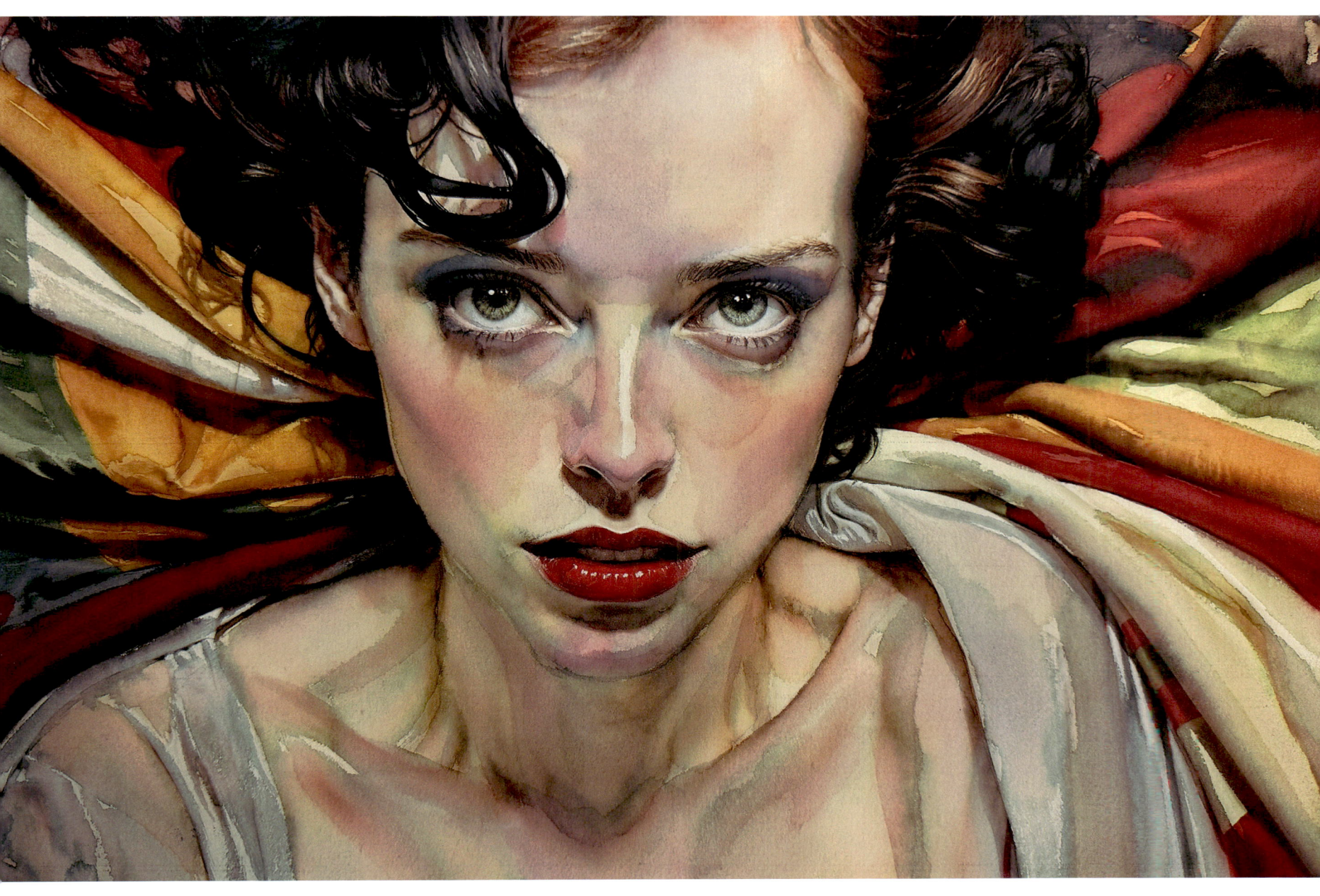

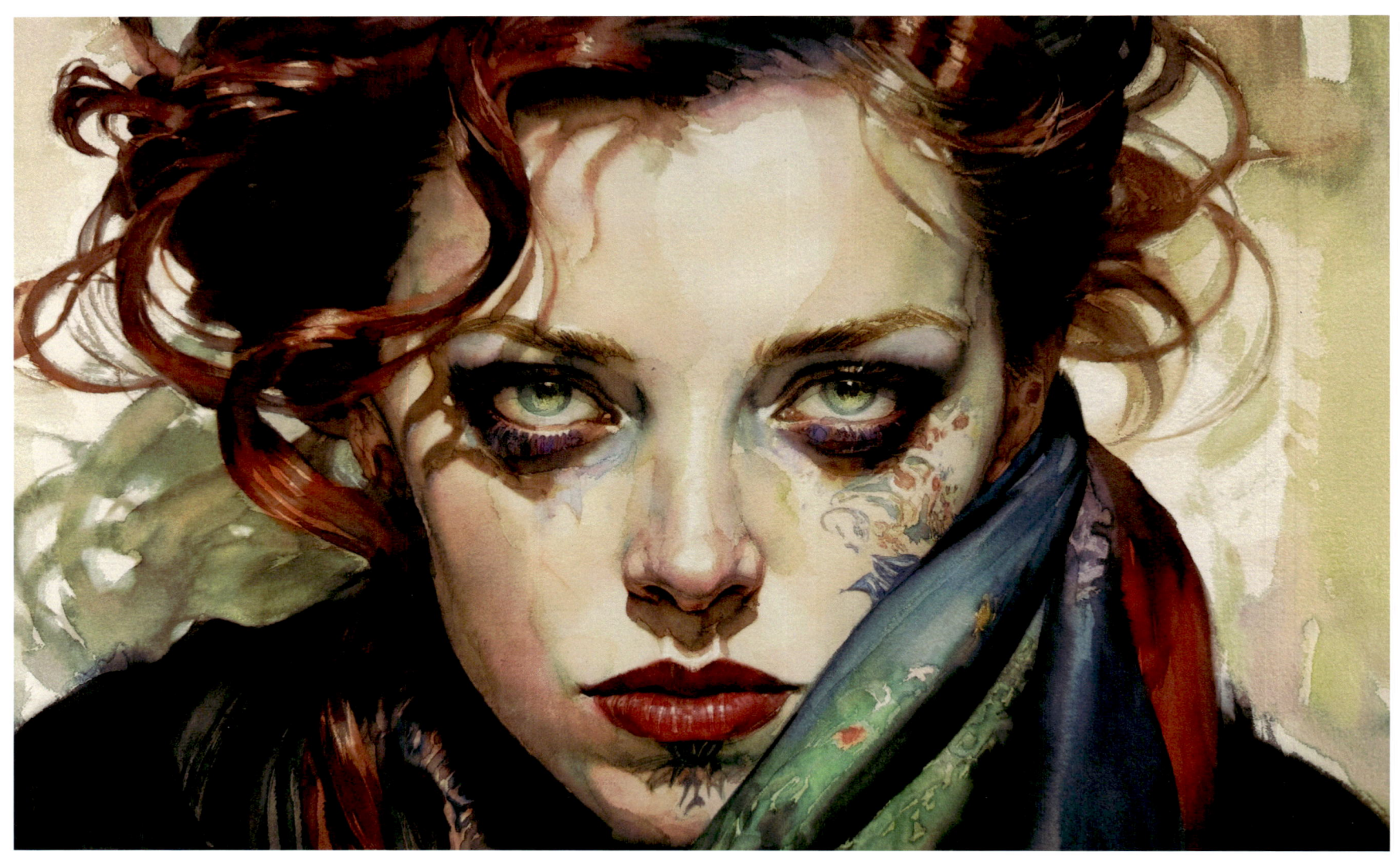

"Rome" | watercolor | 9.25" x 15" | Private Collection

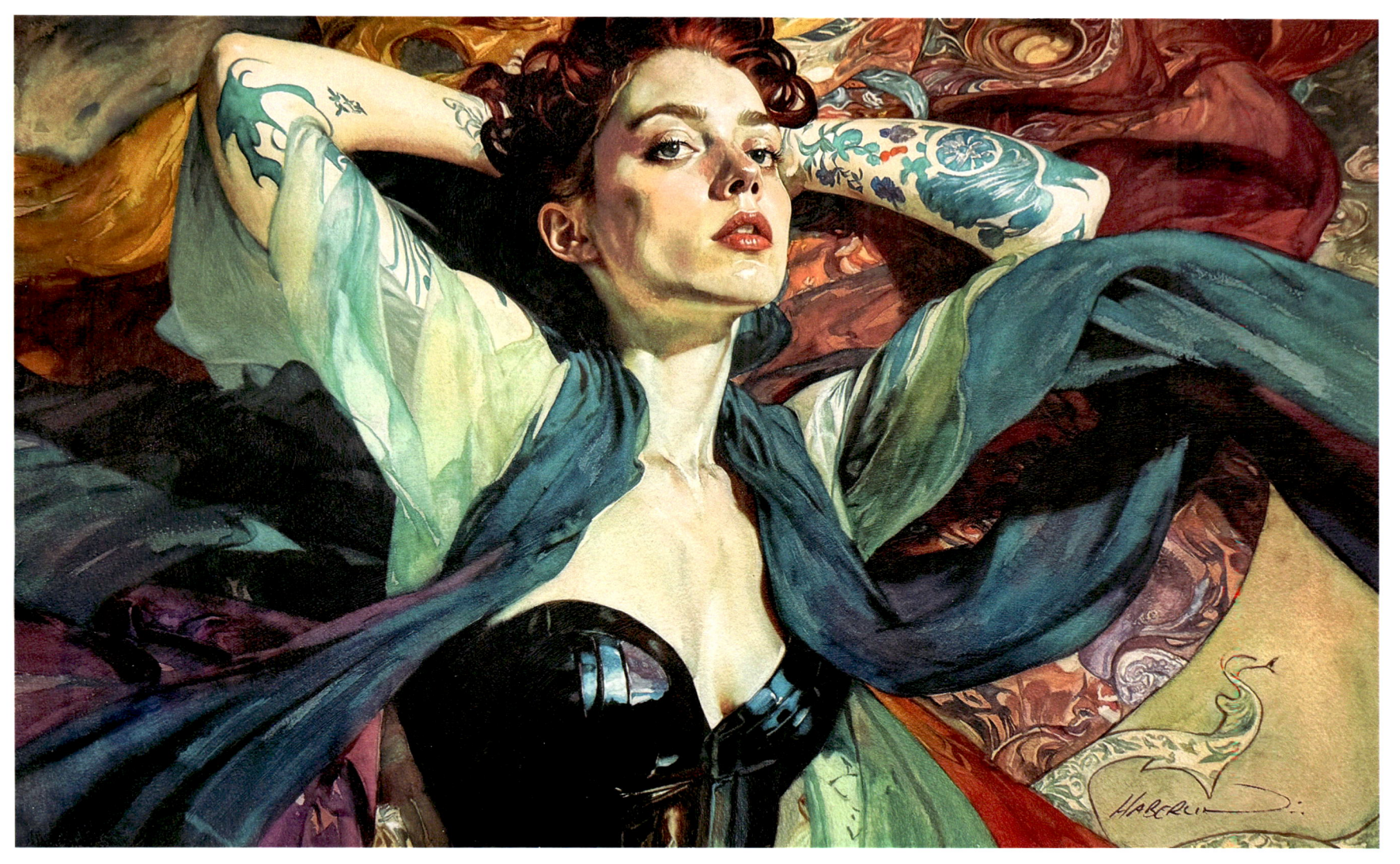

"Sorceress" | watercolor | 18" x 23"

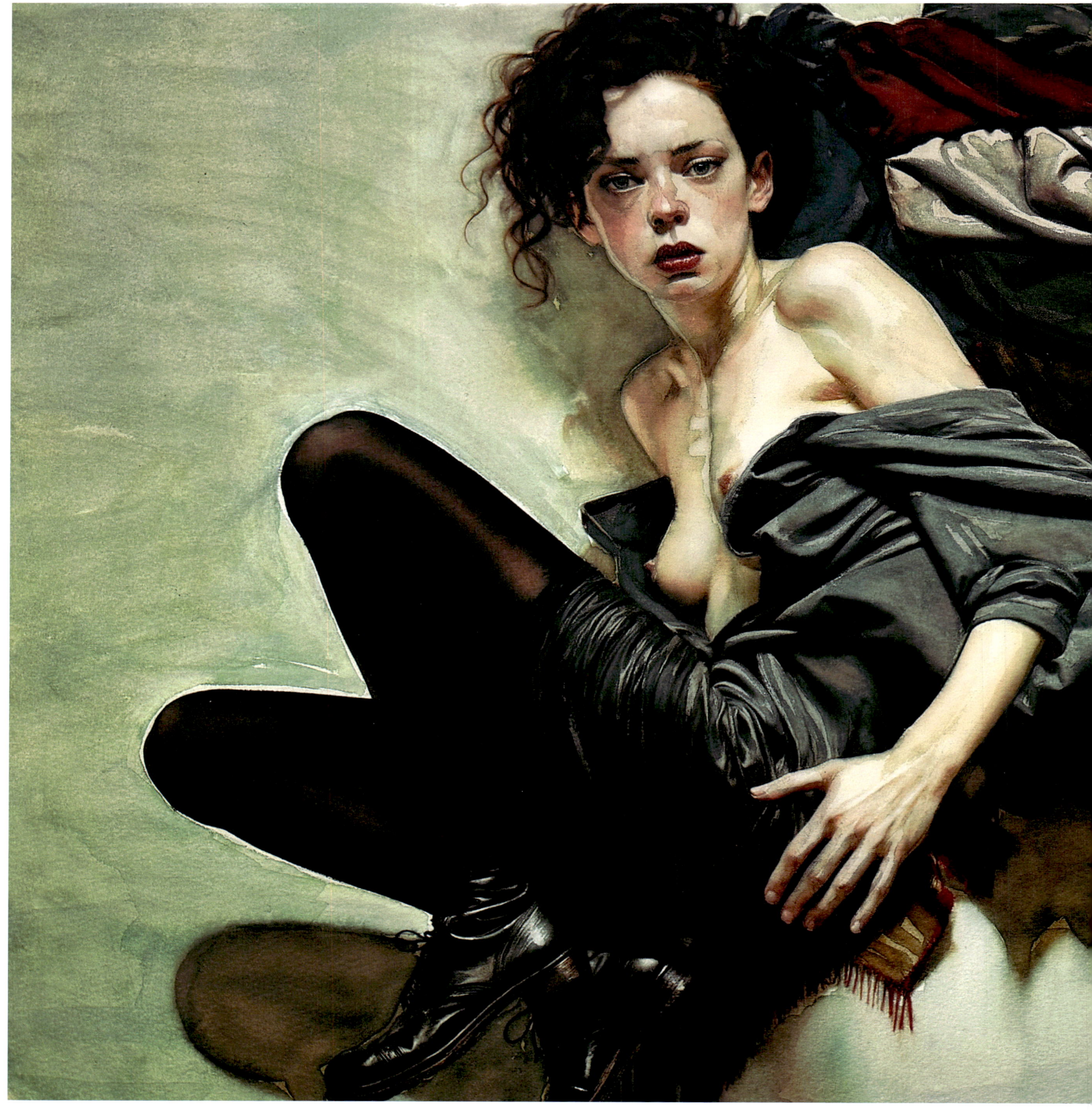

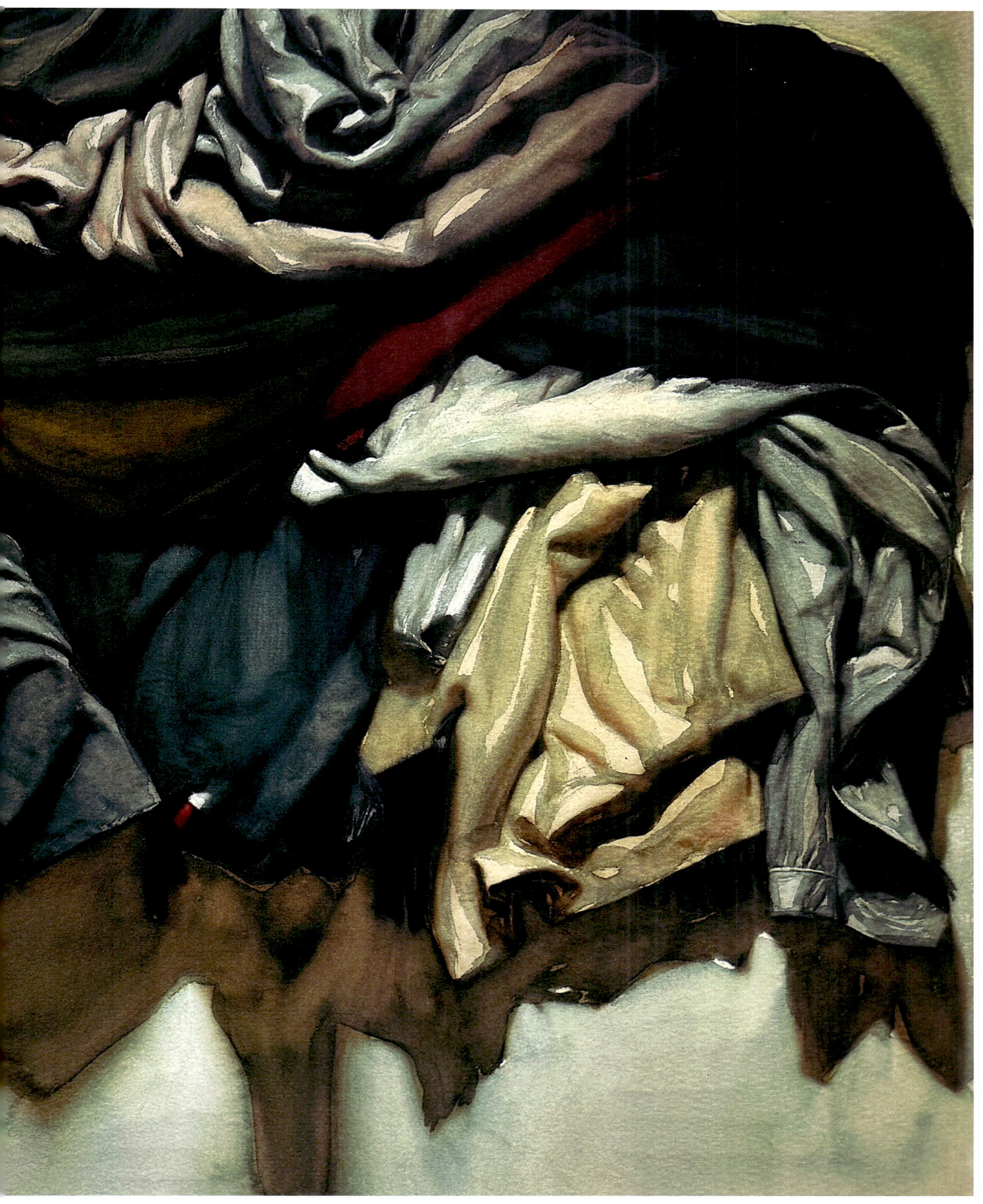

"Unraveled" | watercolor | 12" x 22"

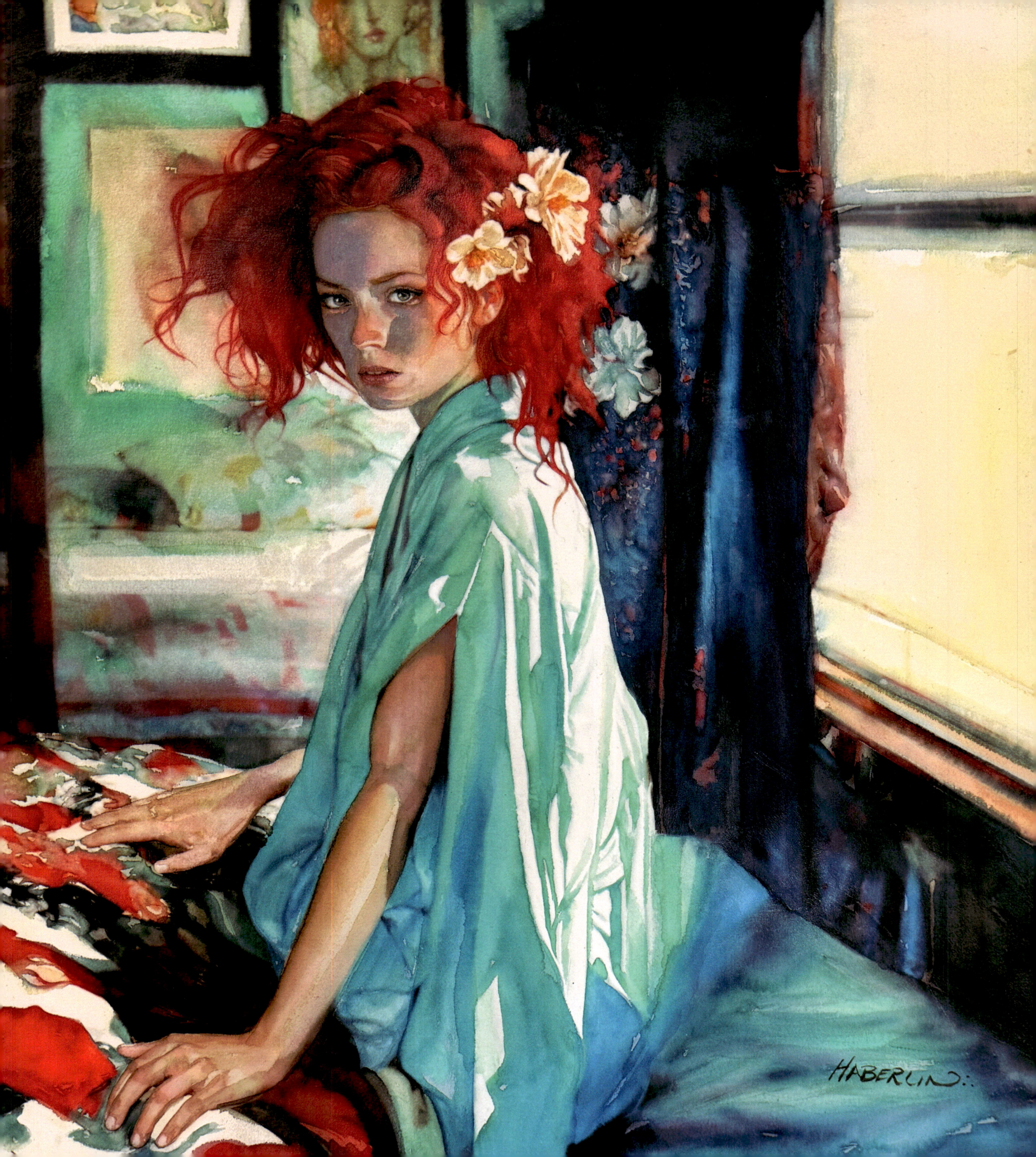

REDS

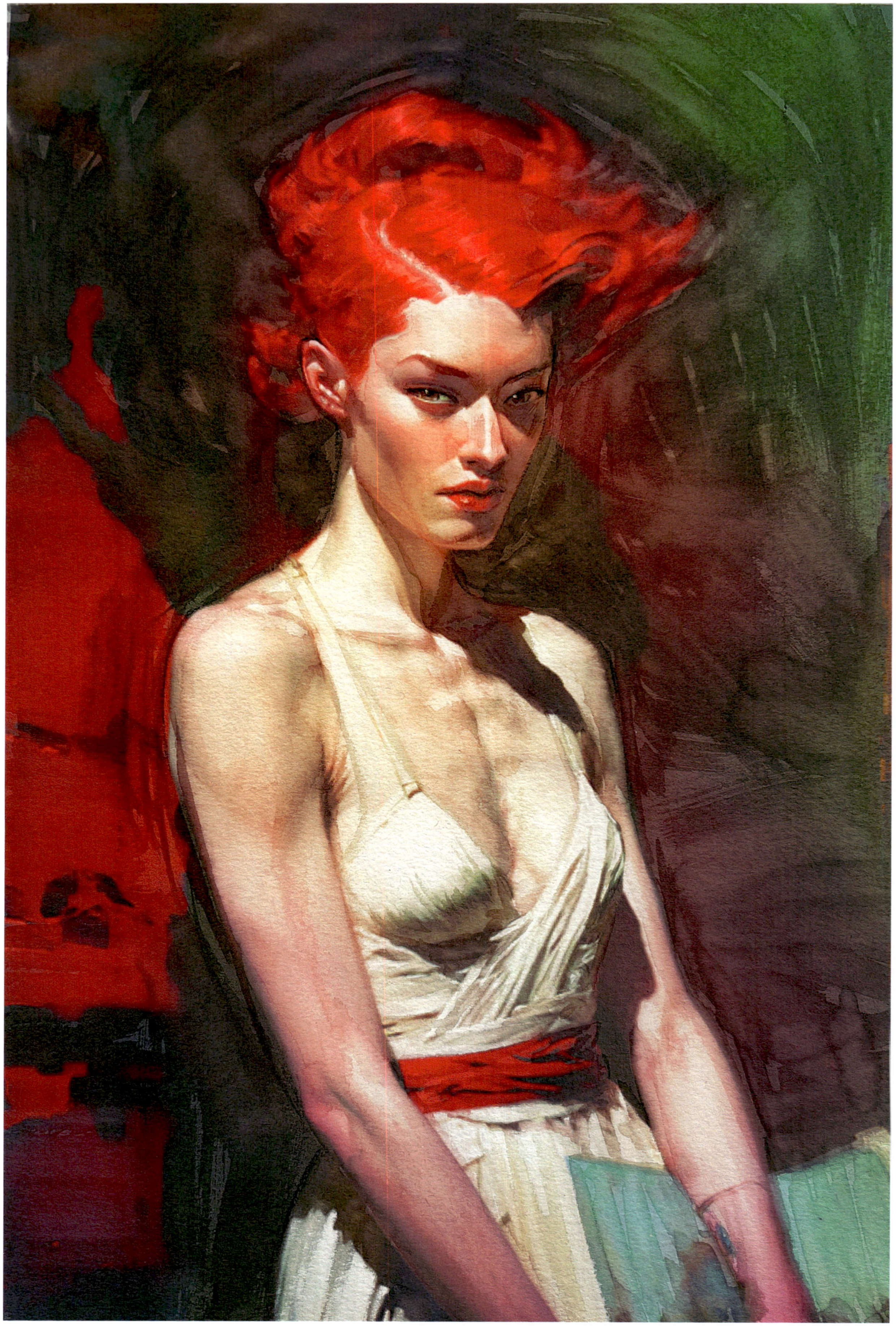

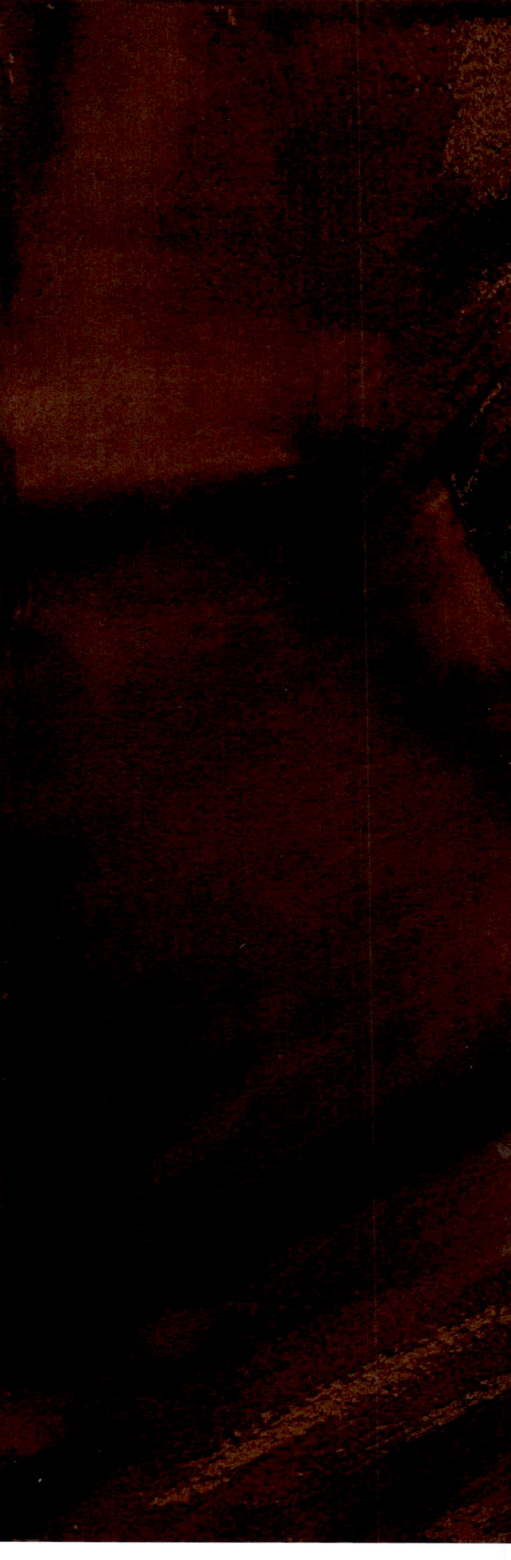

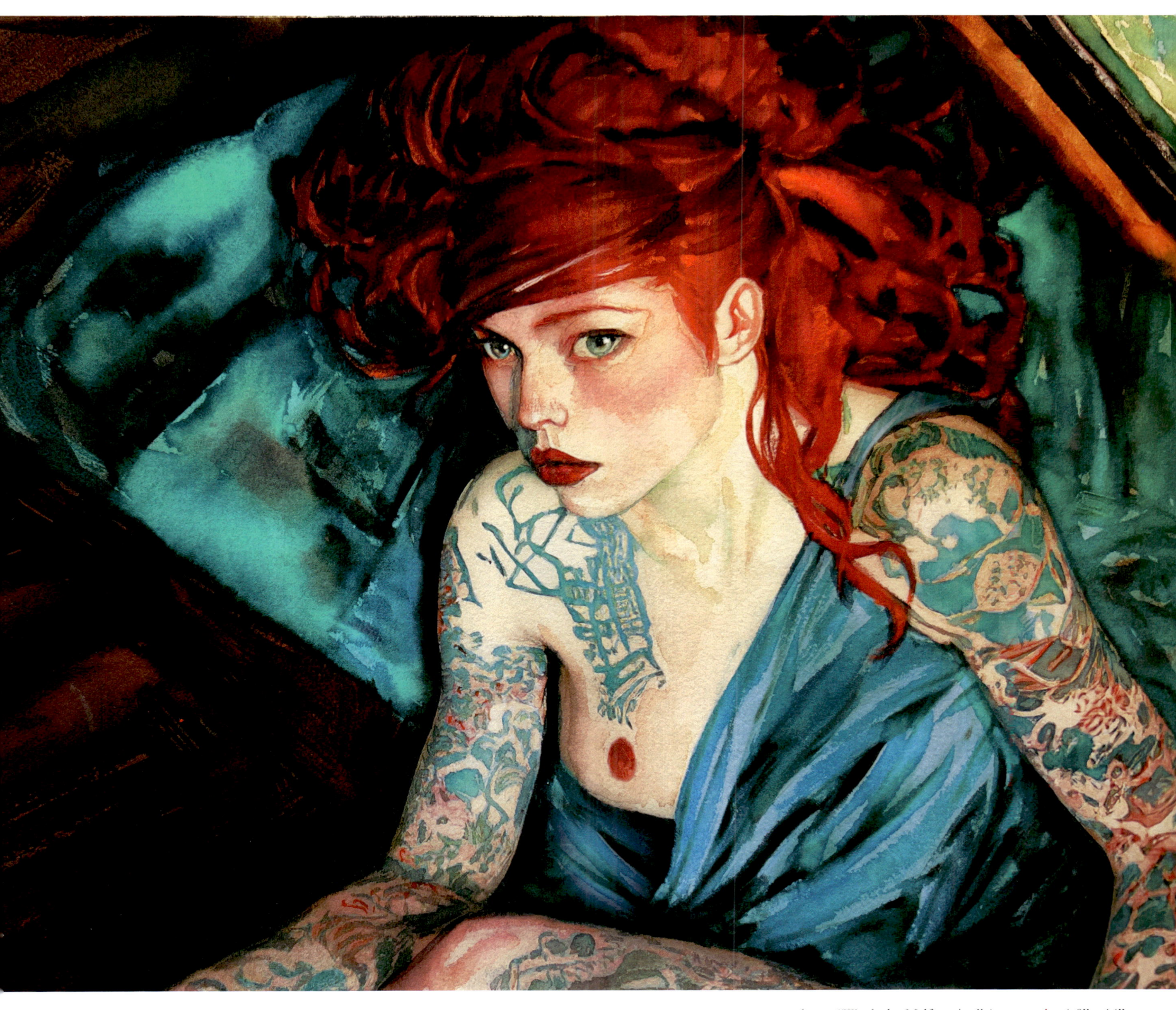

above: "Wardrobe Malfunction" | watercolor | 8" x 14"
opposite: "Selene" | watercolor | 12" x 8"
previous spread: "Peaches" | watercolor | 18" x 18" | Private Collection

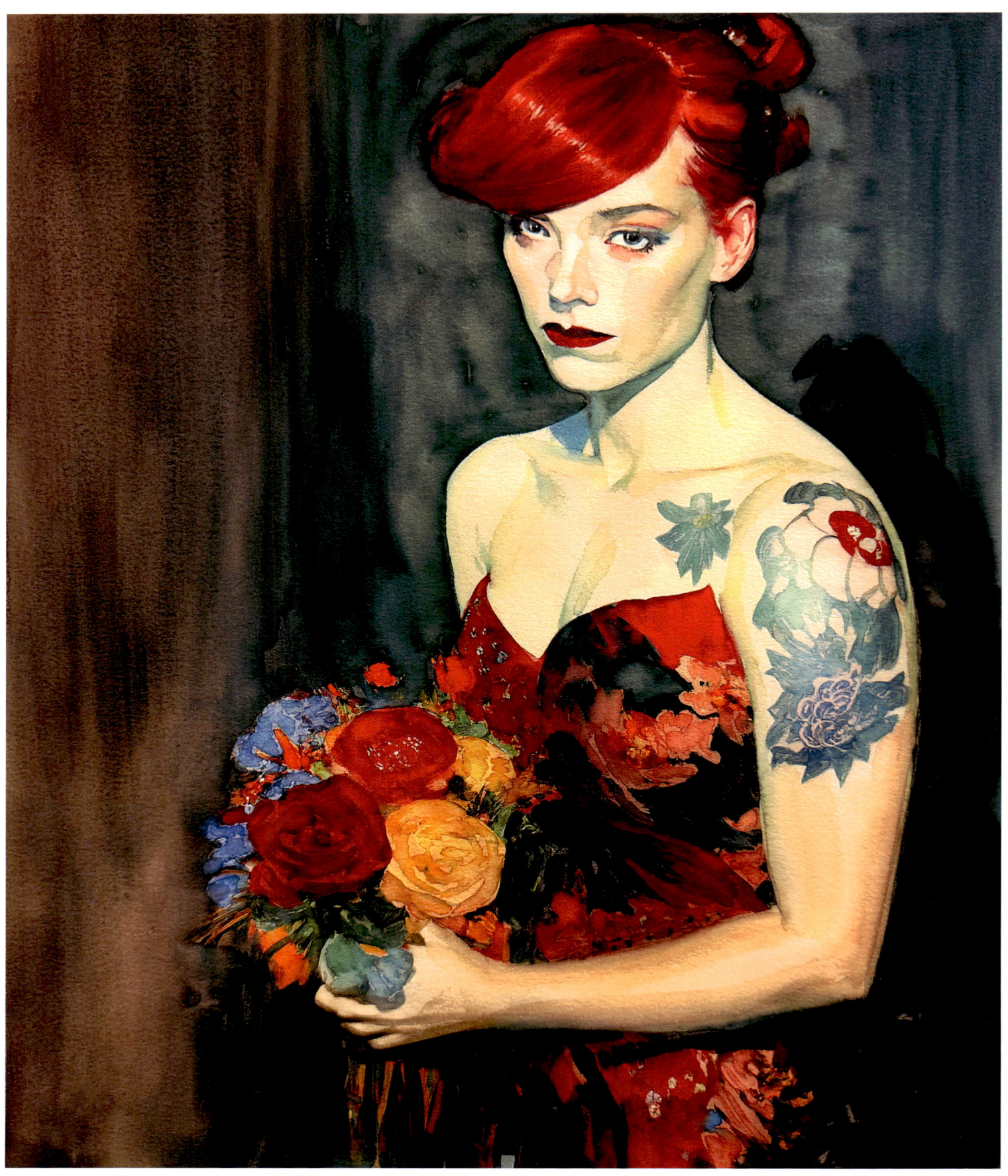

above: "Bouquet" | watercolor | 12" x 8"
opposite: "Just Flowers?" | watercolor | 14" x 9"

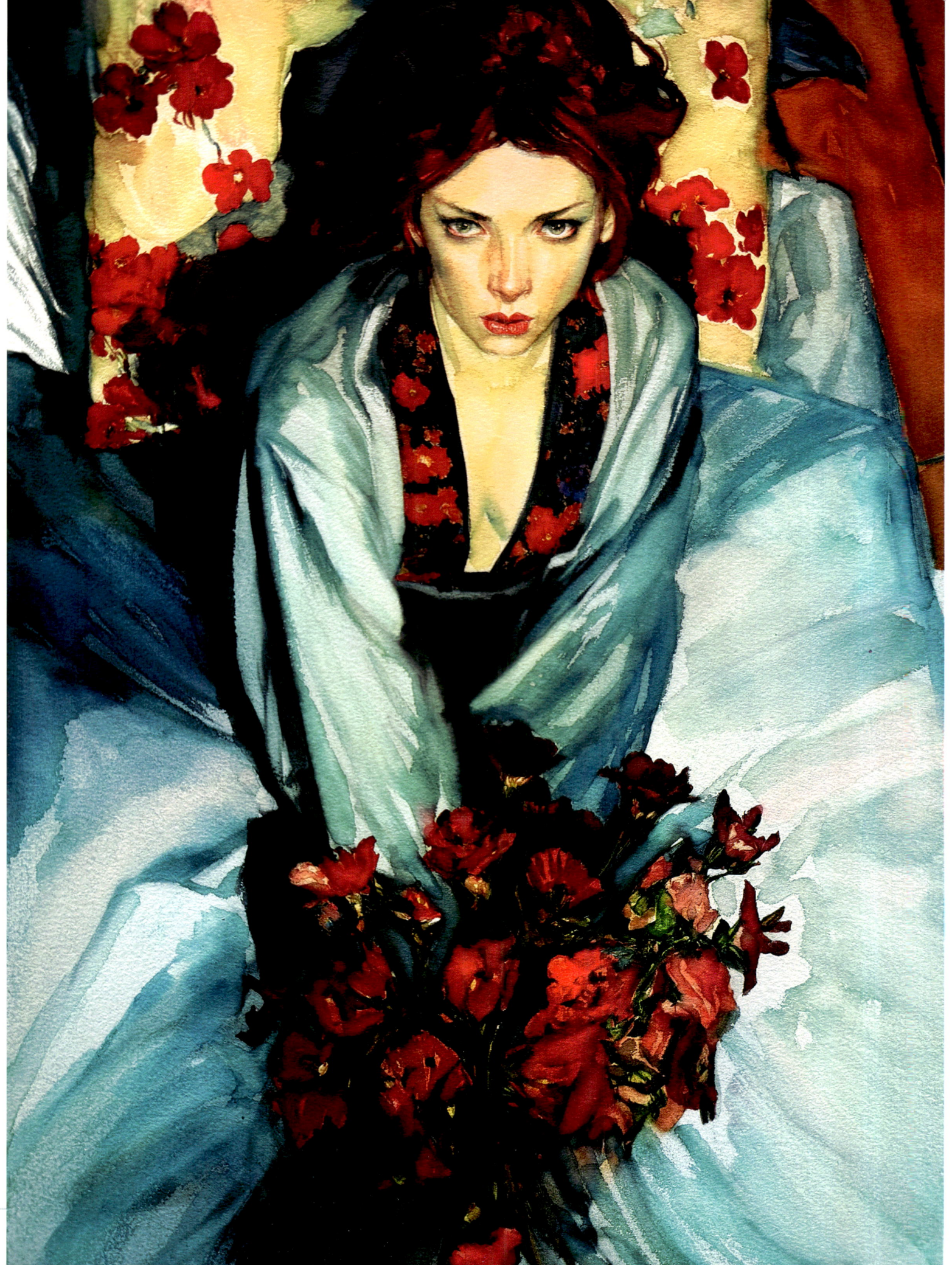

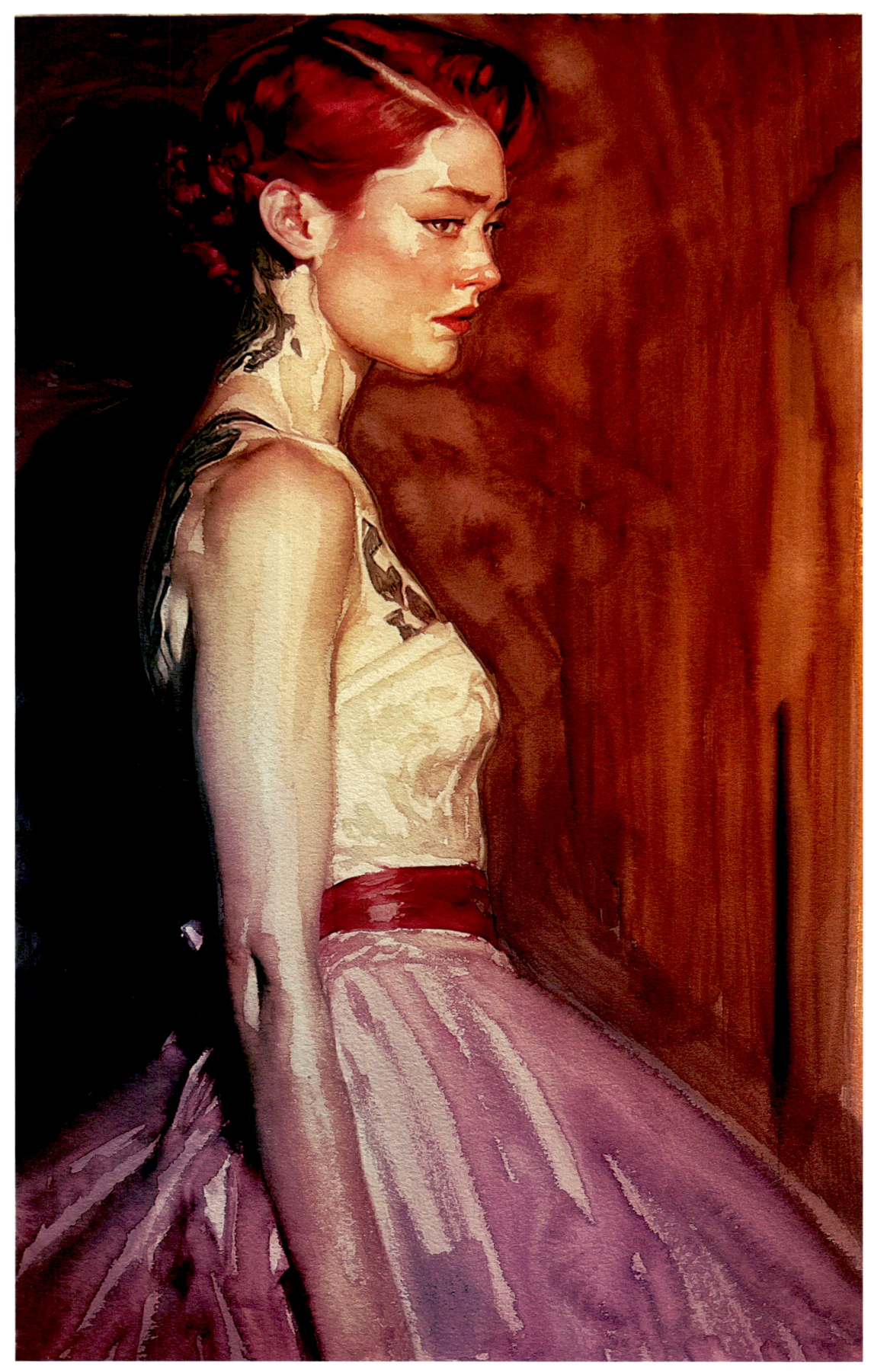

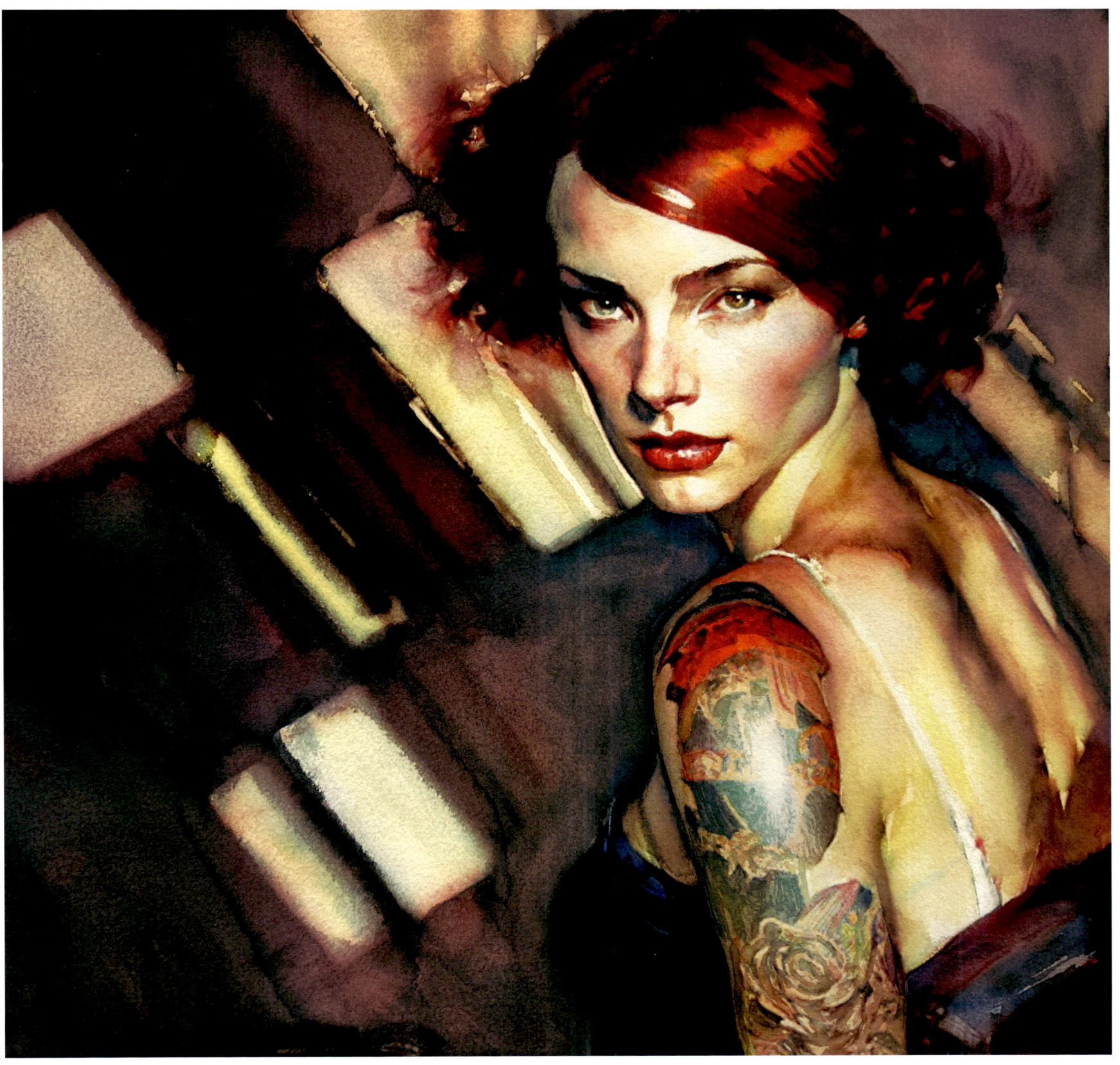

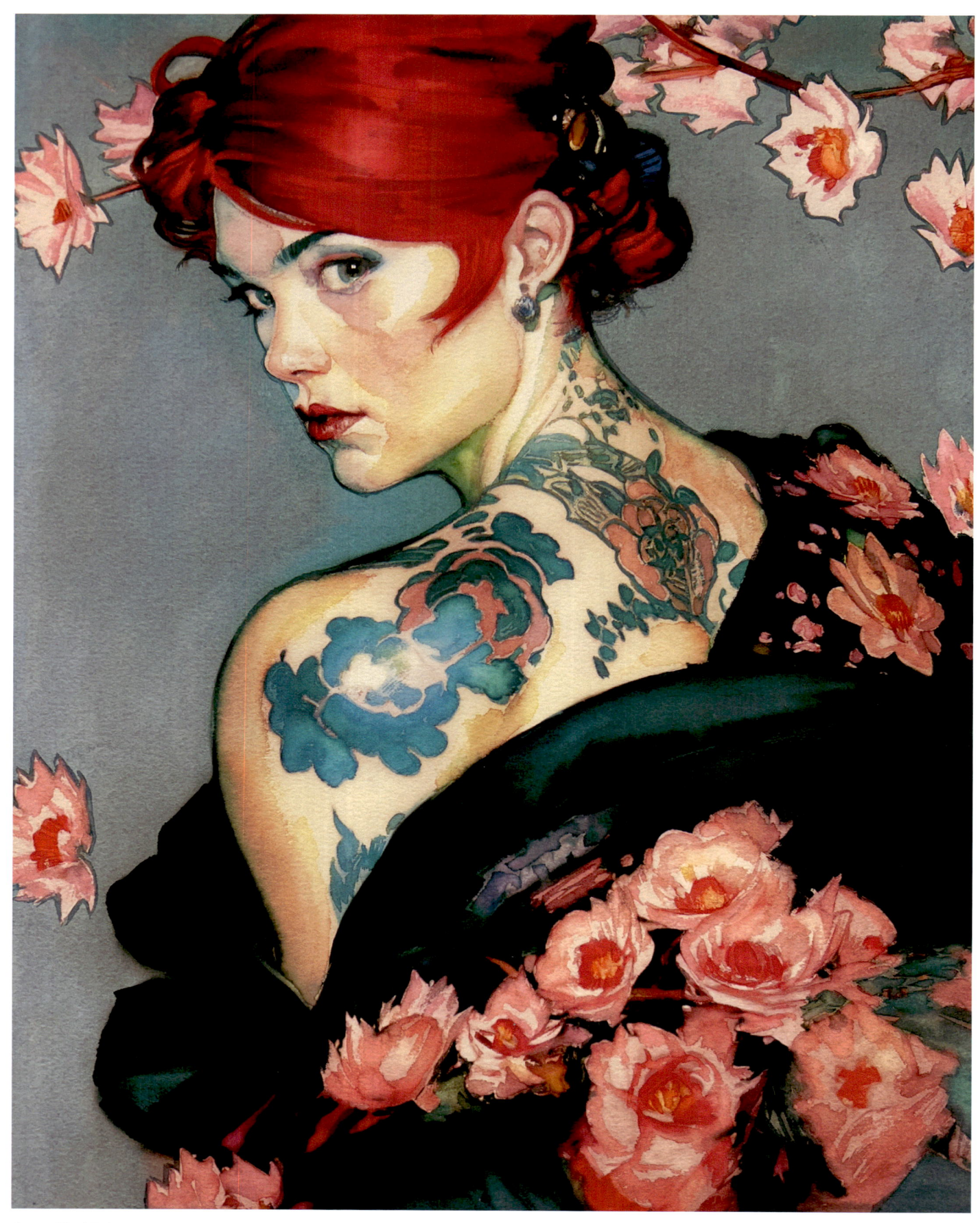

above: "And Who are You?" | watercolor | 13" x 10" | Private Collection
opposite: "Wilma" | watercolor | 10.5" x 10" | Private Collection

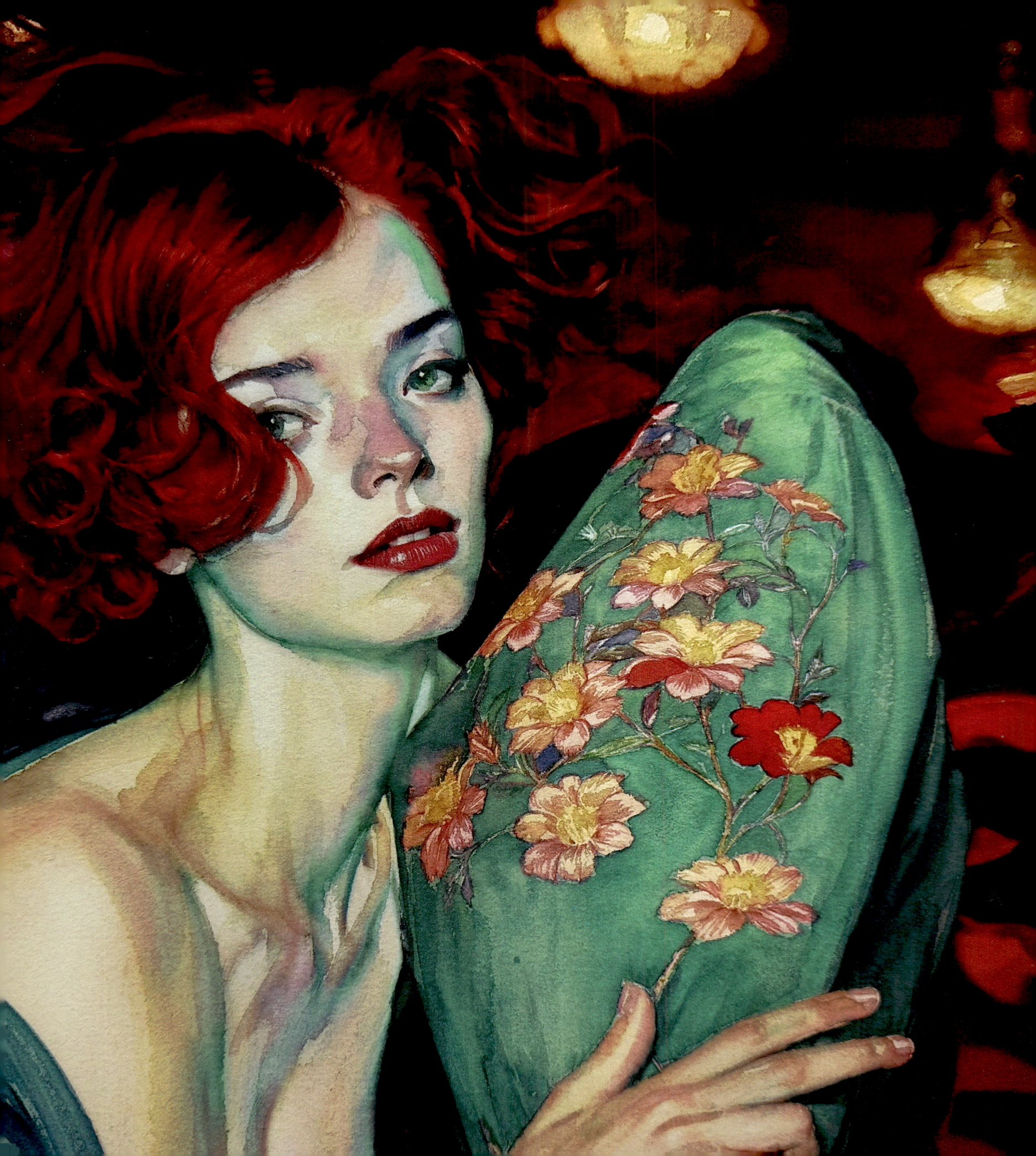

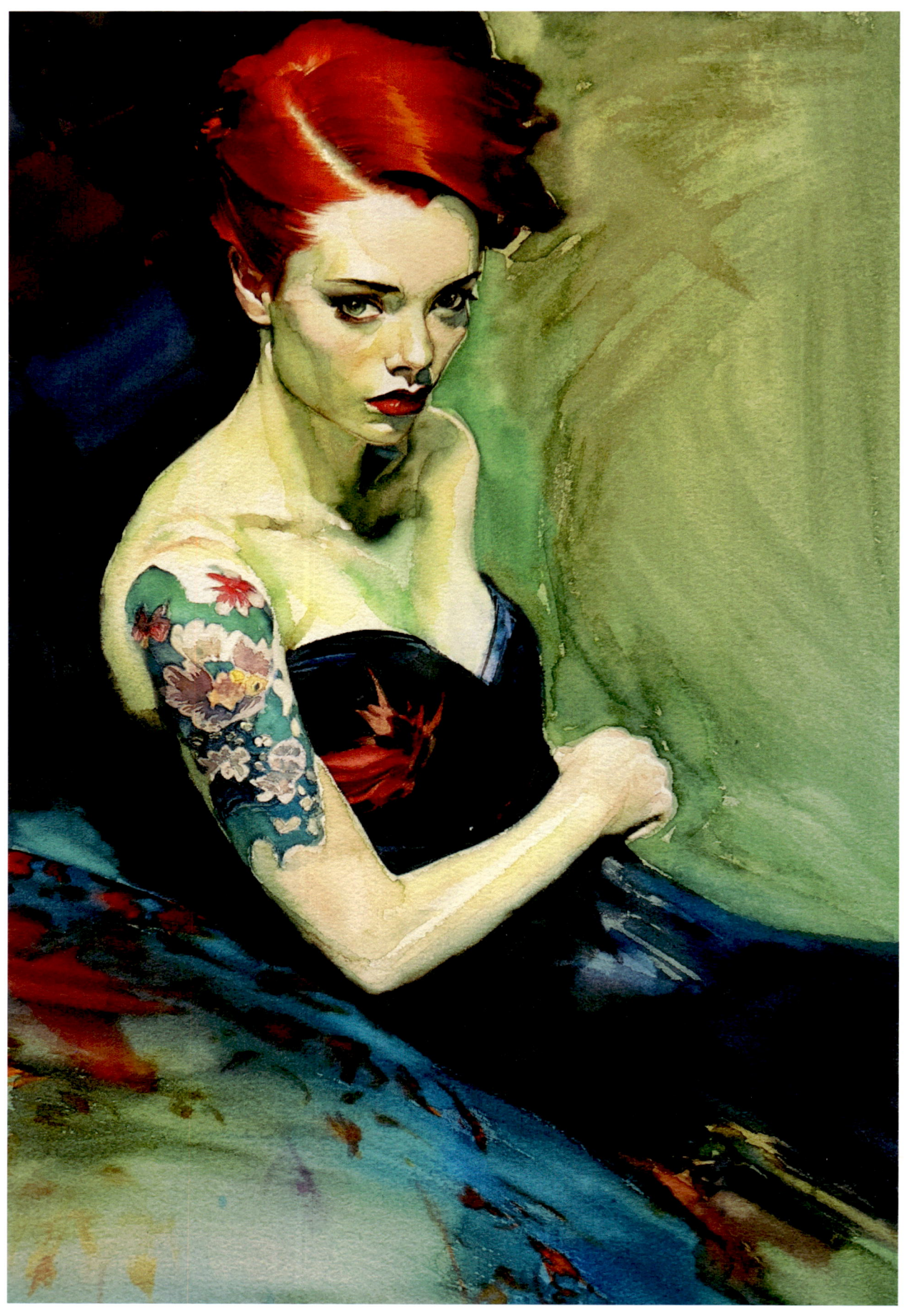

below: "Perfumer" | watercolor | 12" x 12"
opposite: "Jill" | watercolor | 14" x 8" | Private Collection

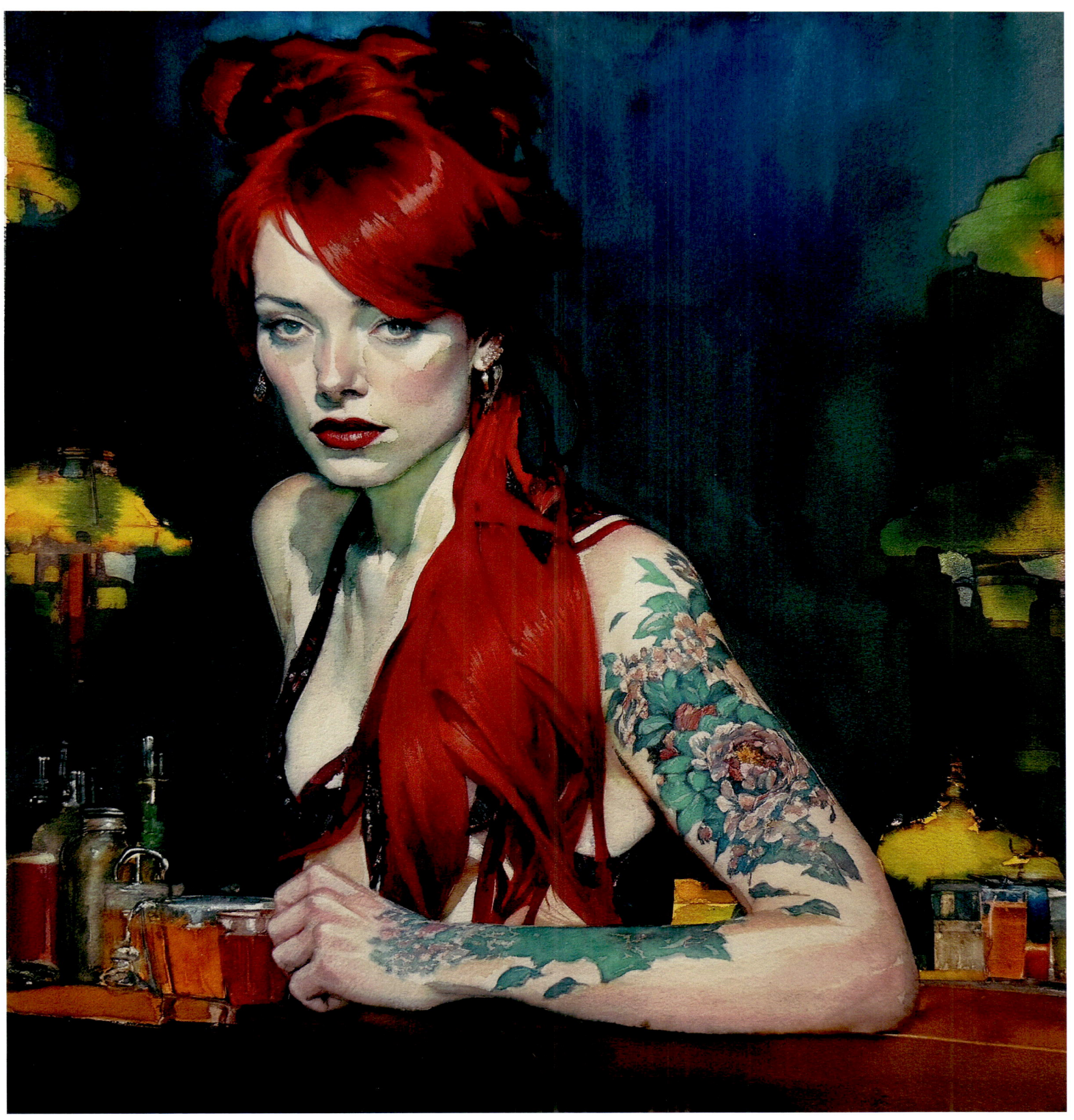

RIPPLES

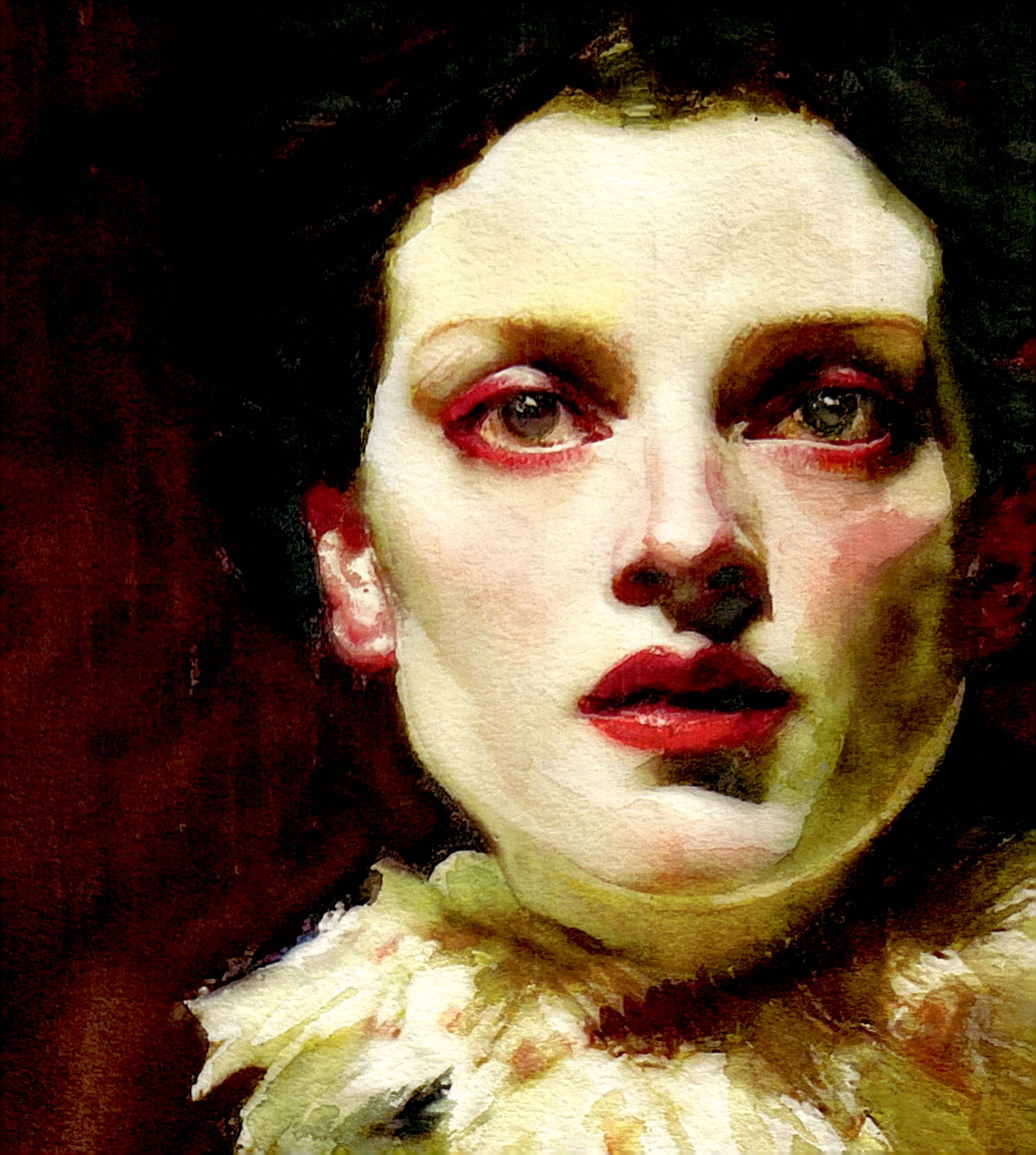

right: "Ruff" | watercolor | 13" x 8"
previous spread: "Ruff" *Detail*
opposite: "Sky" | watercolor | 9" x 6" | Private Collection

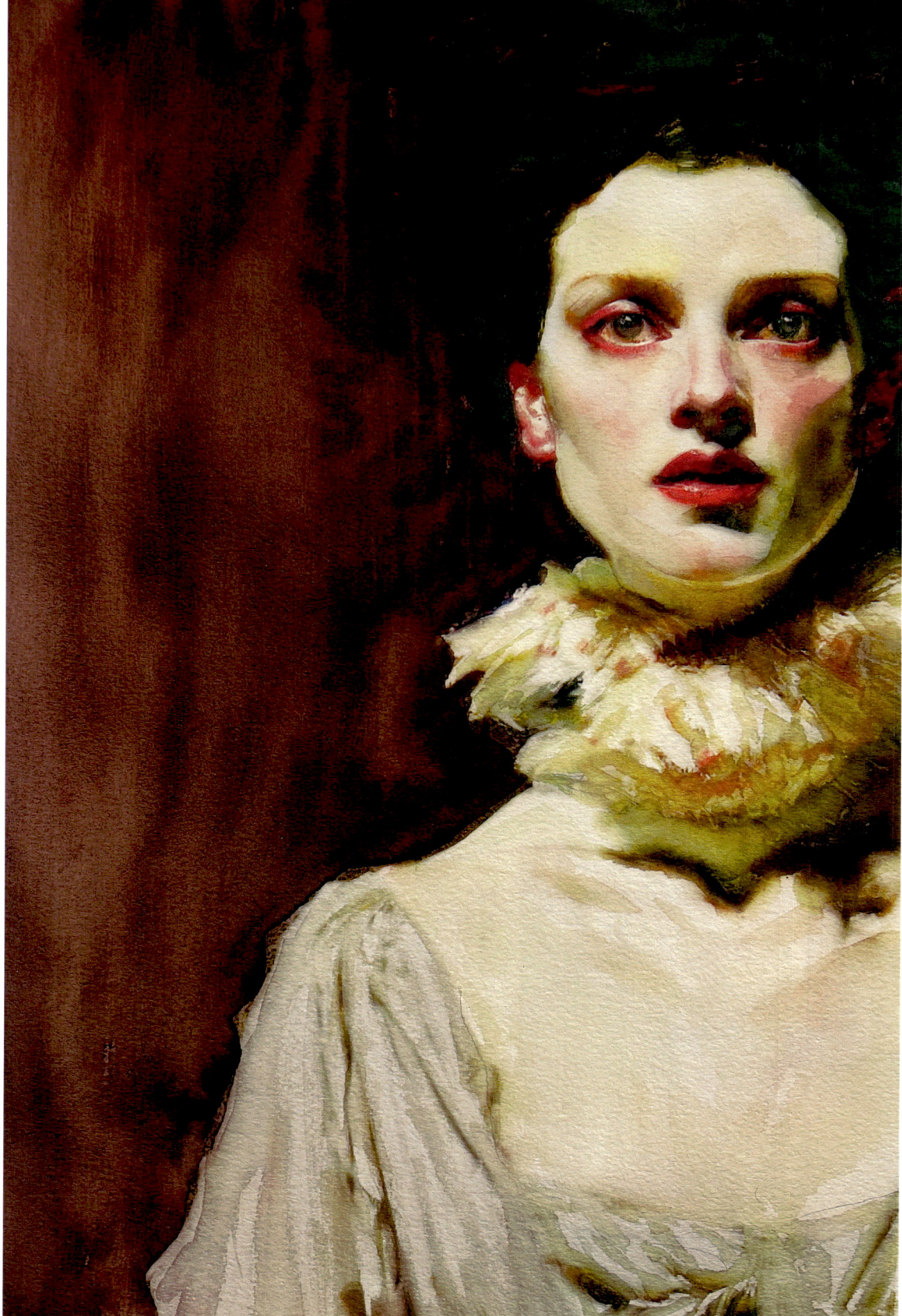

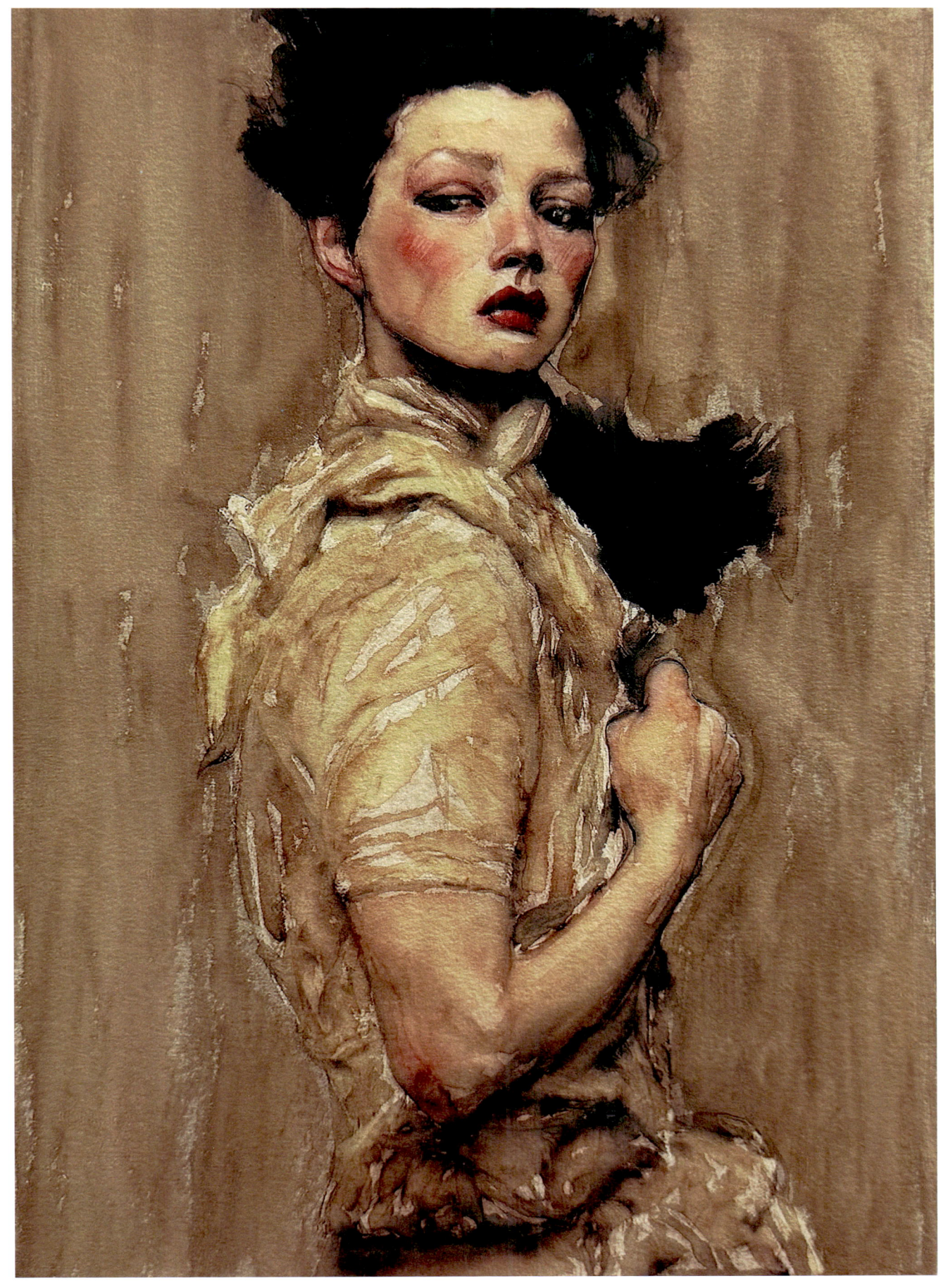

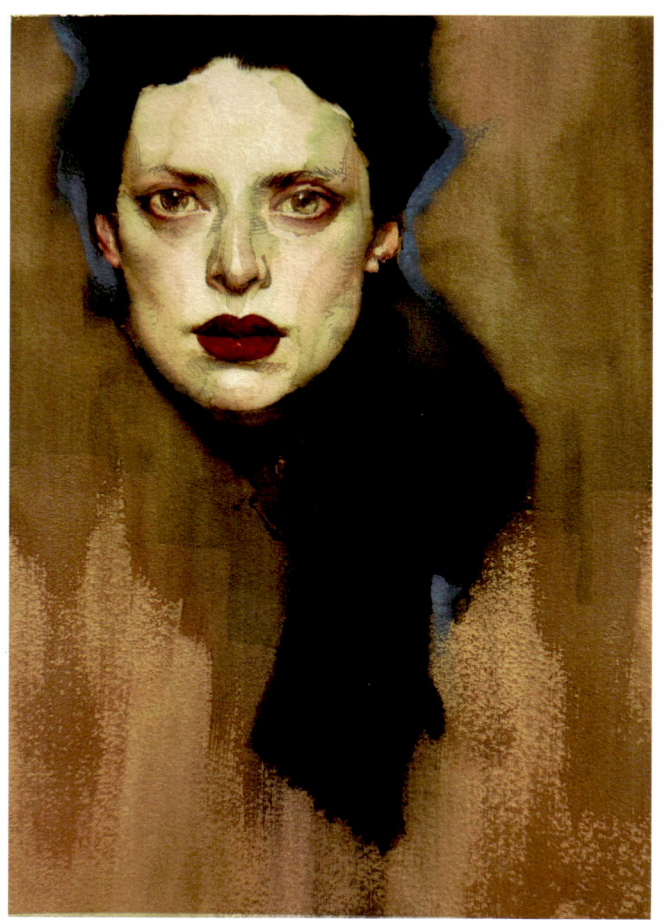

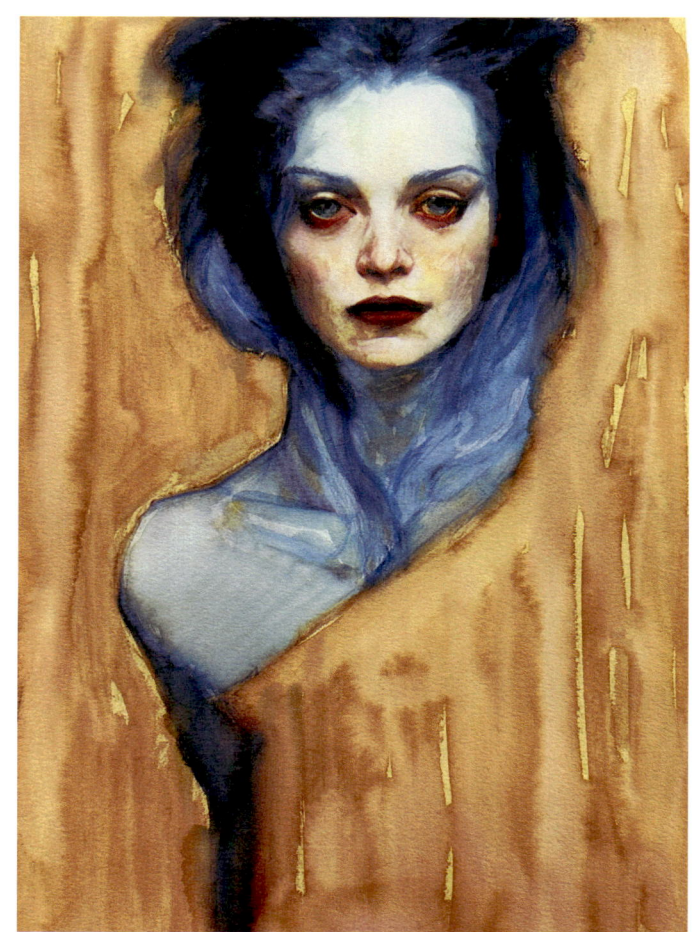

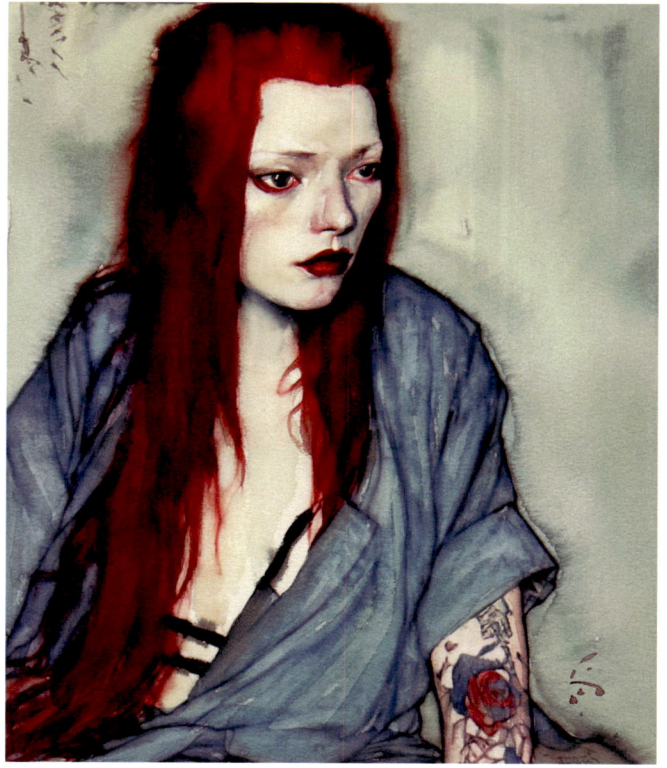

top left: *Study* | watercolor | 10" x 8"
top right: "Aqua" | watercolor   10" x 8" | Private Collection
left: "Robe" | watercolor | 8" x 6"
opposite: "Sheila" | oil on canvas | 24" x 18"

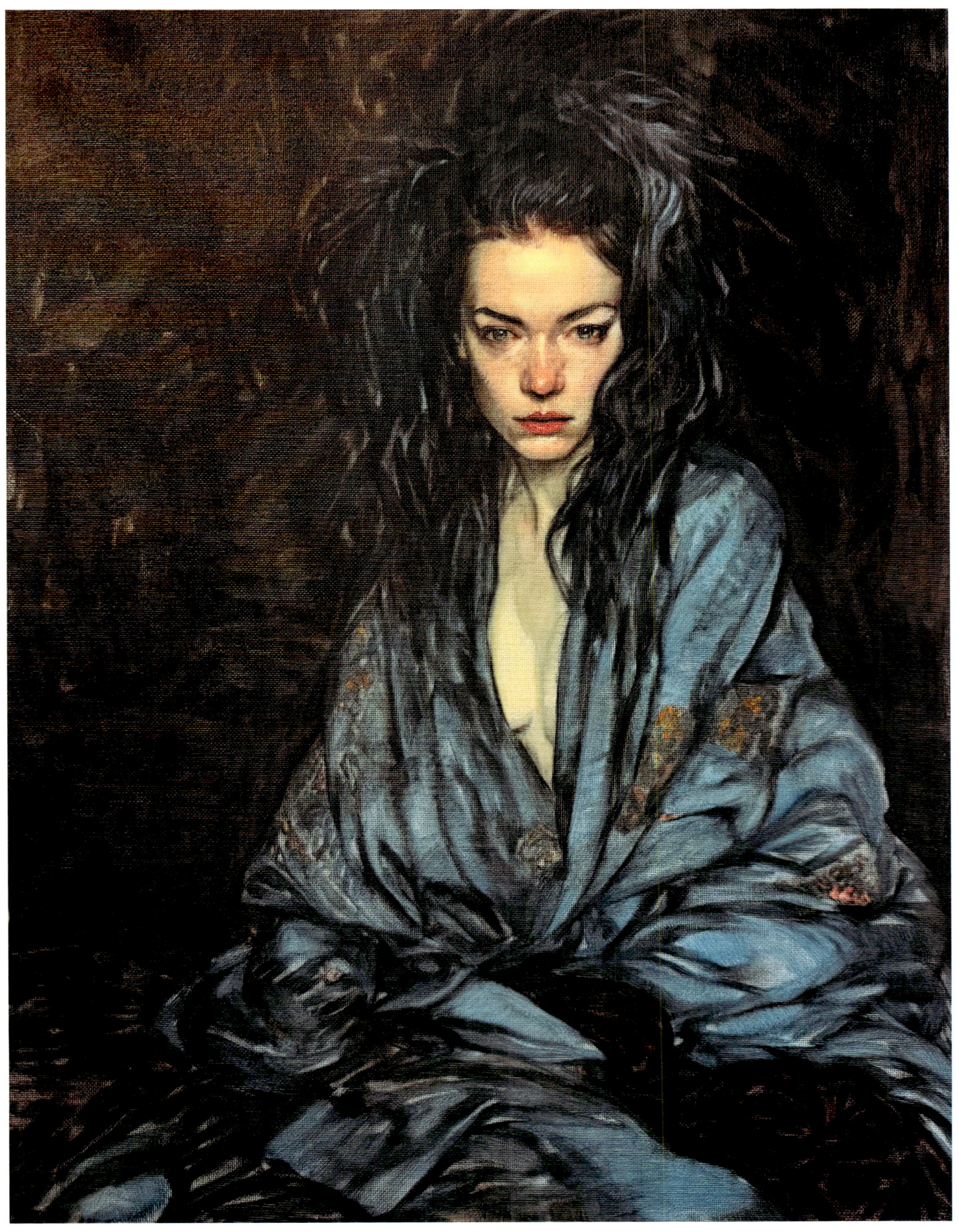

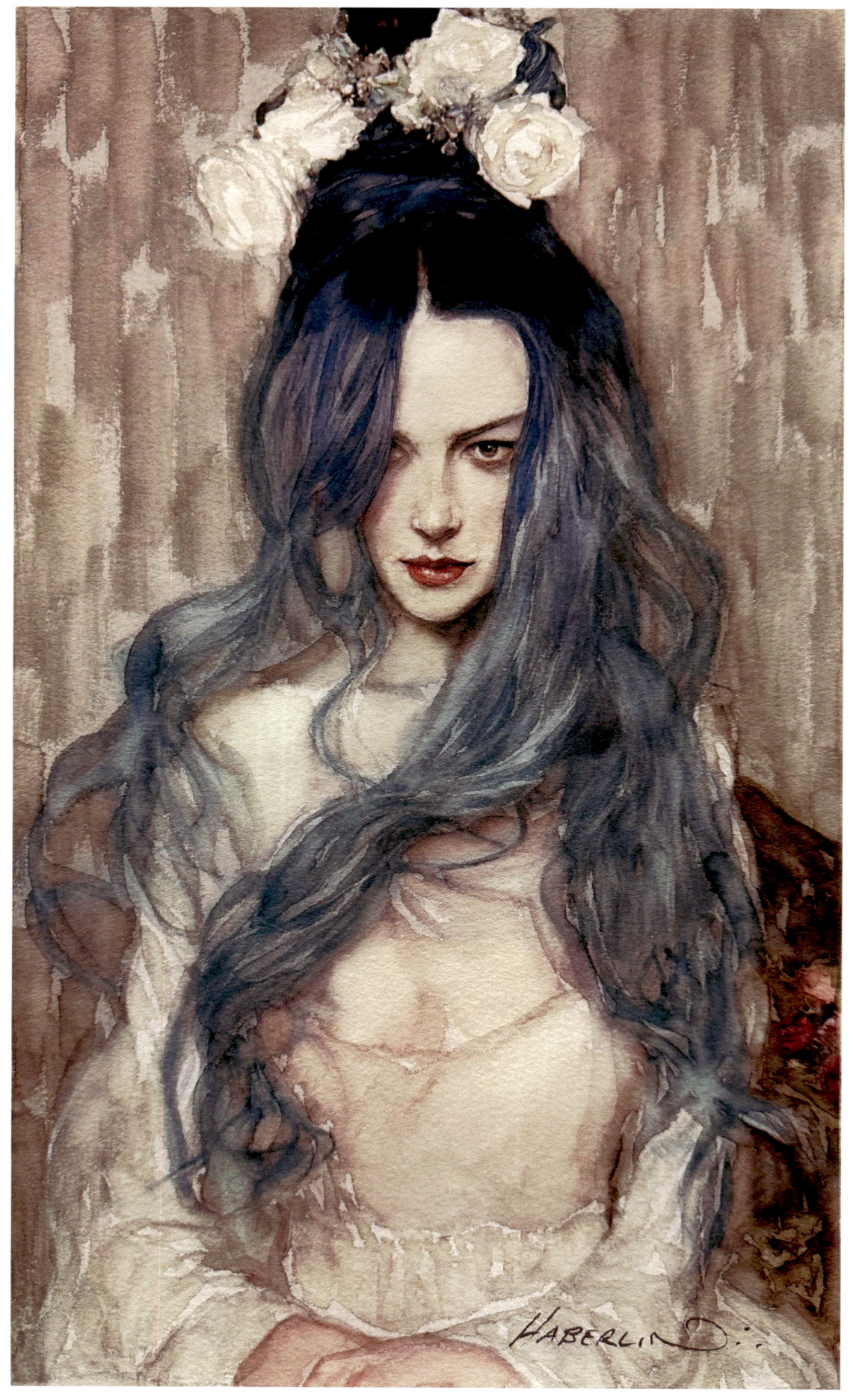

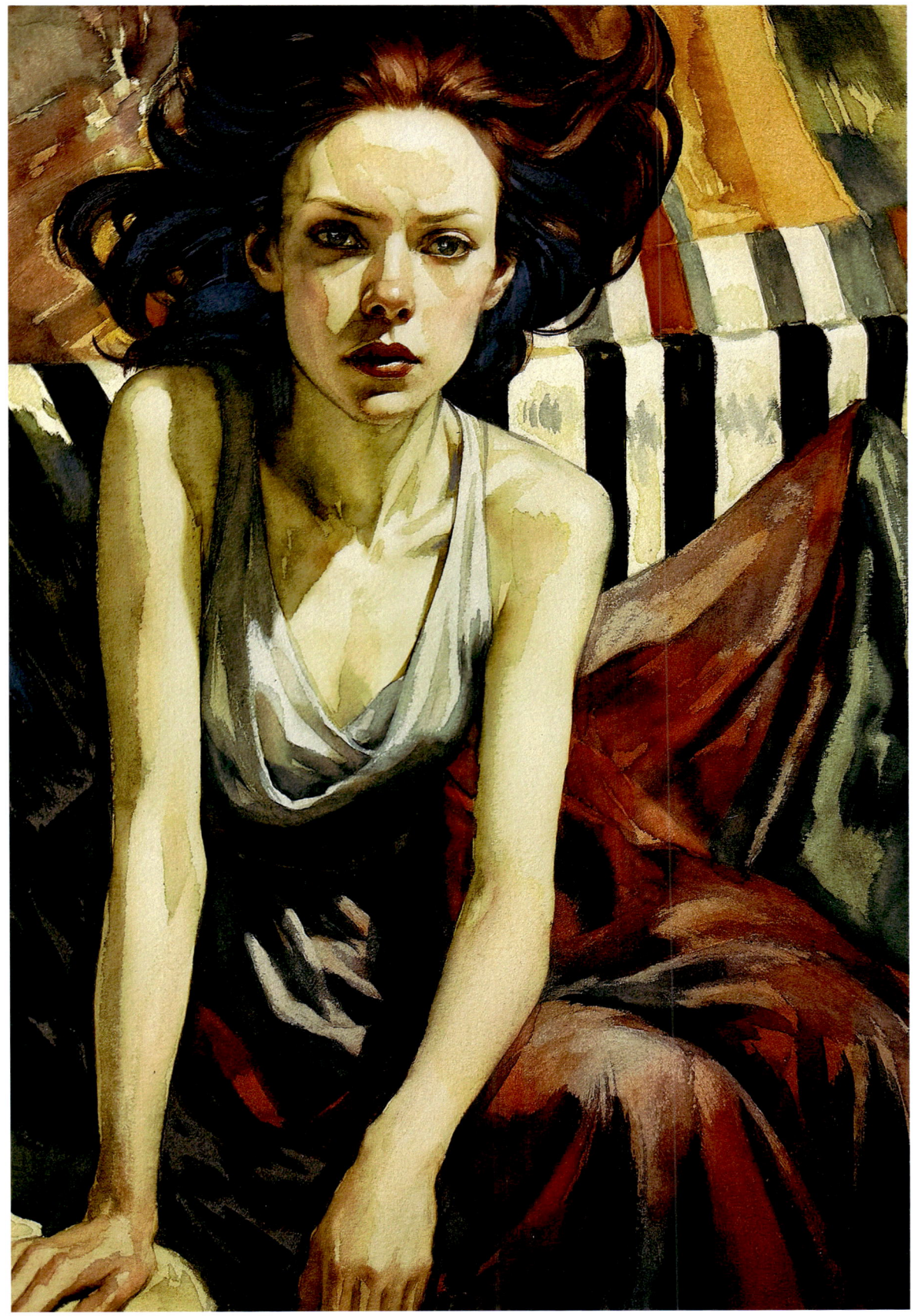

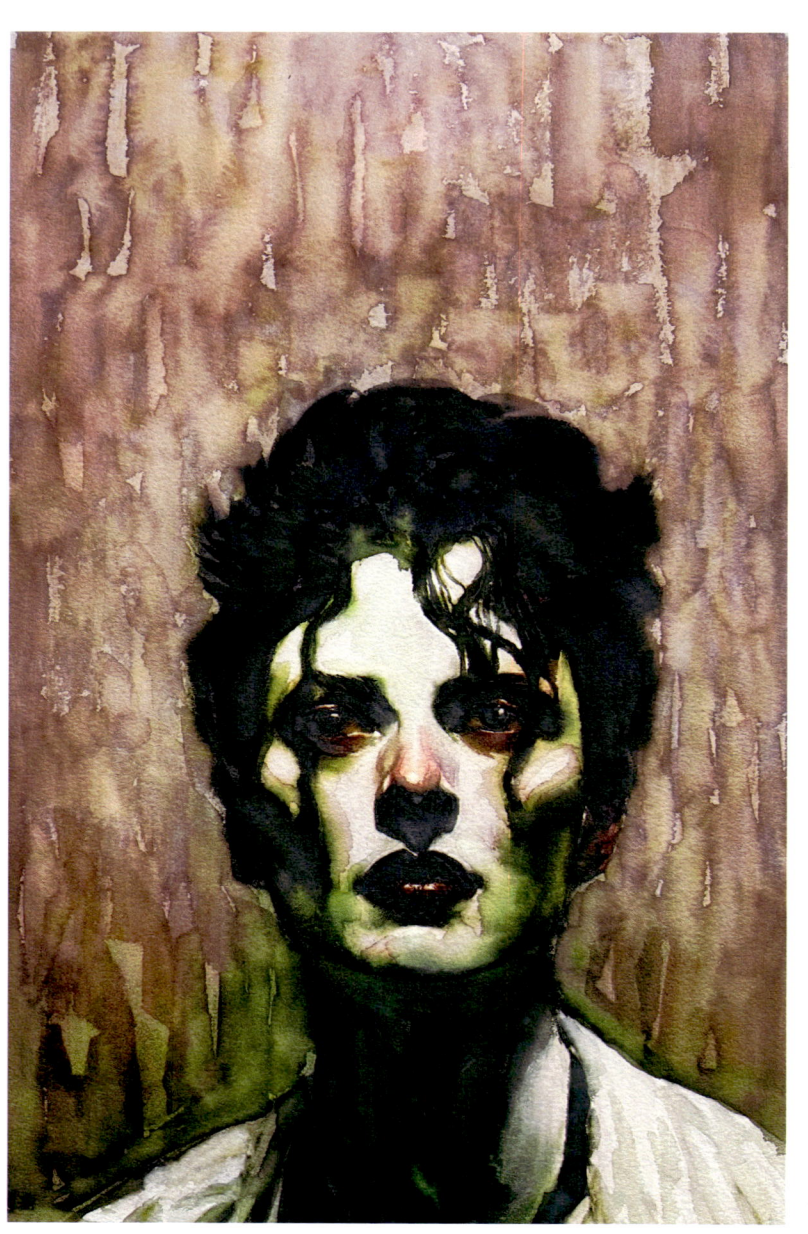

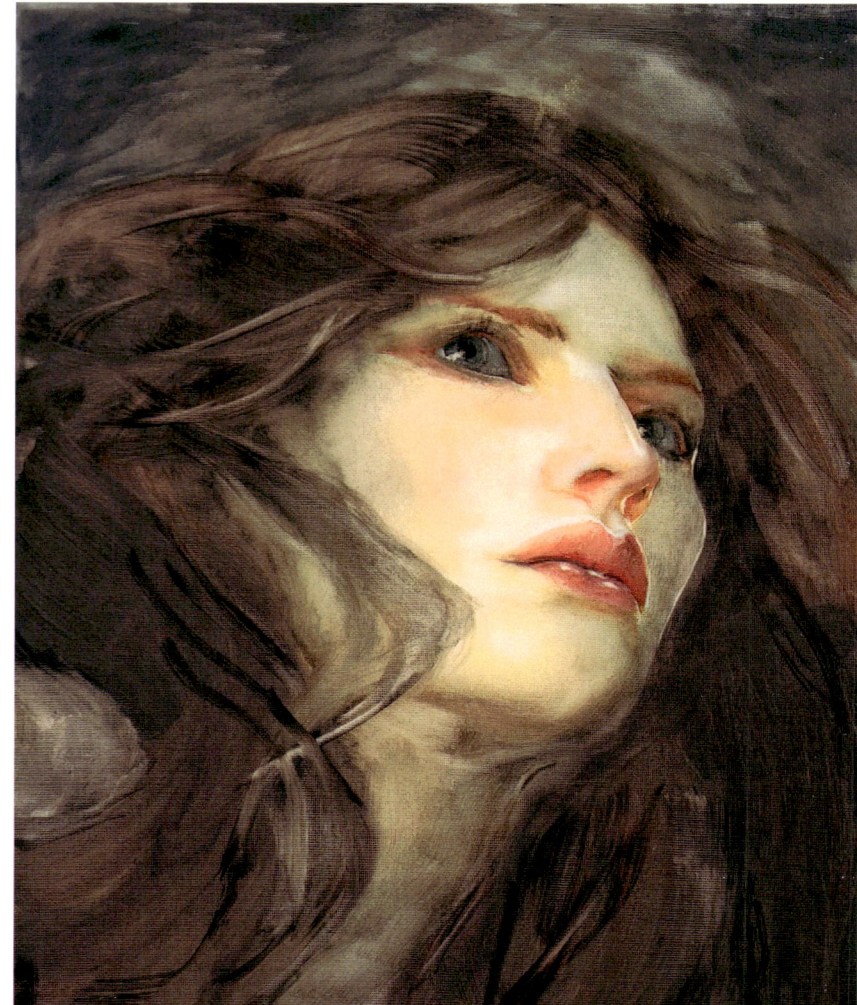

above left: "Stuck" | watercolor | 14" x 7"
above right: "Rosetti" | oil on canvas | 30" x 20"
opposite: "The Dark of Night" | watercolor | 13" x 7"

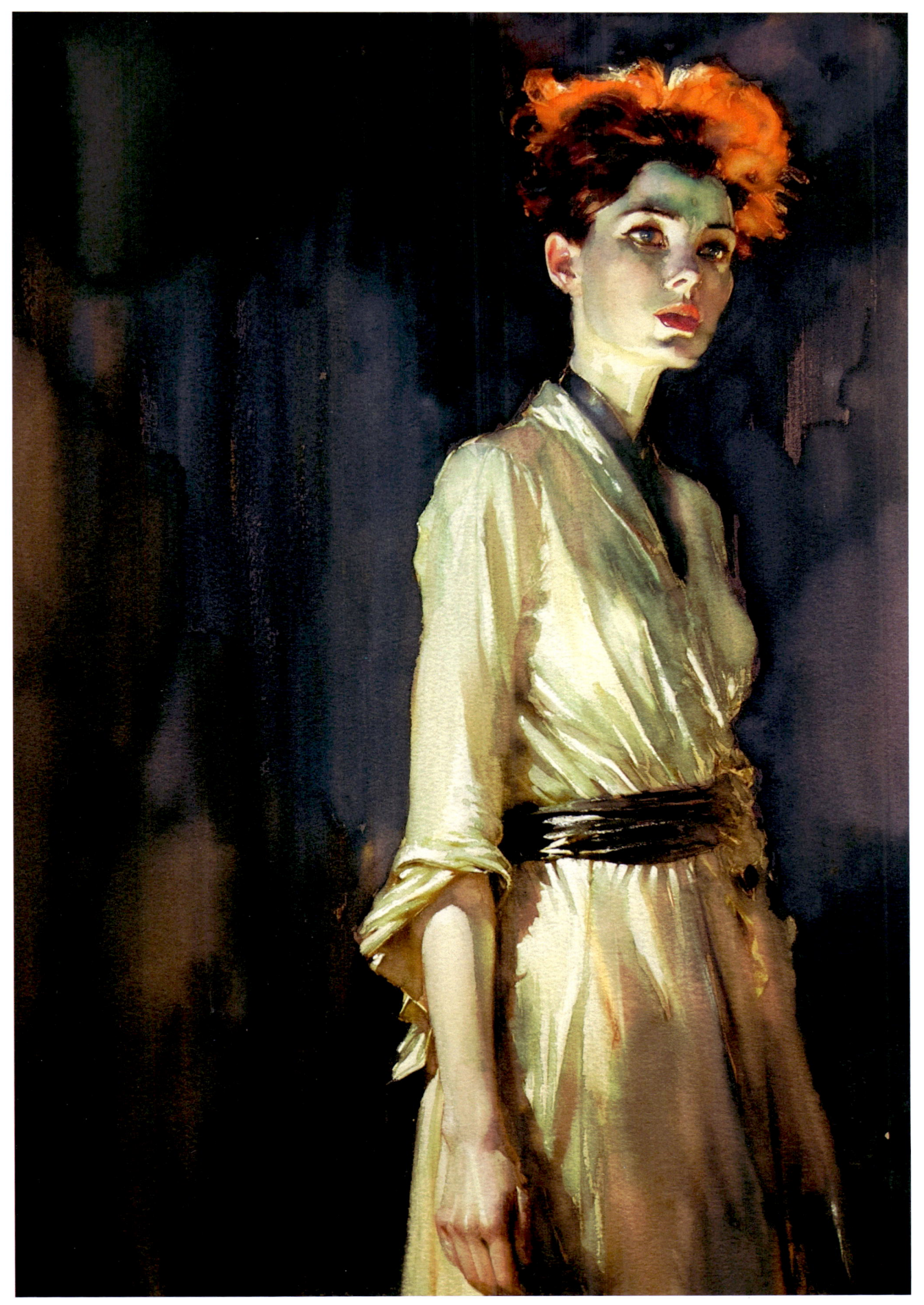

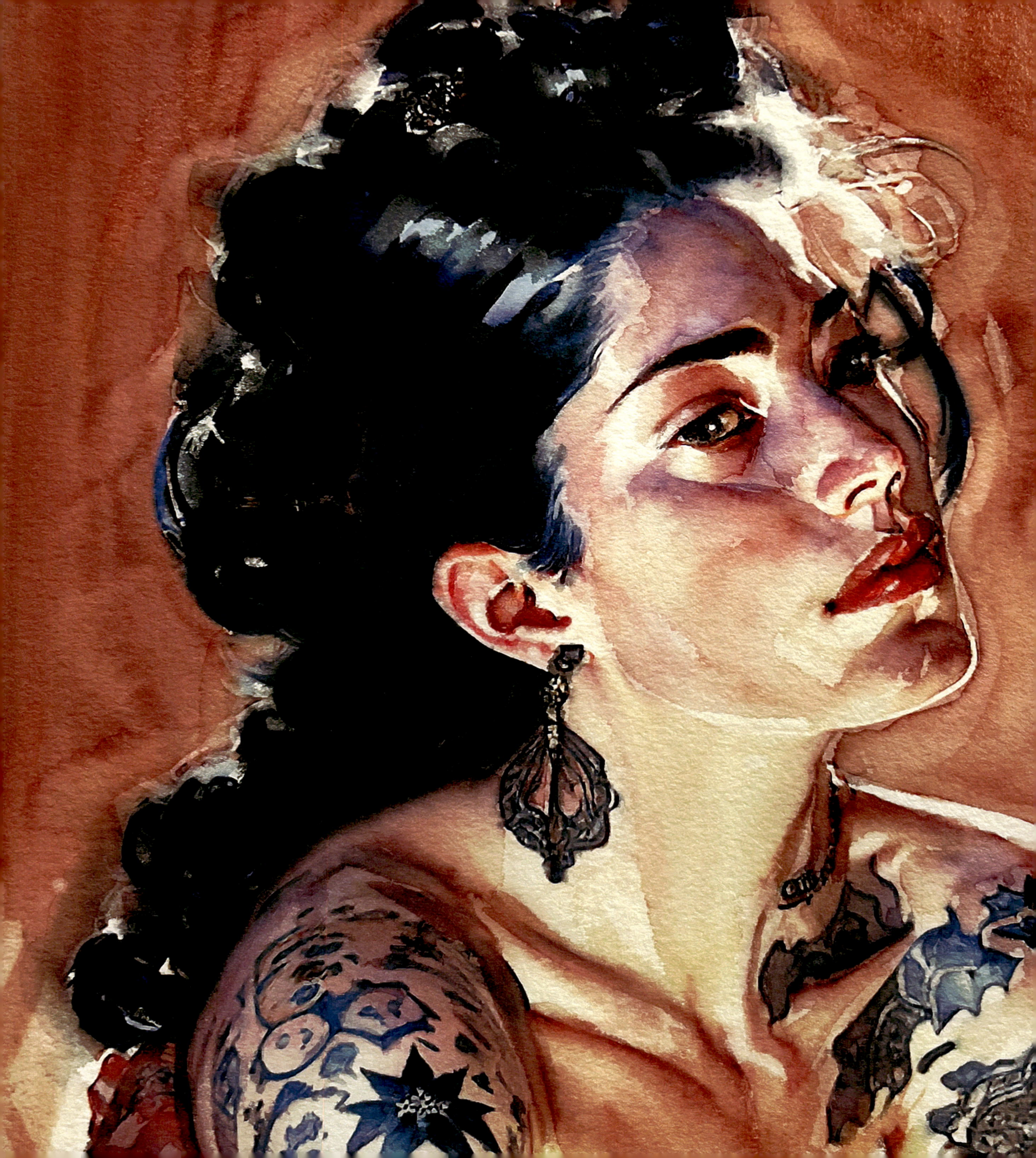

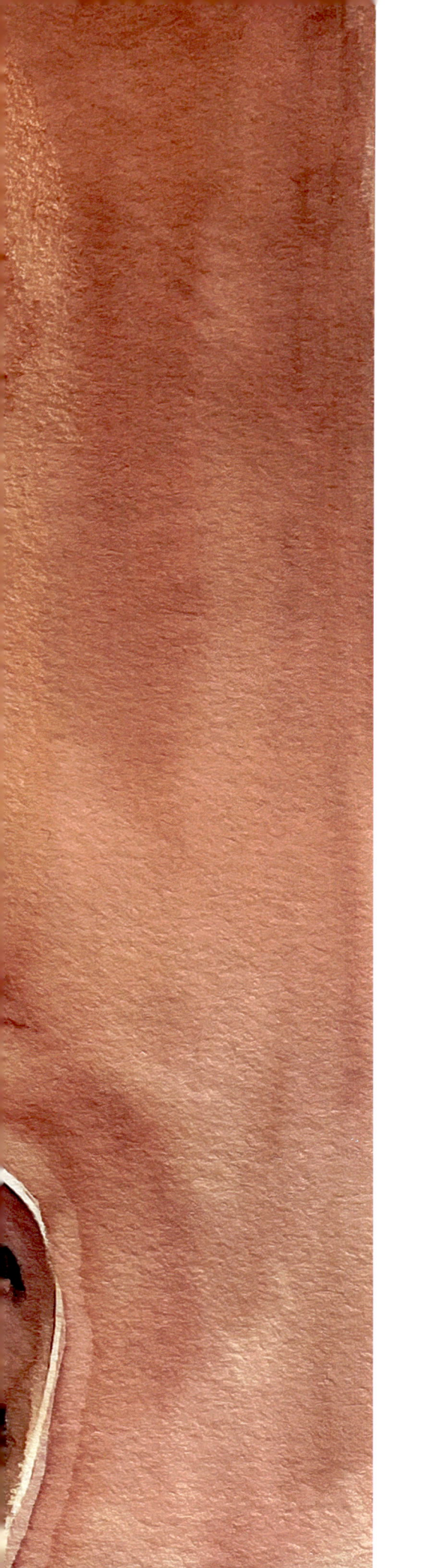

INK

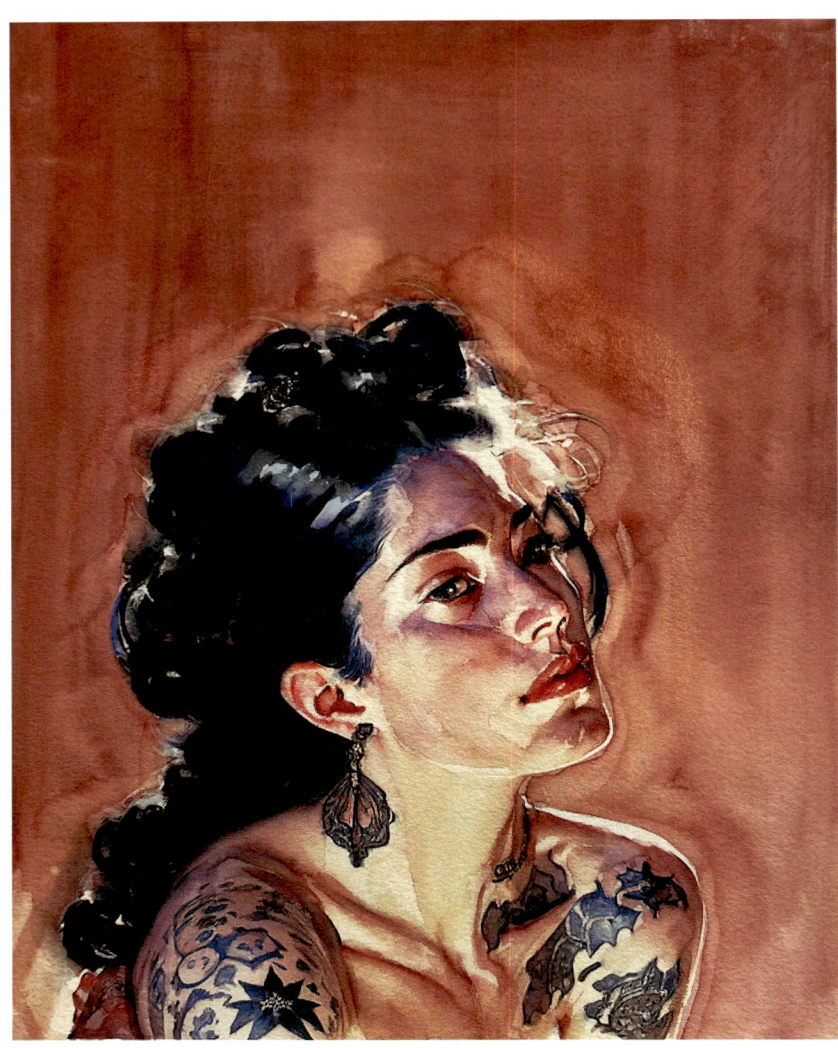

above: "Newly" | watercolor | 12" x 7"
previous spread: "Newly" *Detail*

"Turquoise" | watercolor | 13" x 7" | Private Collection

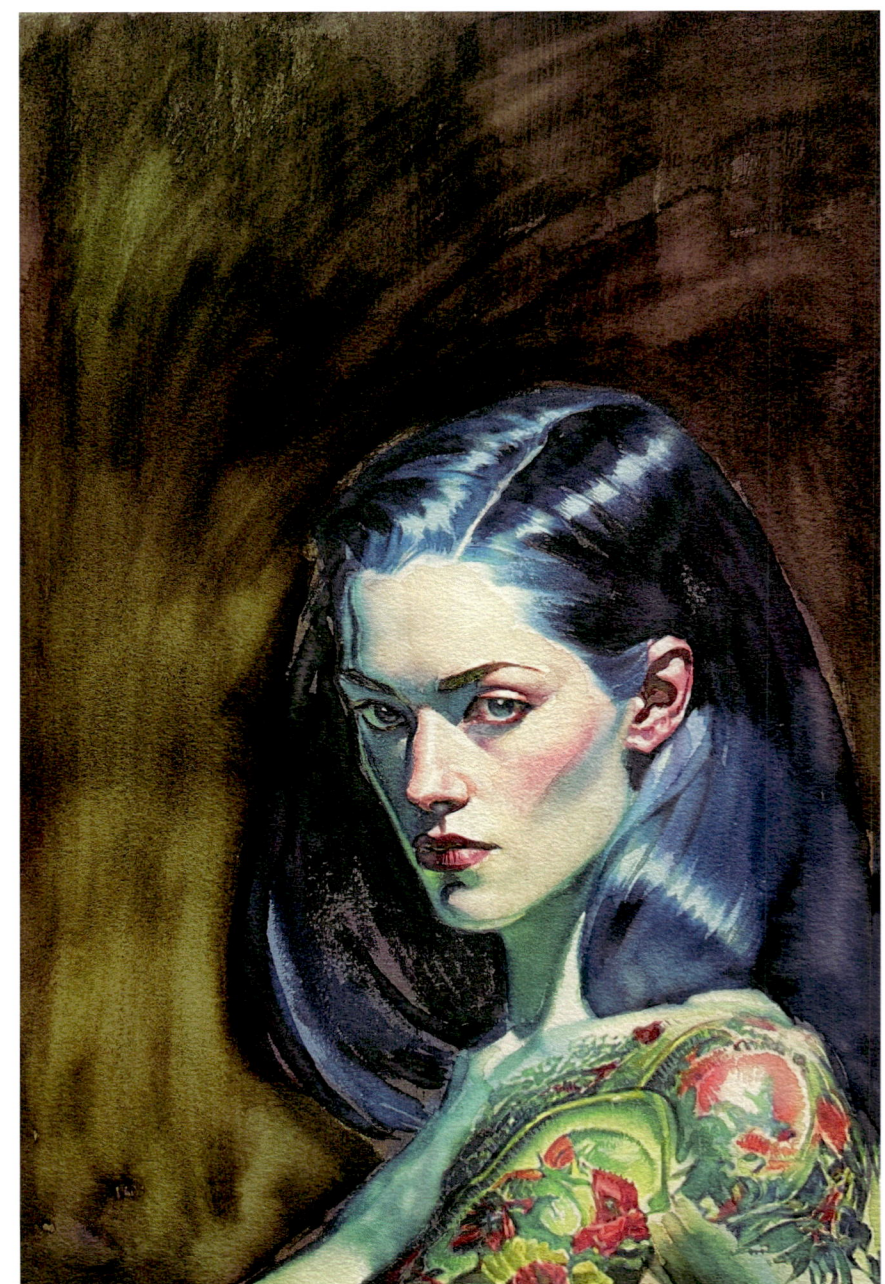

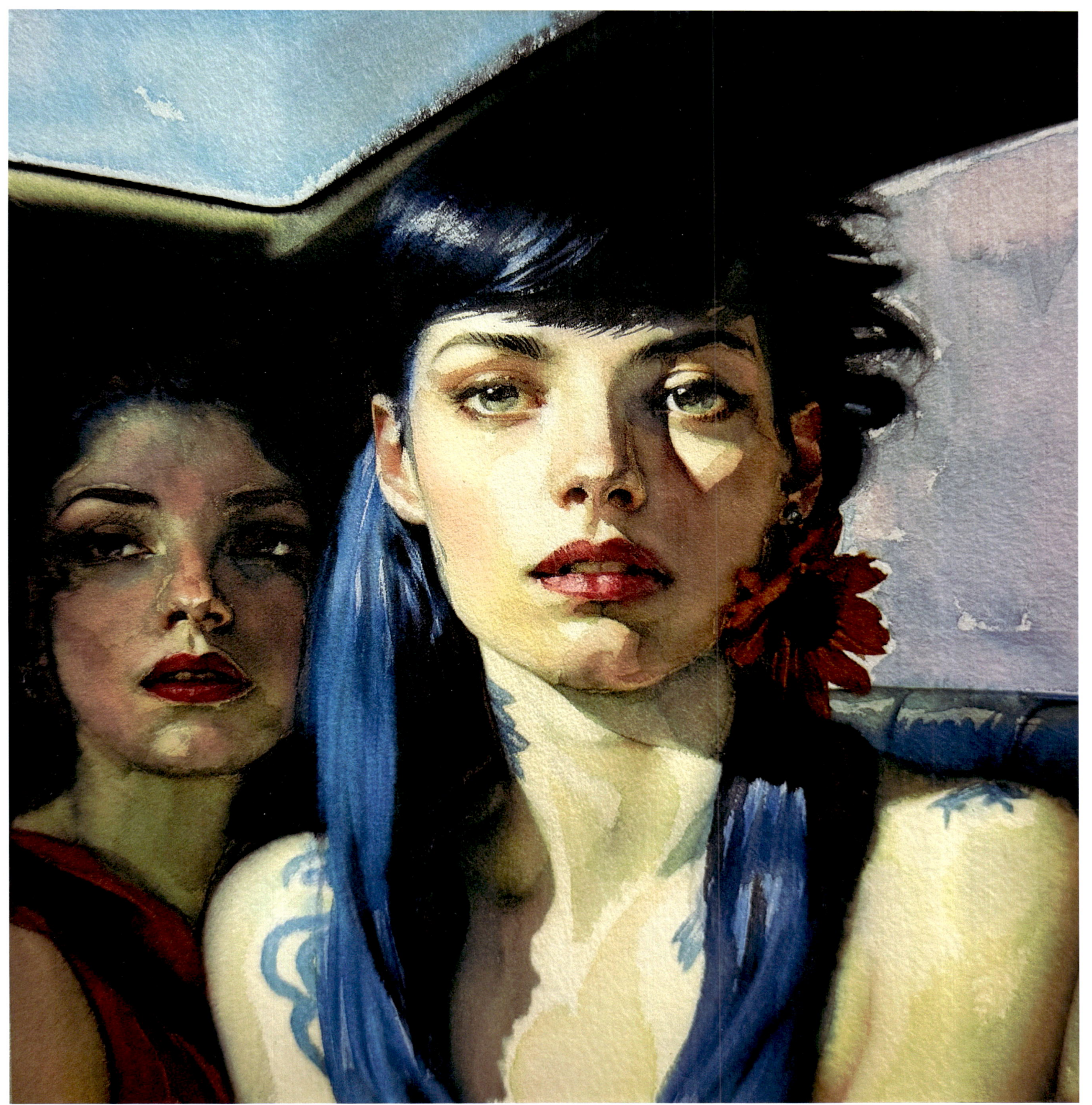

"Time to Go" | watercolor | 9" x 6" | Private Collection

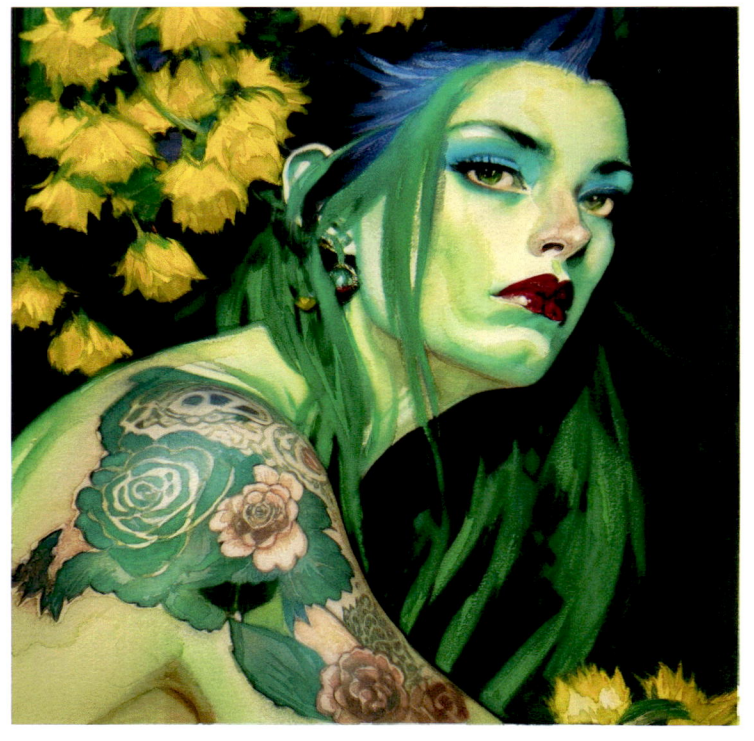

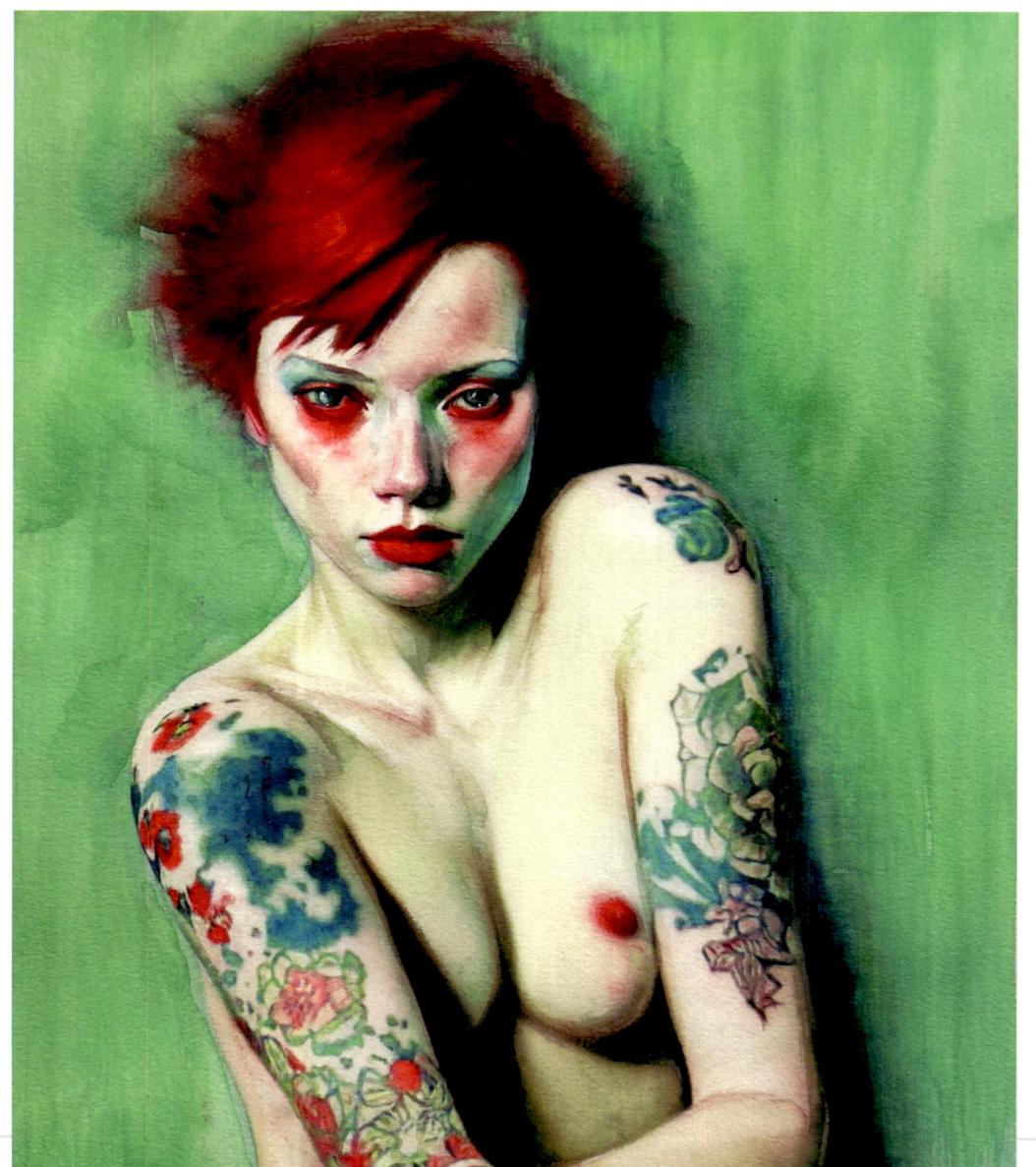

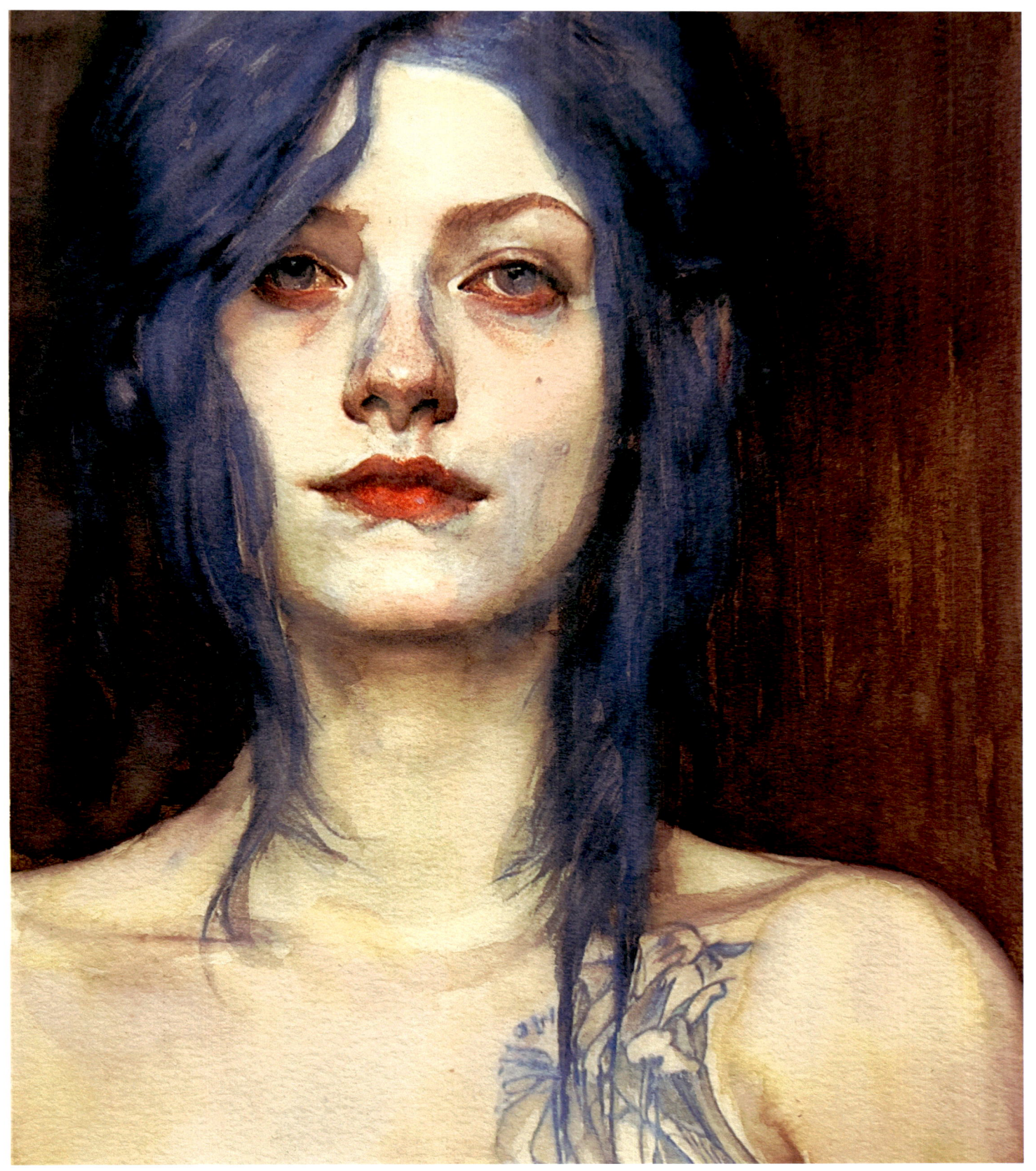

above: "Steph" | watercolor | 10" x 8" | Private Collection
opposite top: "Chrissy" | watercolor | 8" x 8" | Private Collection
opposite bottom: "Christmas" | watercolor | 11" x 8" | Private Collection

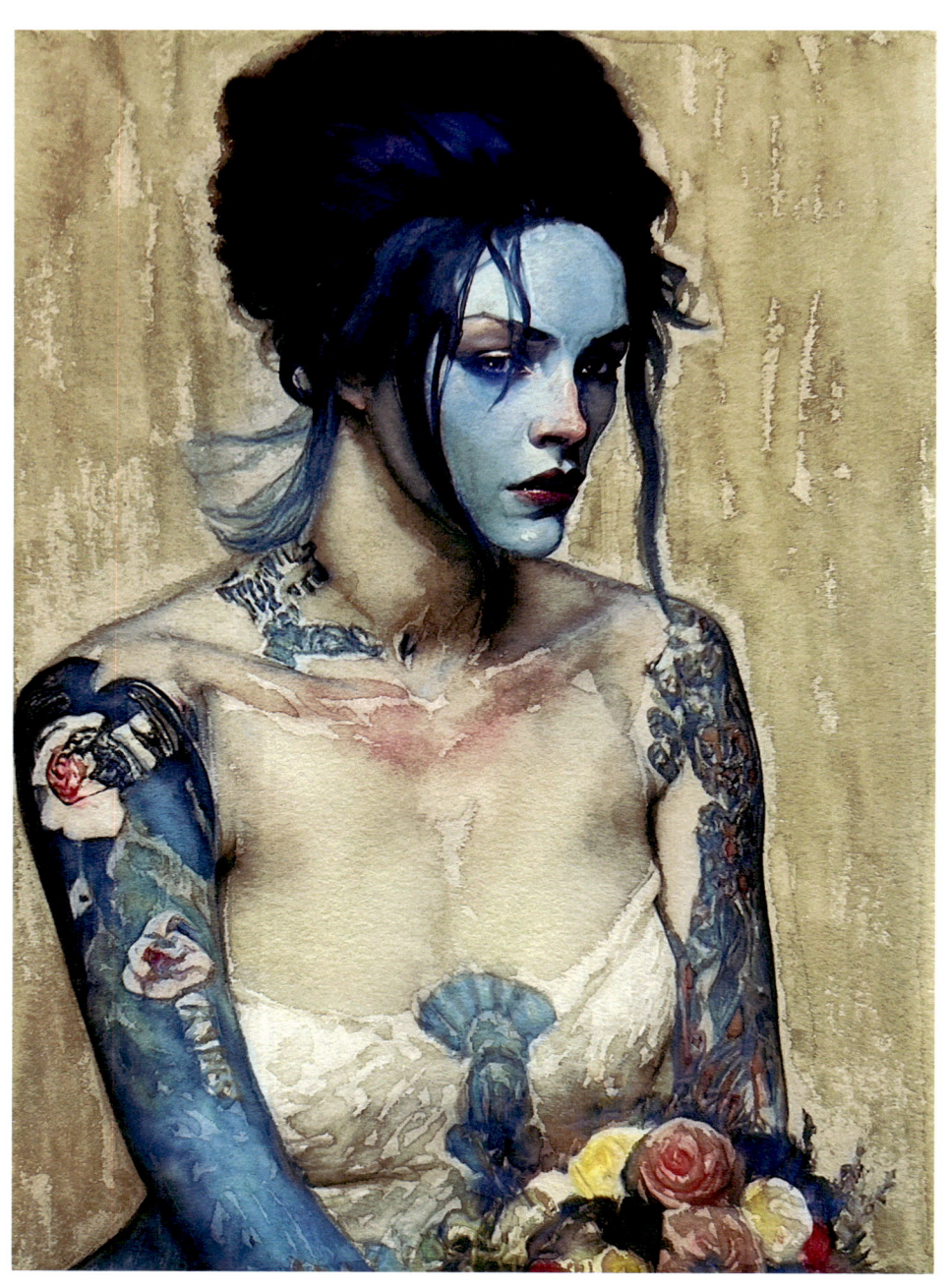

above: "Jen - Blue" | watercolor | 8" x 5" | Private Collection
opposite: "Robin 2" | watercolor | 12" x 7"

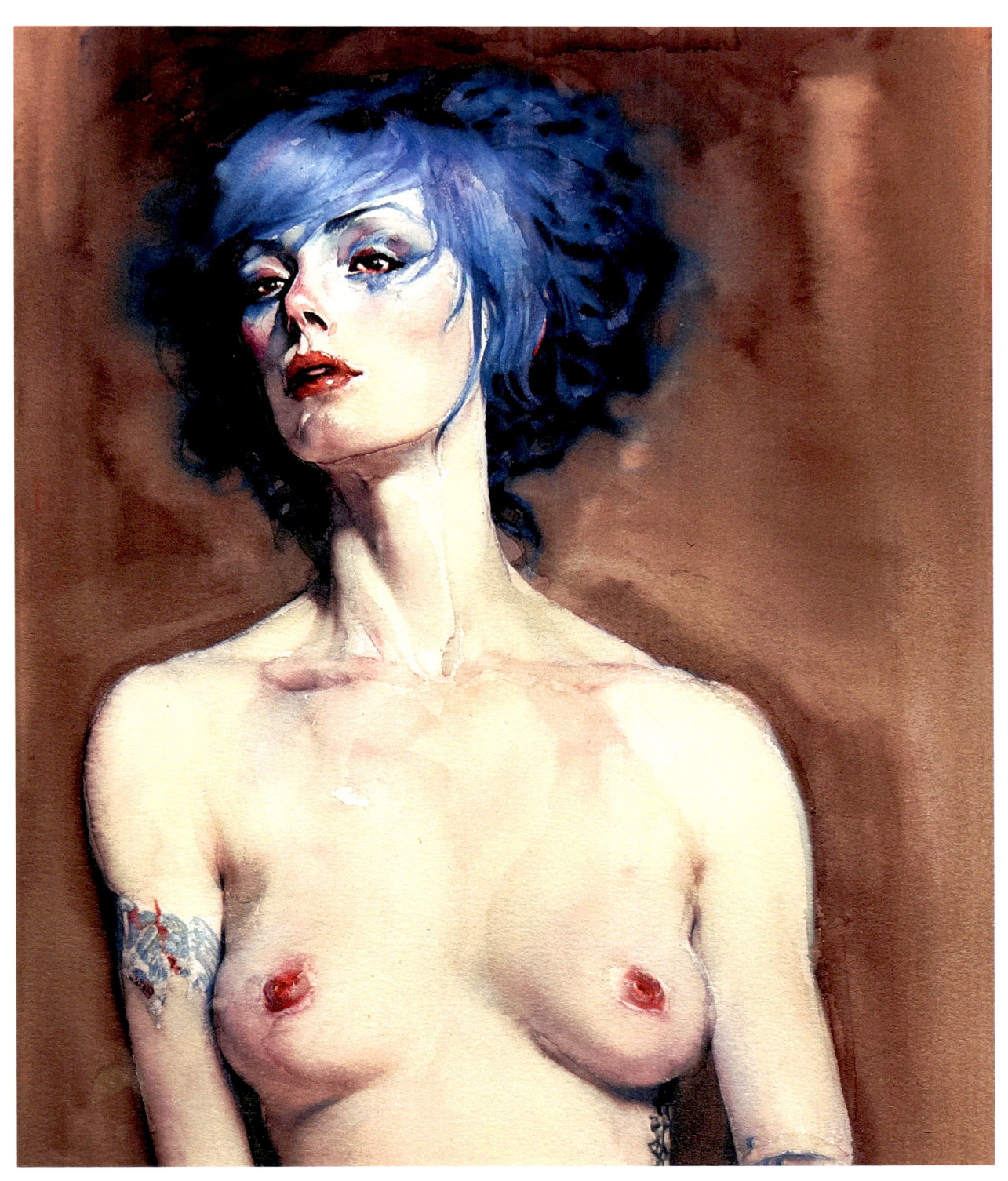

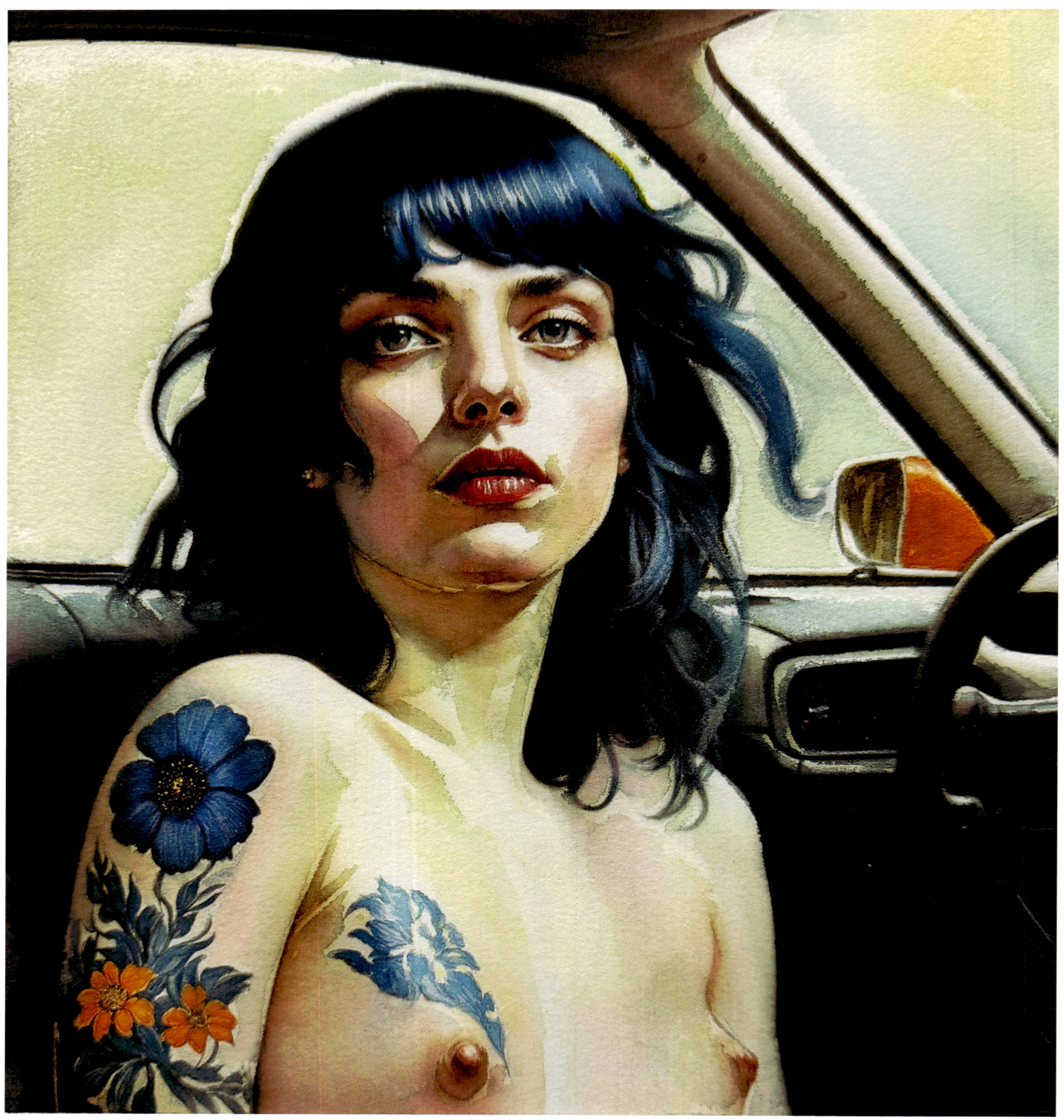

"Let's Drive" | watercolor | 14" x 10" | Private Collection

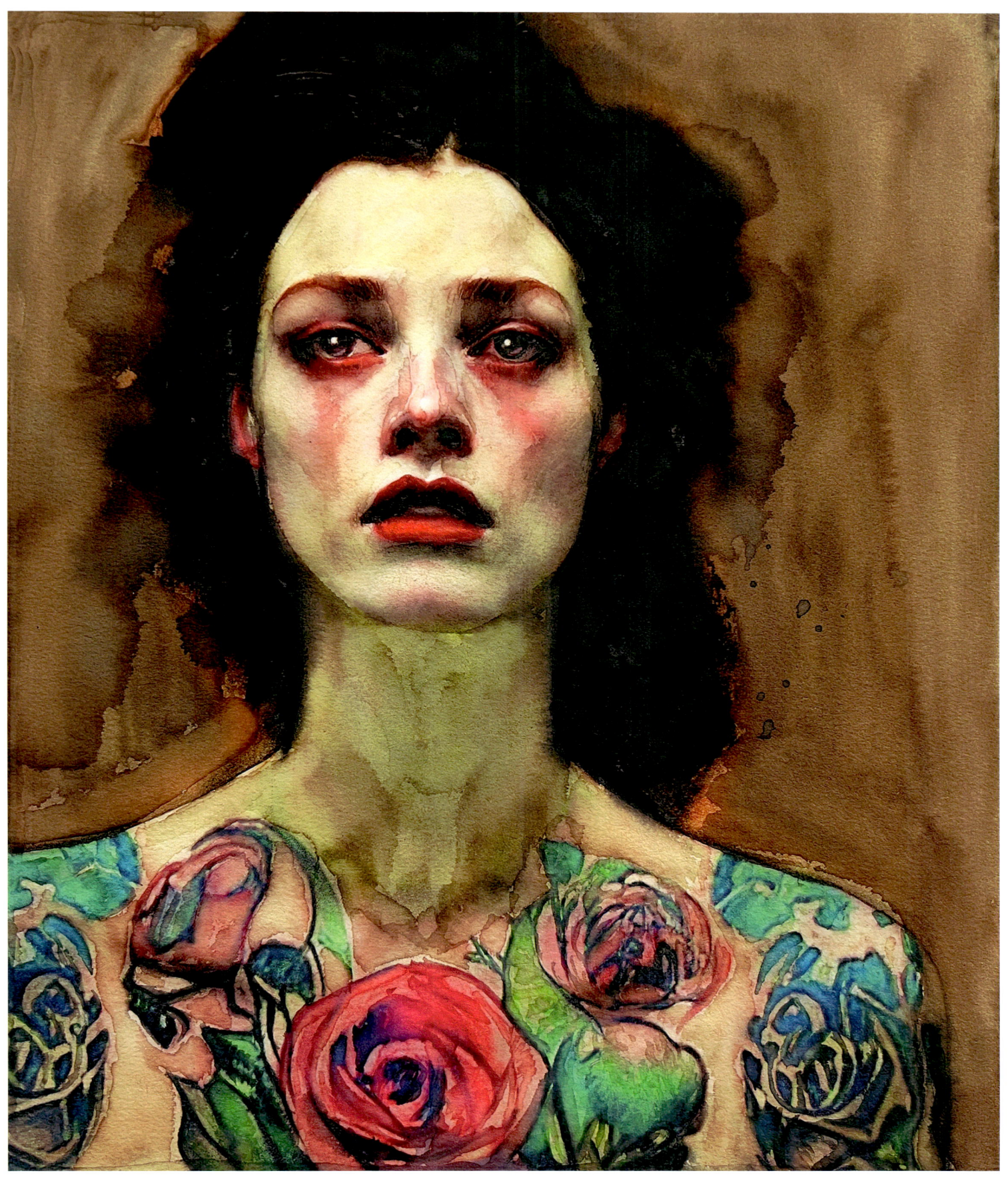

"Naya" | watercolor | 12" x 9" | Private Collection

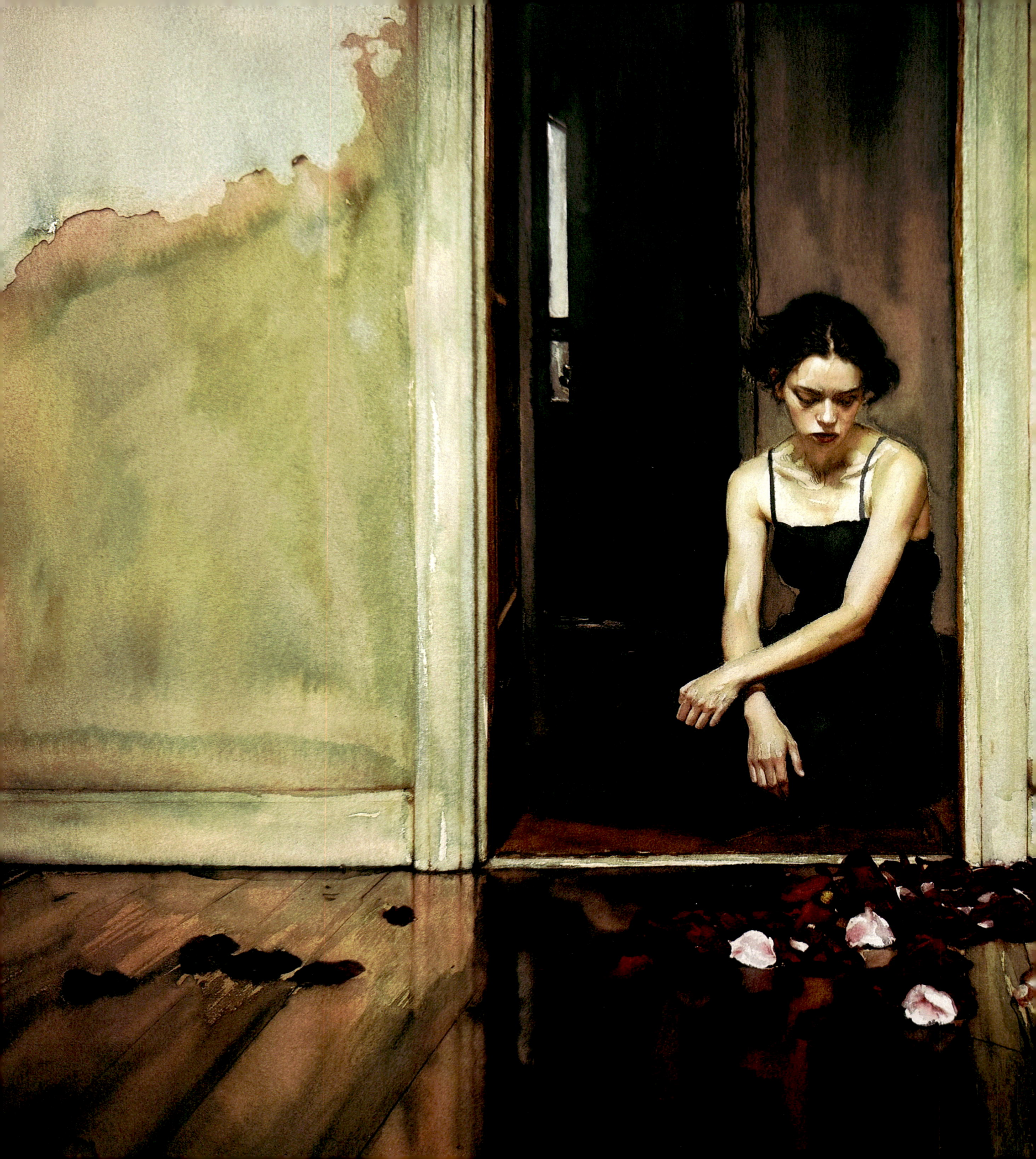

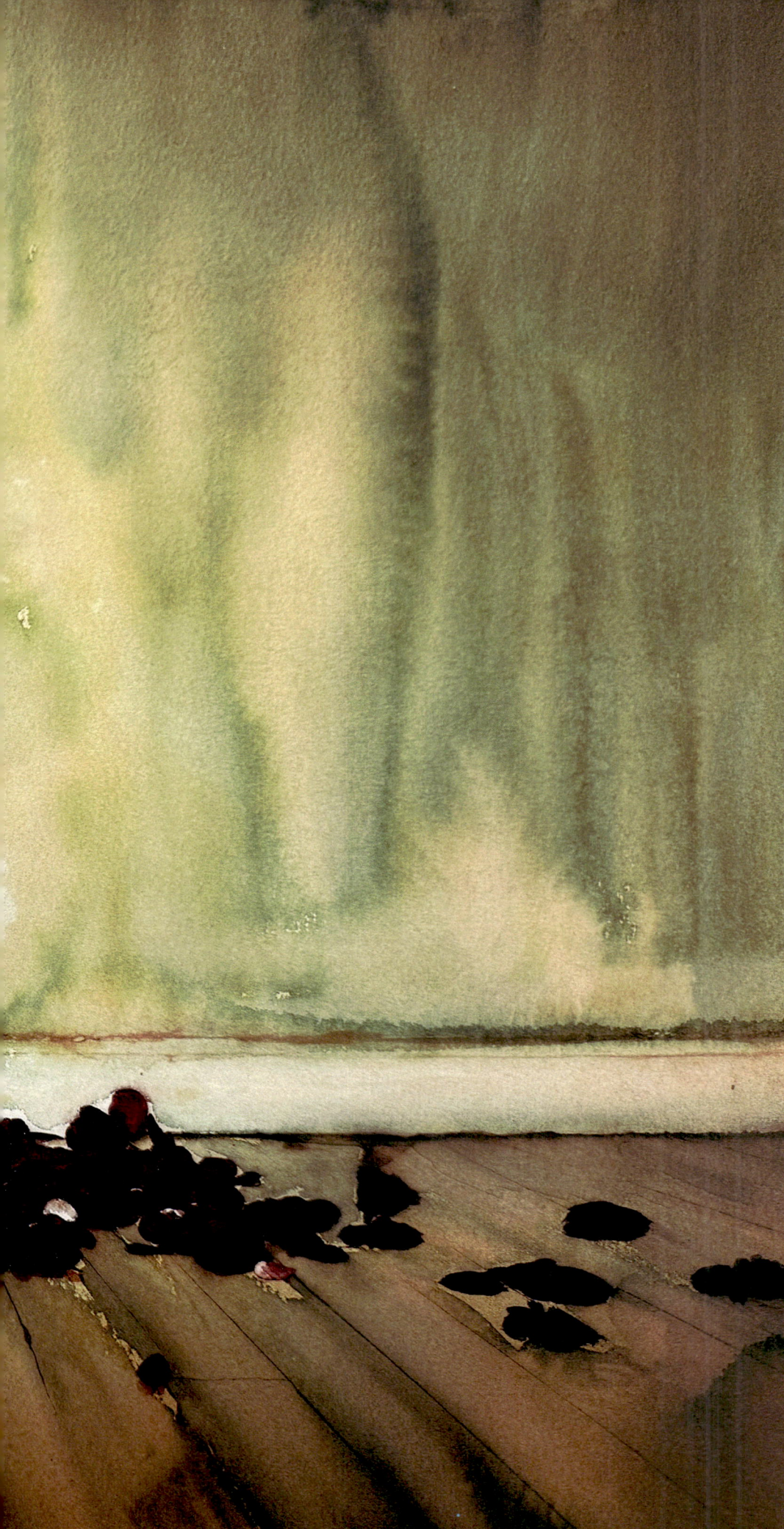

ROOMS

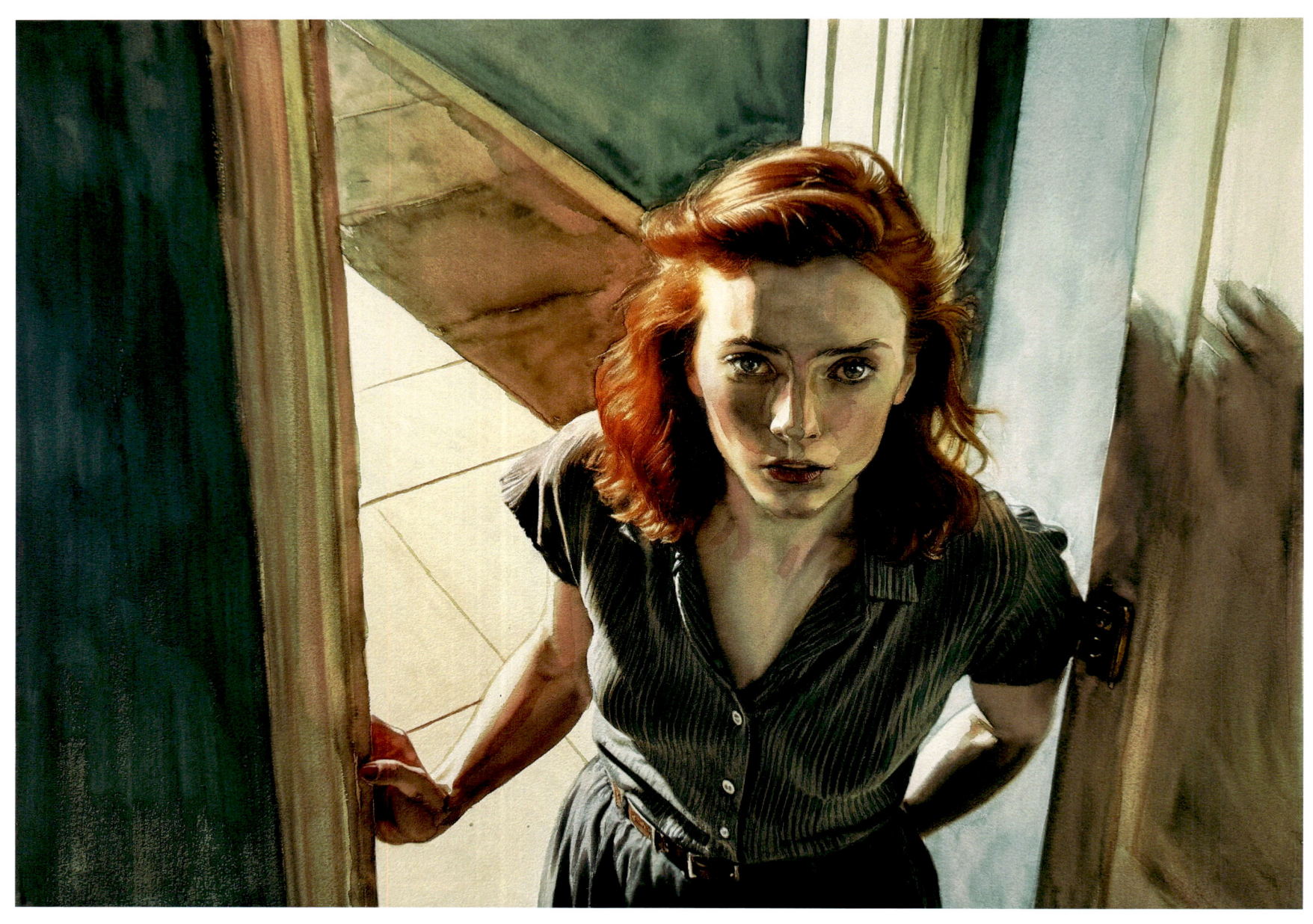

above: "Doorway 2" | watercolor | 20" x 30"
opposite: "Abstract" | watercolor | 22" x 16" | Private Collection
previous spread: "Cascade" | watercolor | 18" x 22" | Private Collection

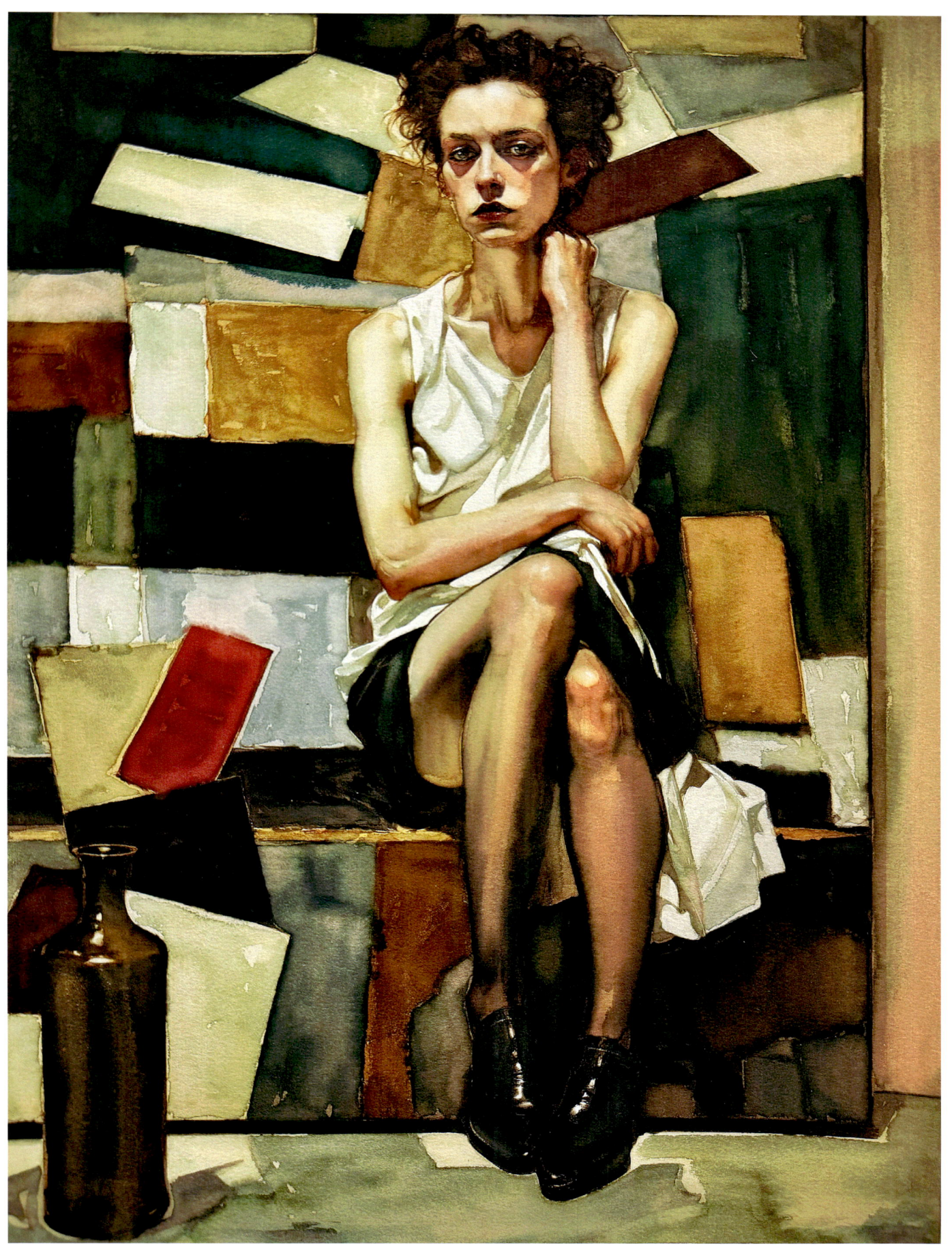

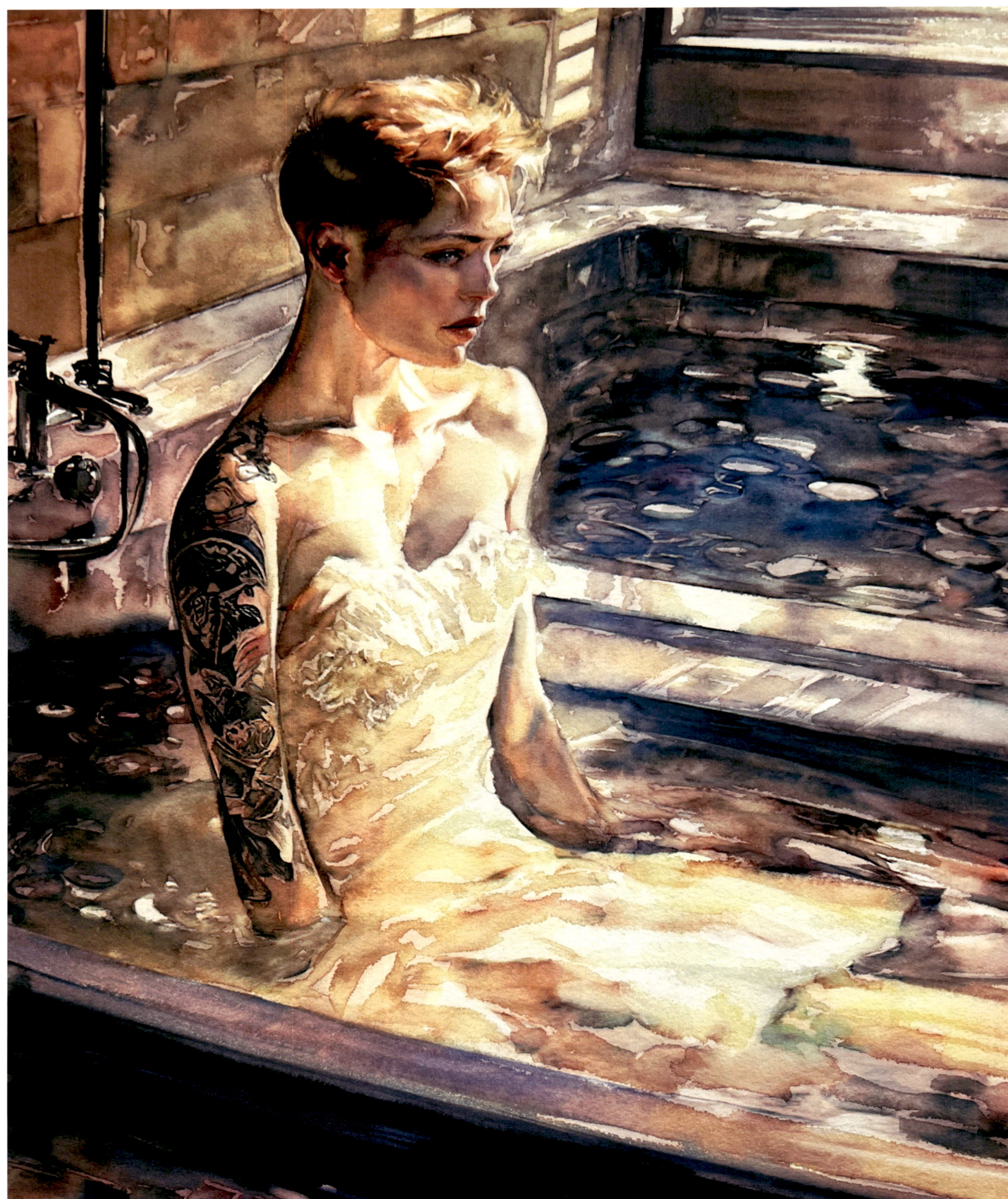

below: "After Party" | watercolor | 20" x 24" | Private Collection
opposite: "Bride Bath" | watercolor | 12" x 8"

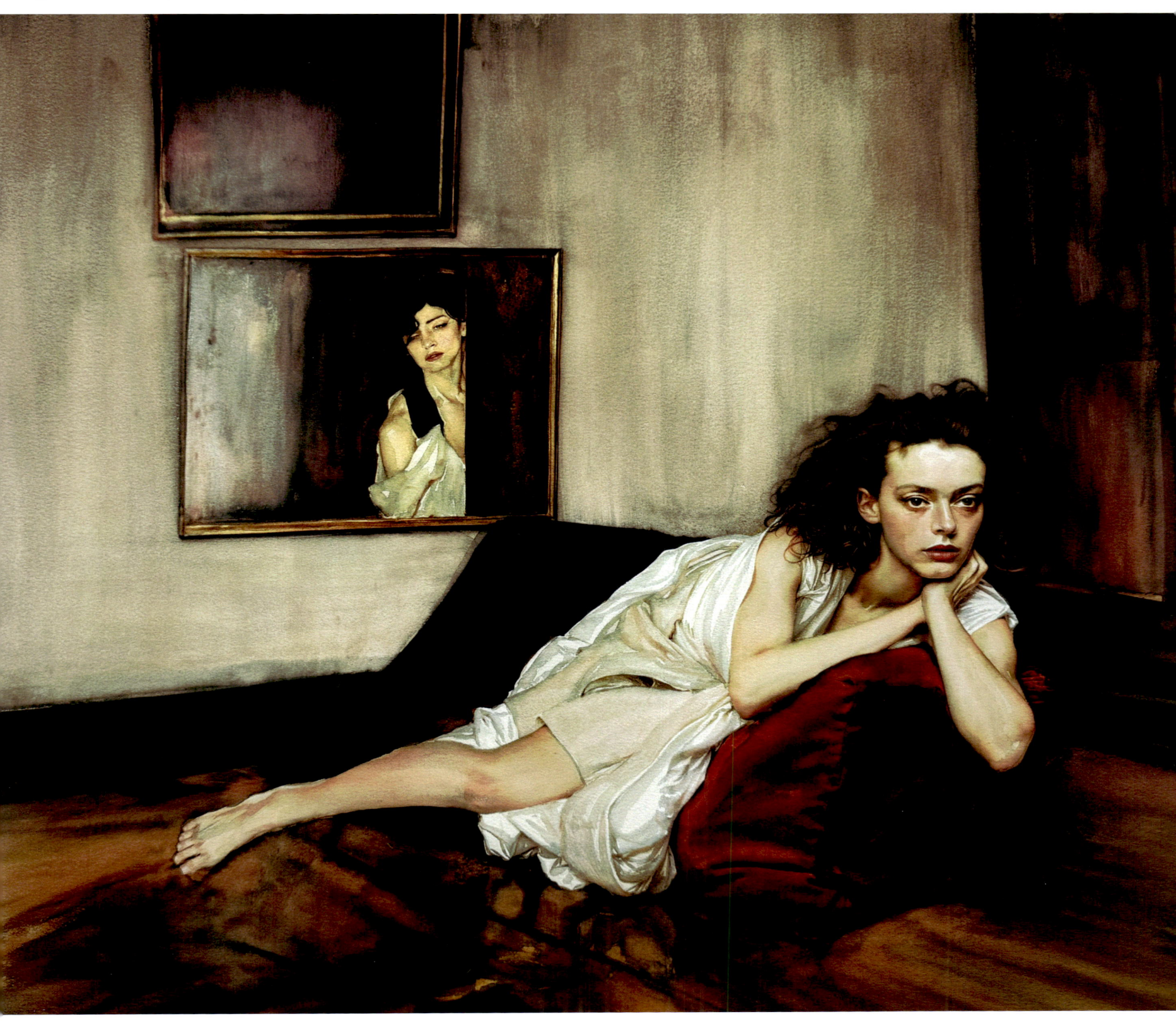

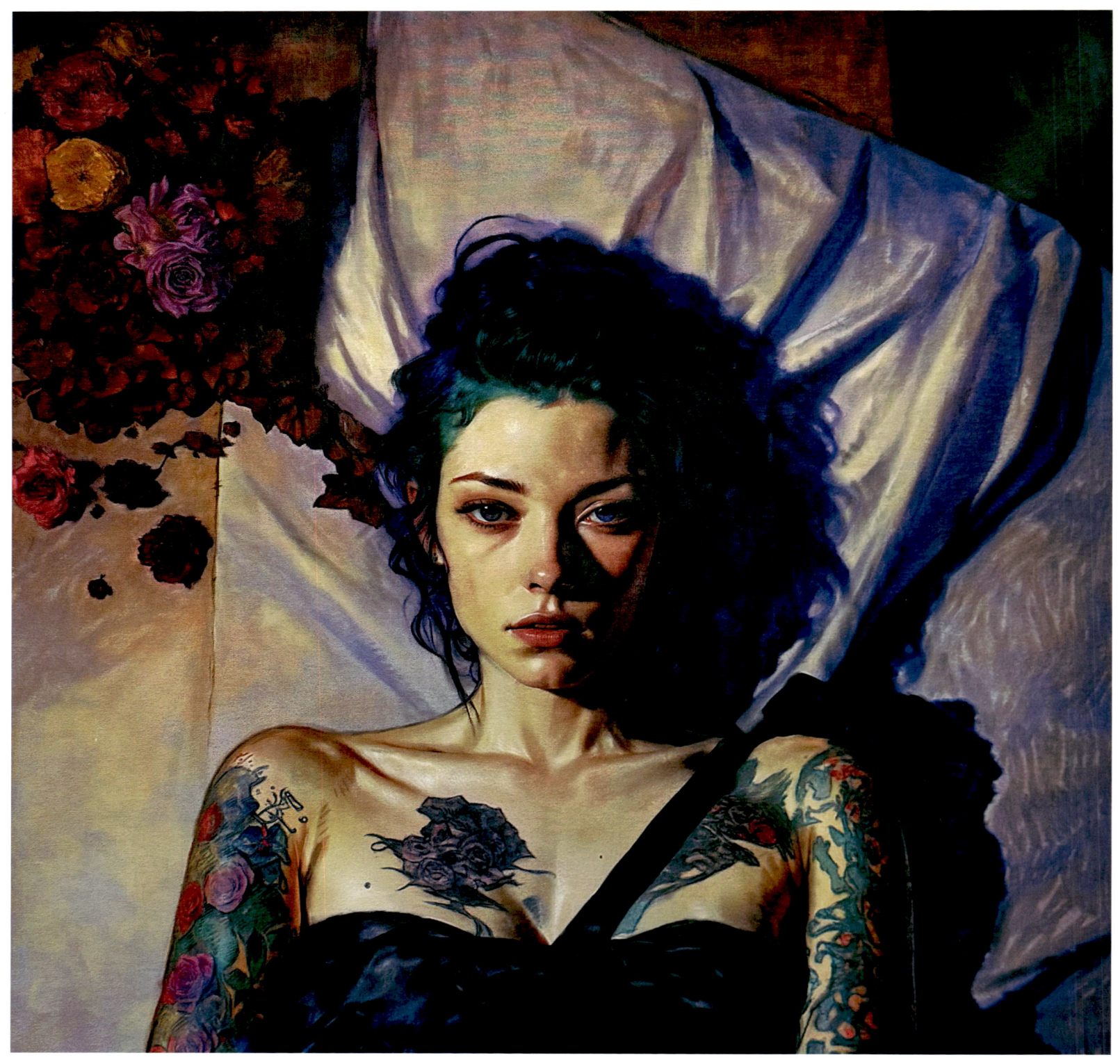

above: "Bed Head" | oil on canvas | 32" x 32" | Private Collection
opposite: "Silk" | watercolor | 14" x 8" | Private Collection

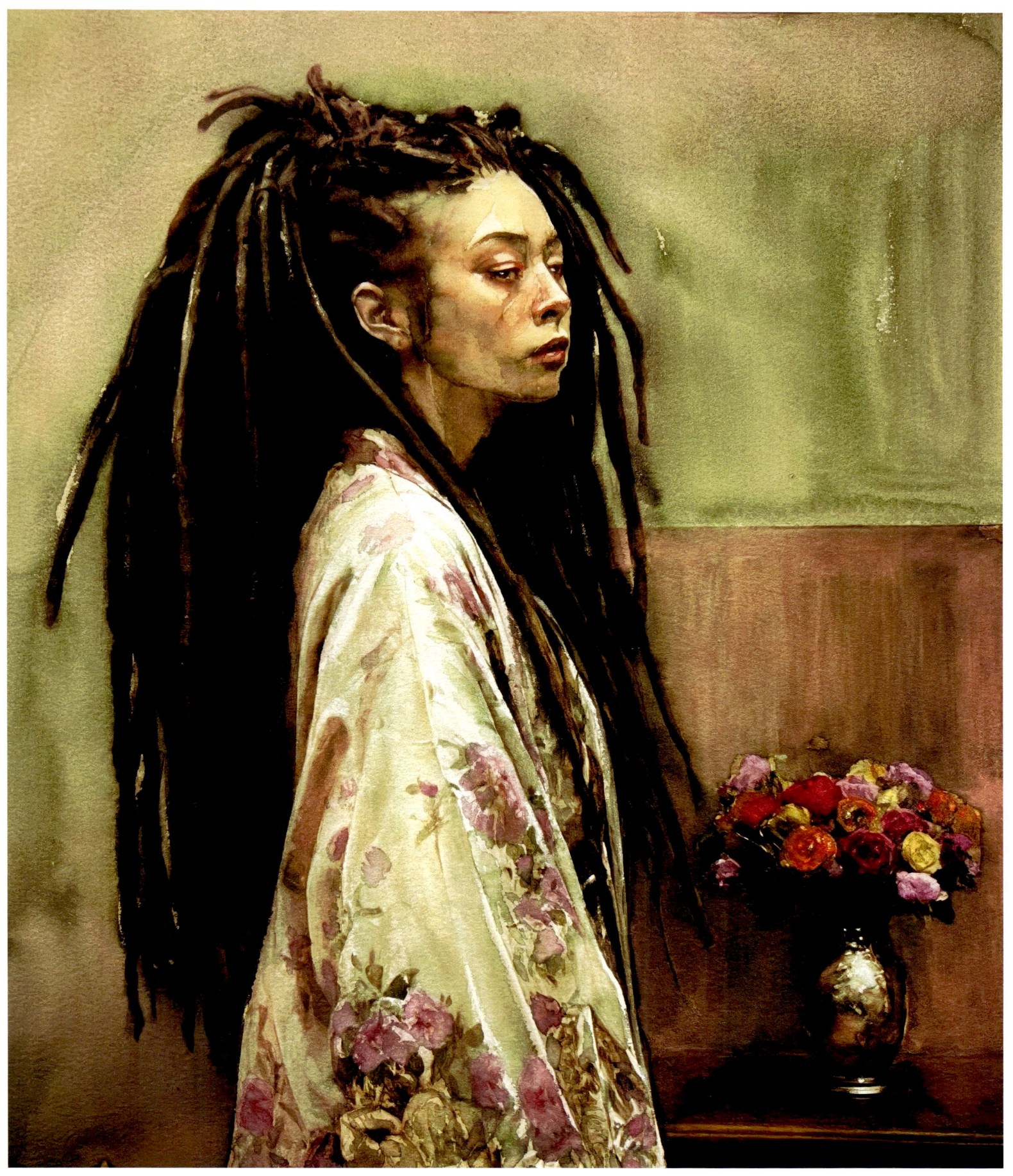

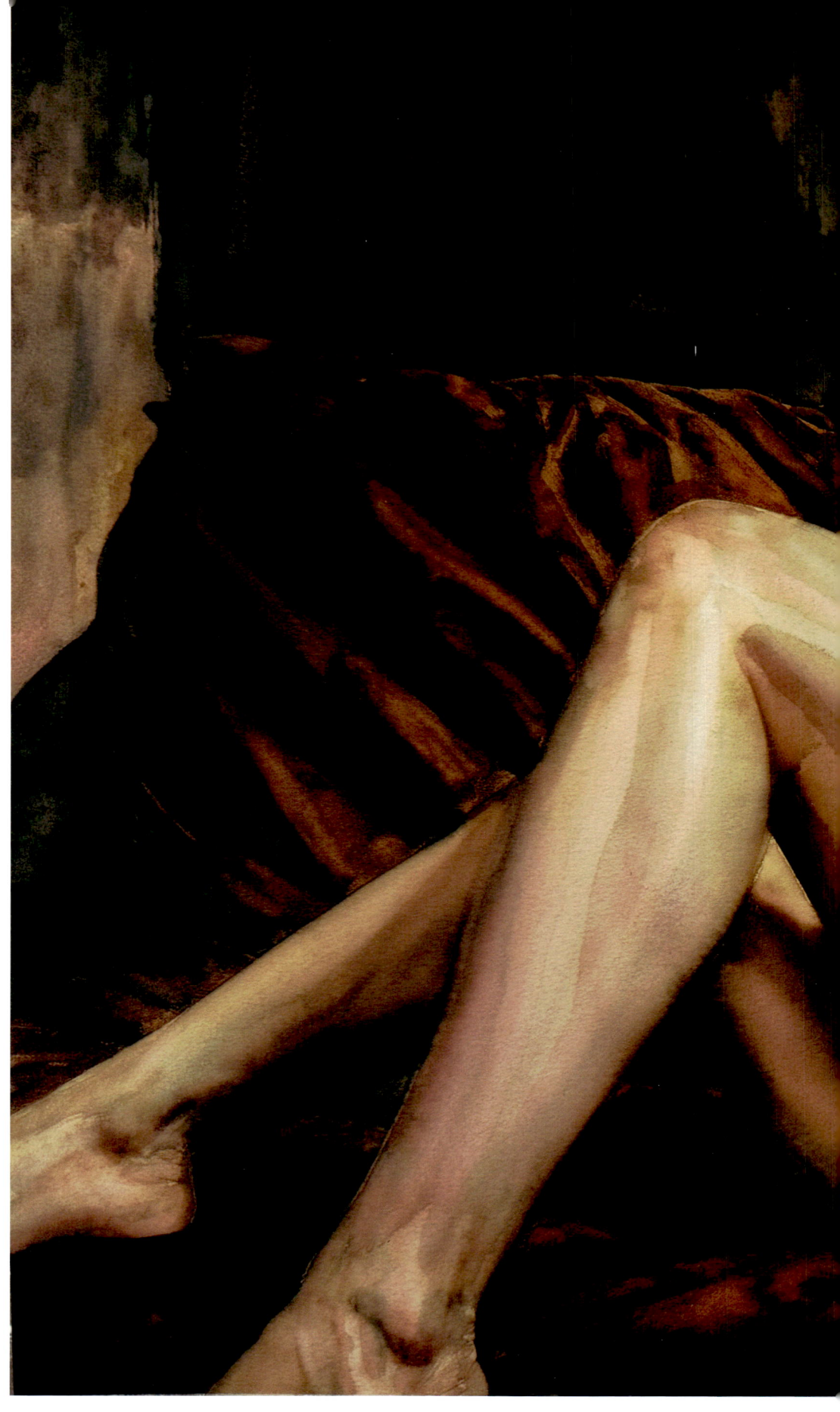

"And so it Goes" | watercolor | 13" x 21" | Private Collection

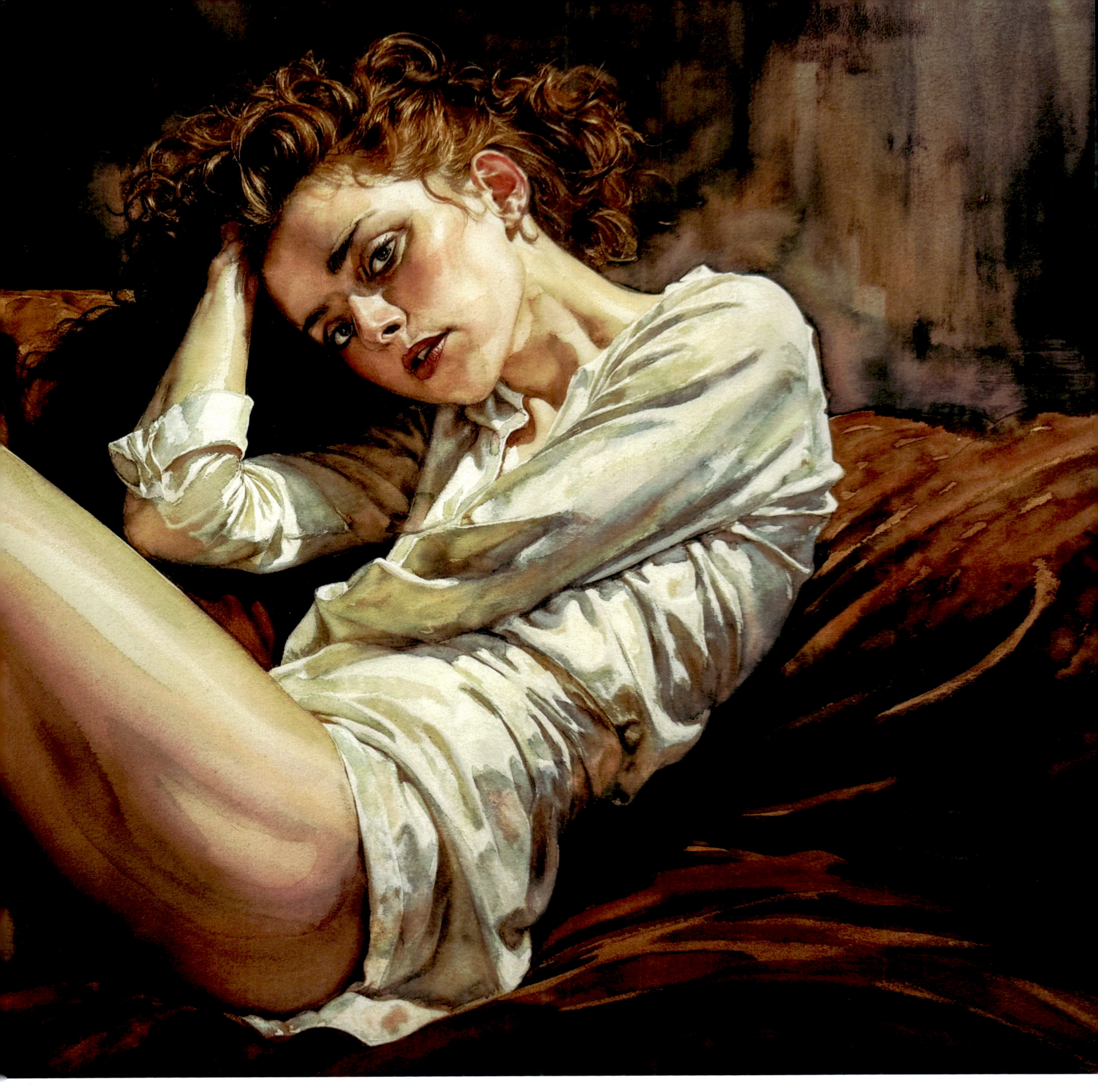

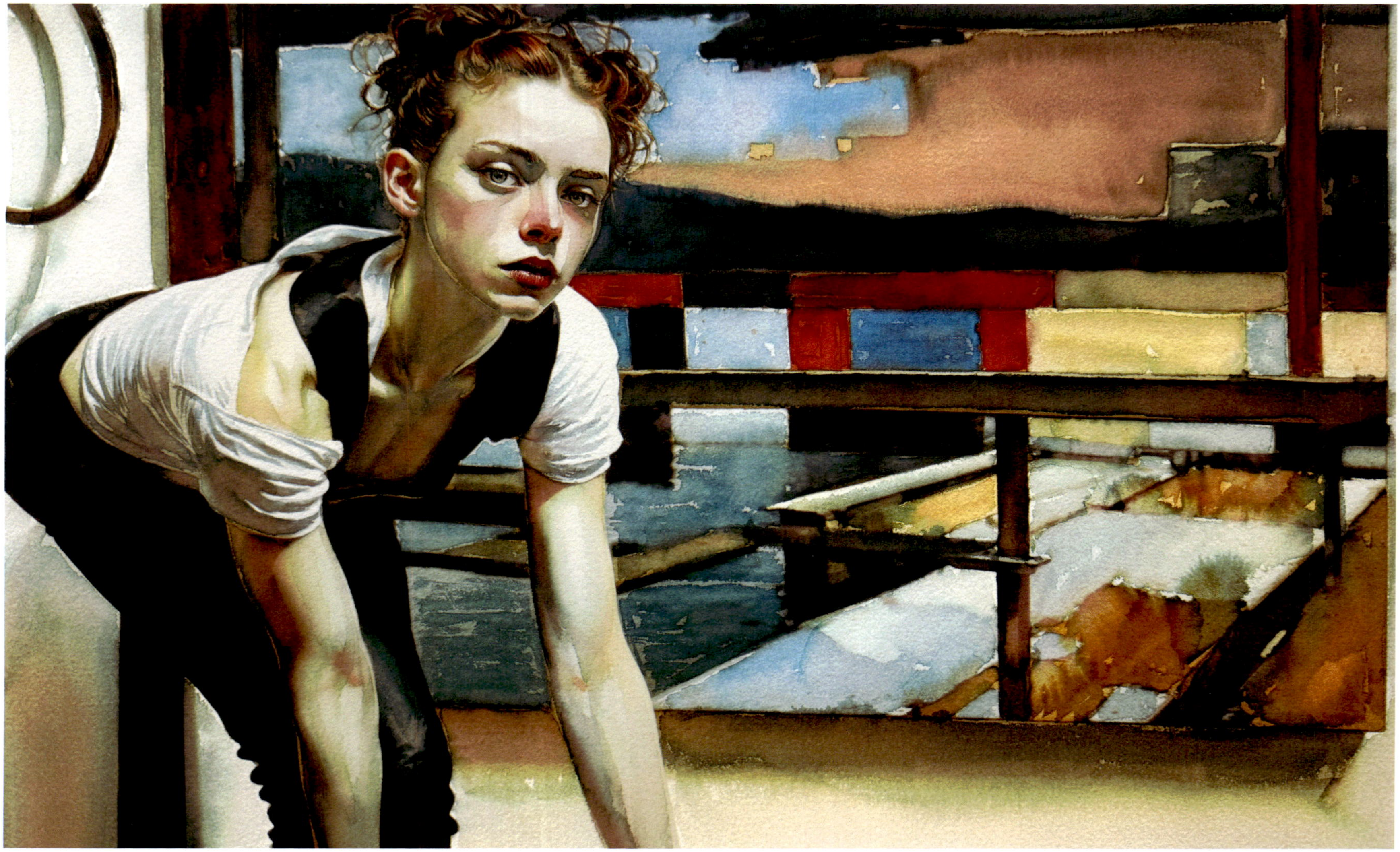

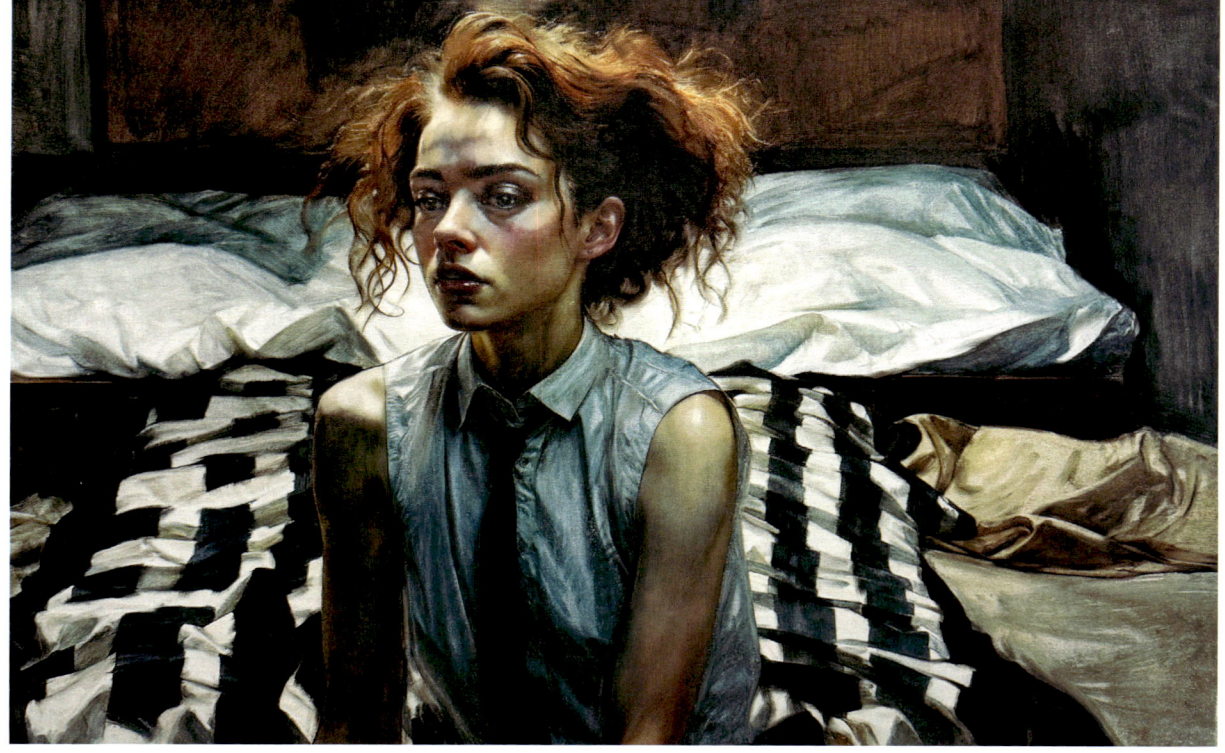

above: "Patches" | watercolor | 13" x 18" | Private Collection

left: "You Make It" | oil on canvas | 24" x 37"

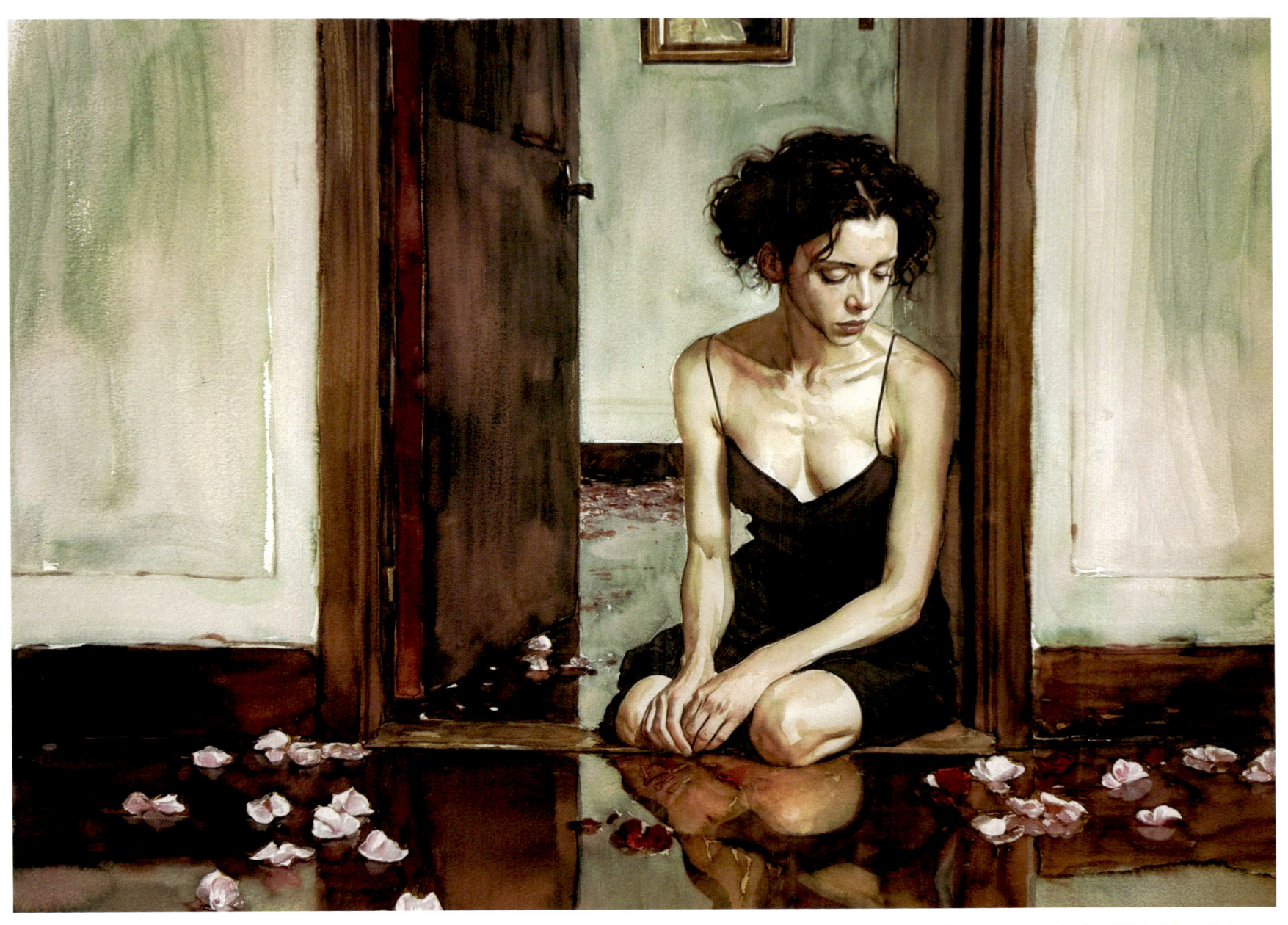

"Cascade" | watercolor | 14" x 18" | Private Collection

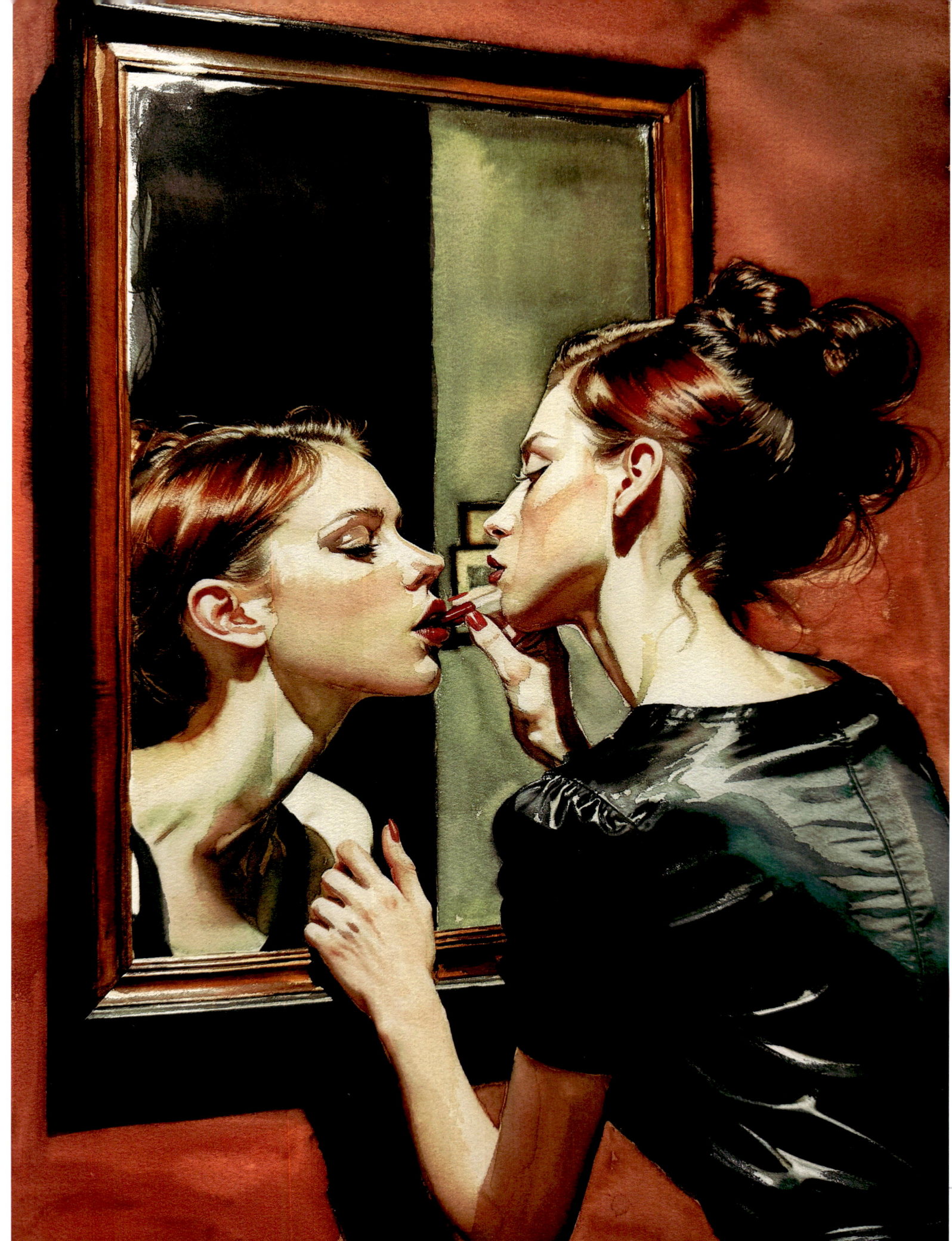

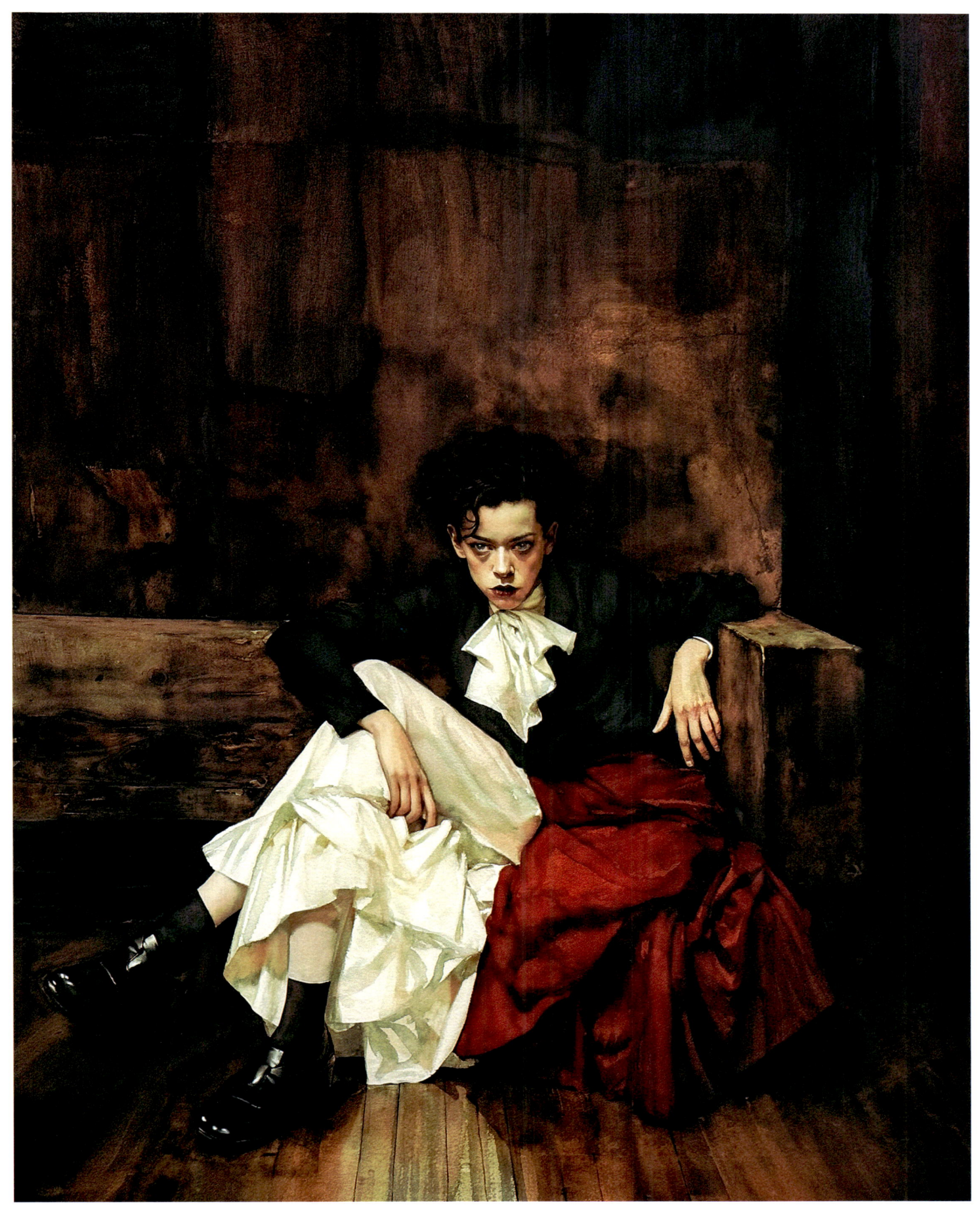

above: "Going Out" | watercolor | 24" x 18" | Private Collection
opposite: "Lipstick" | watercolor | 15" x 10" | Private Collection

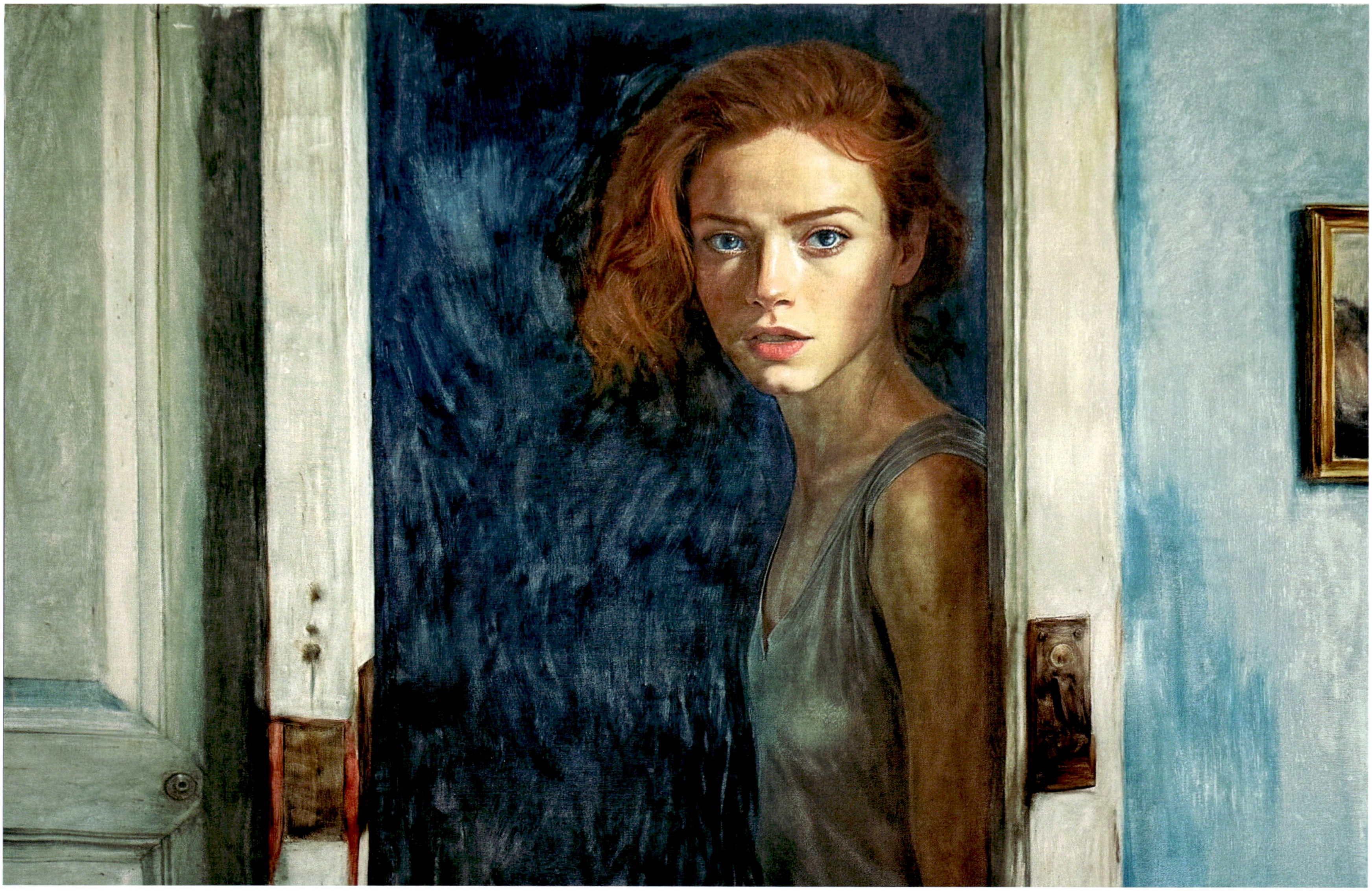

above: "Blue Door" | oil on canvas | 27" x 38" | Private Collection
below: "Doorway" | watercolor | 14" x 18" | Private Collection
opposite: "Last Look" | watercolor | 20" x 16"

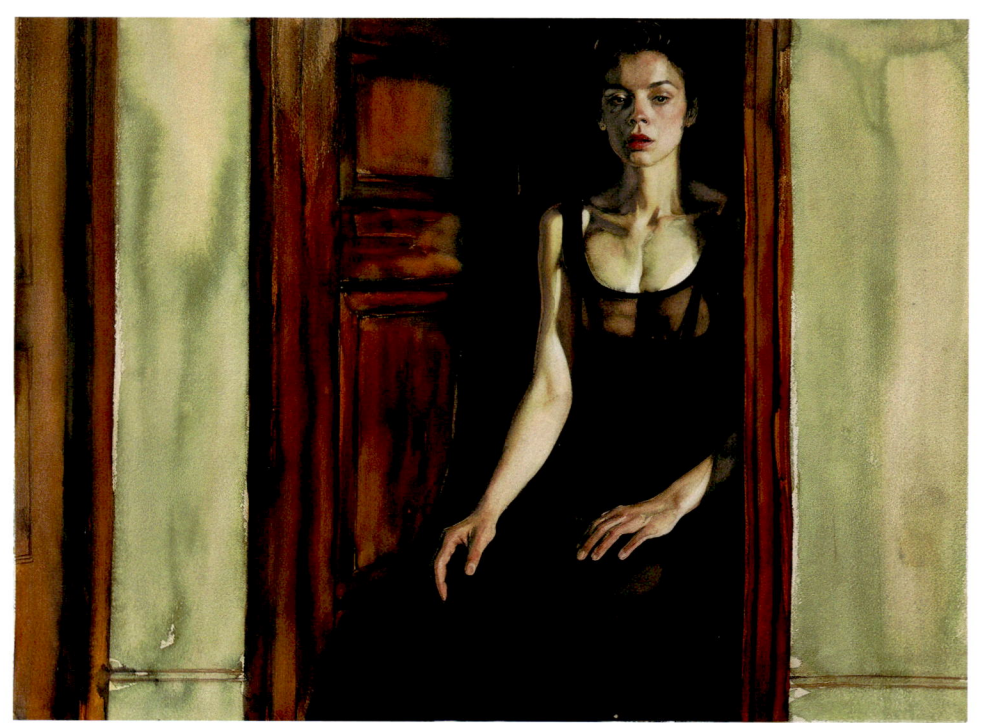

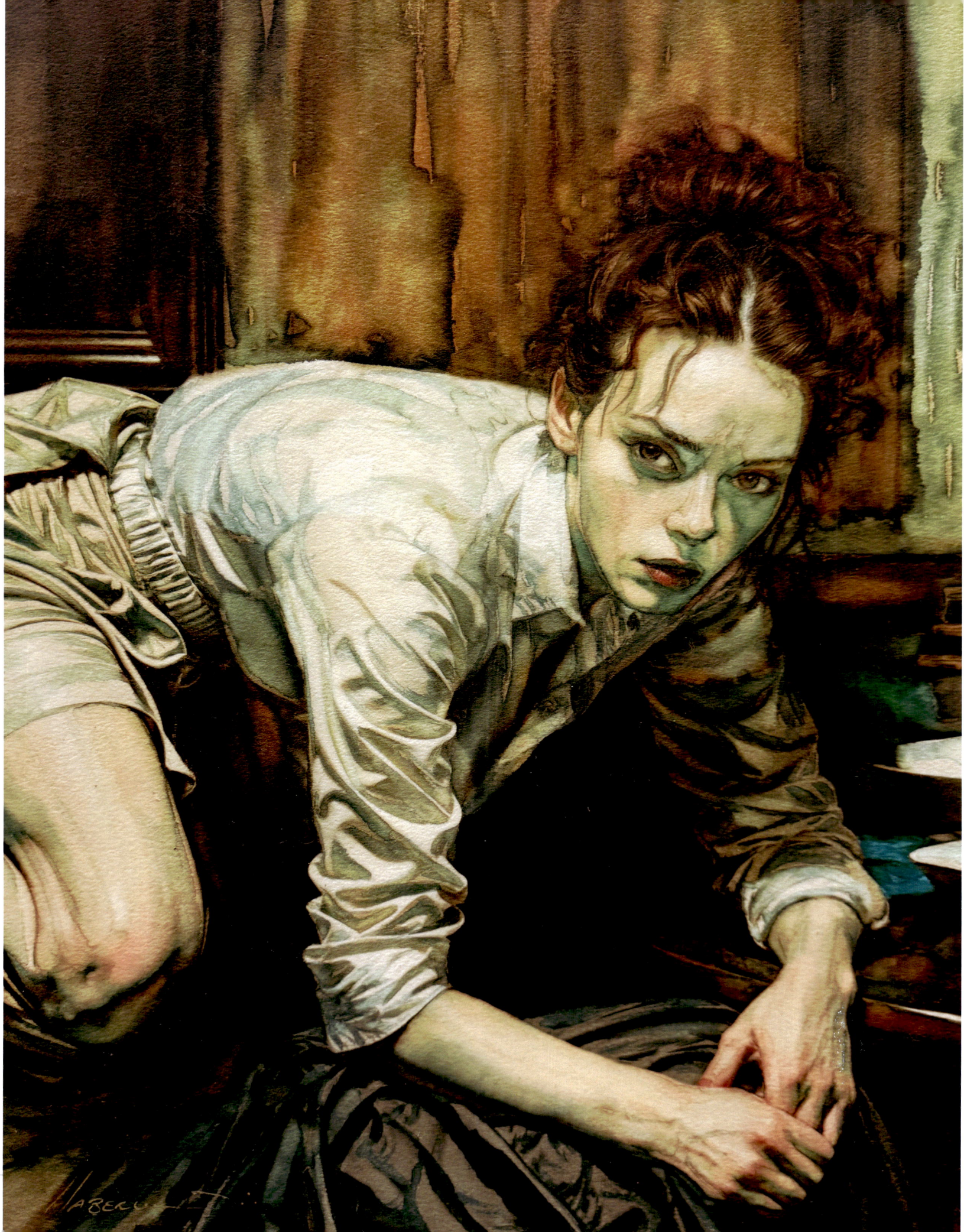

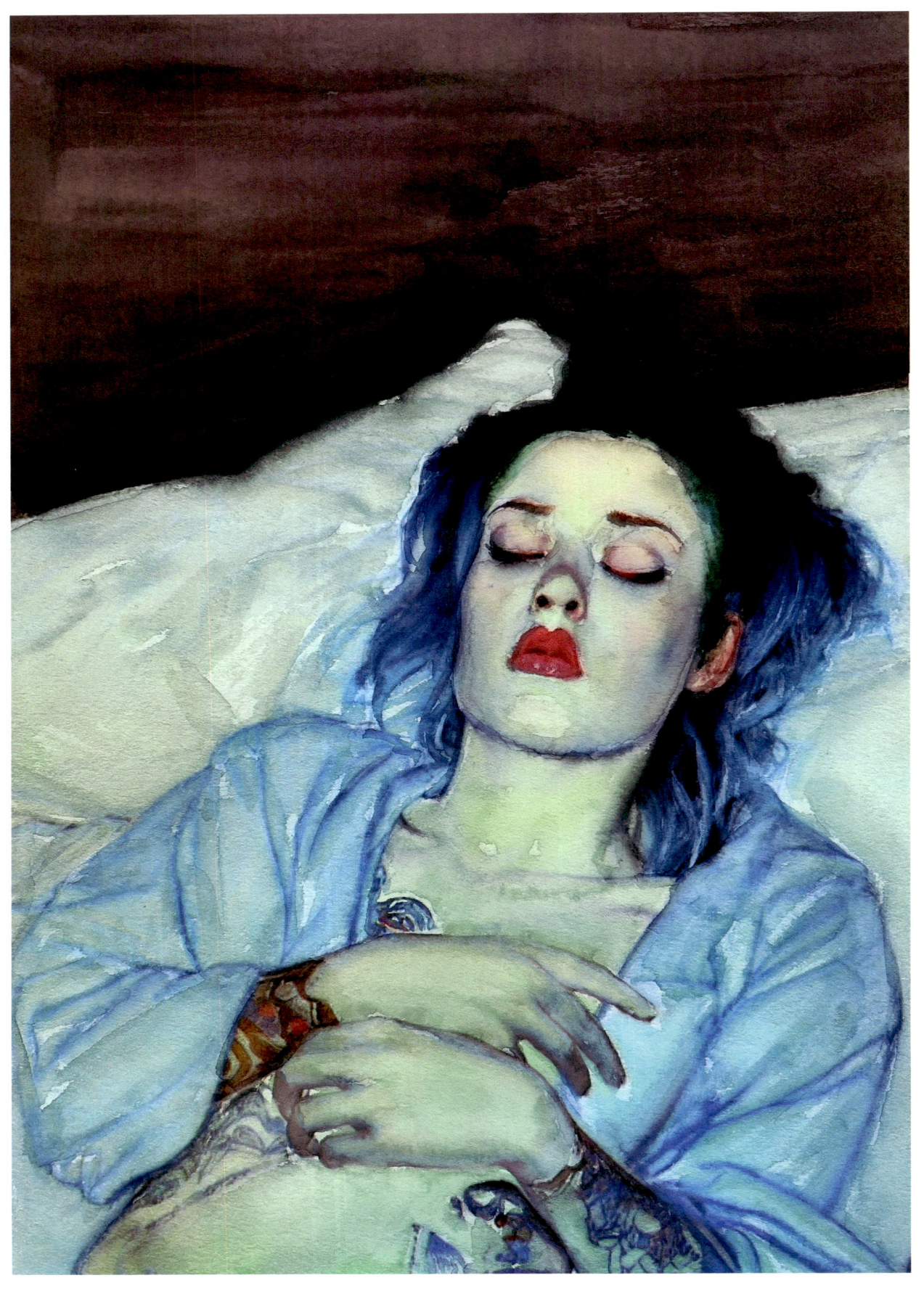

above: "To Dream" | watercolor | 14" x 8"
opposite: "Eileen" | watercolor | 12" x 9" | Private Collection

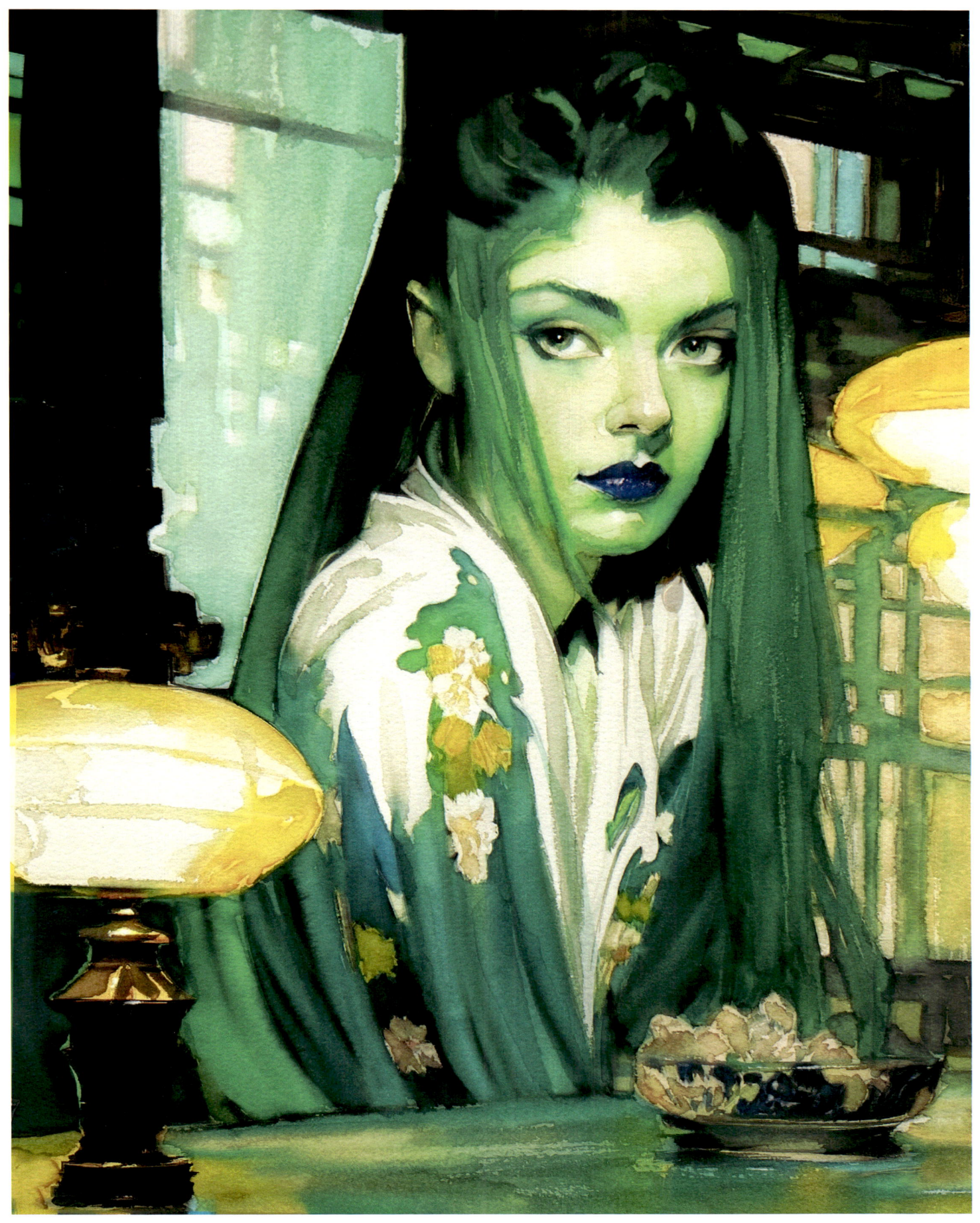

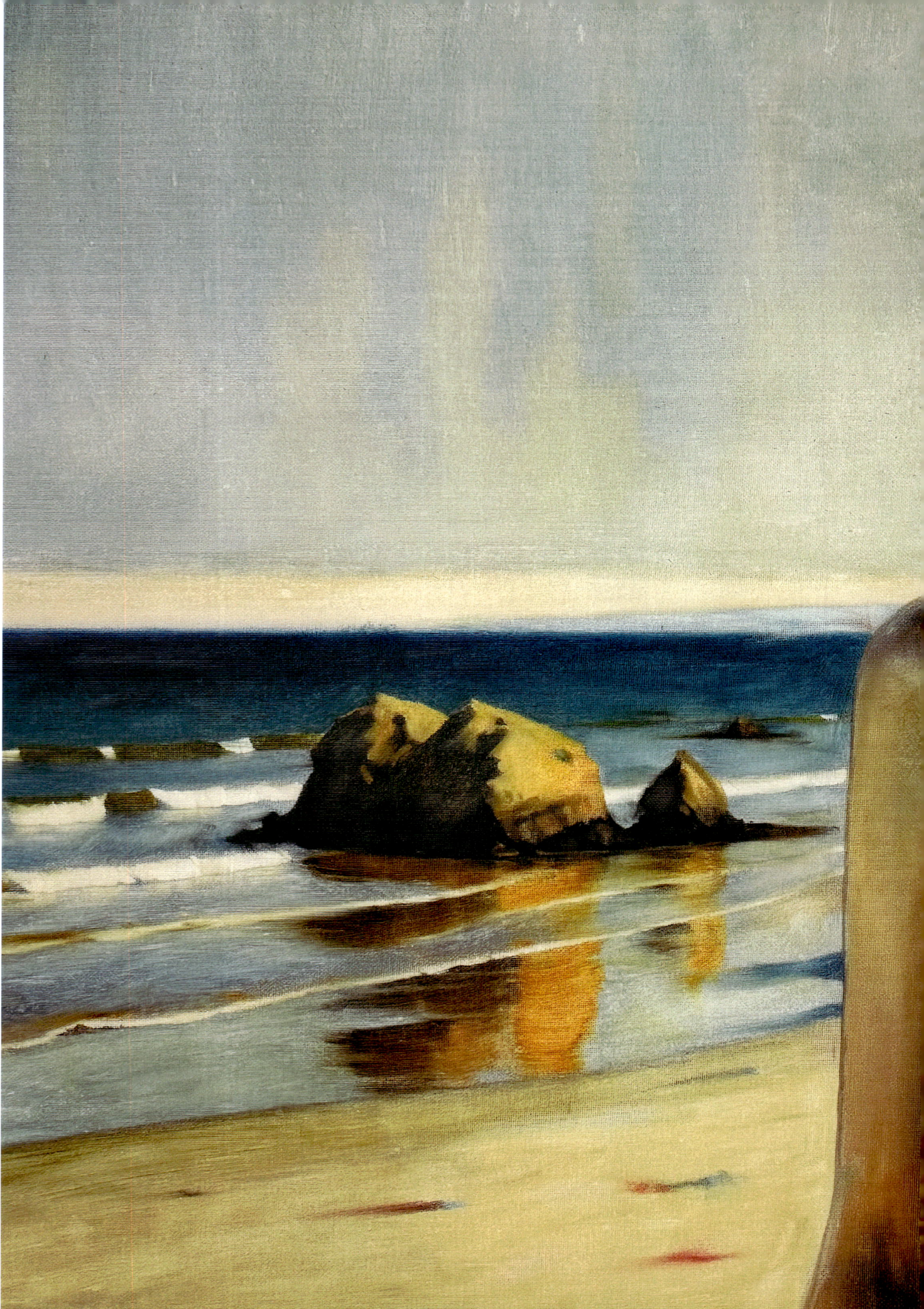

CHARM

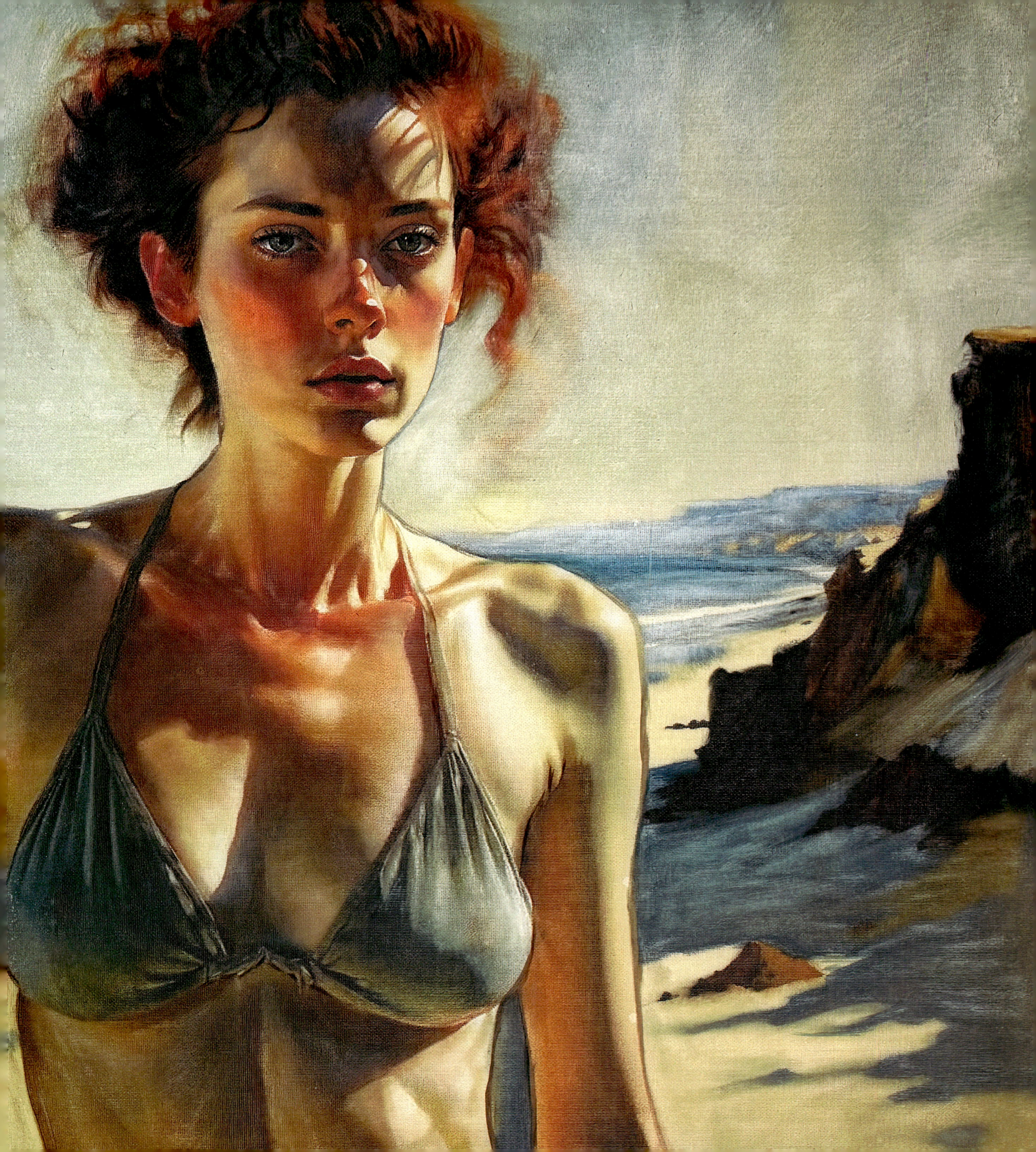

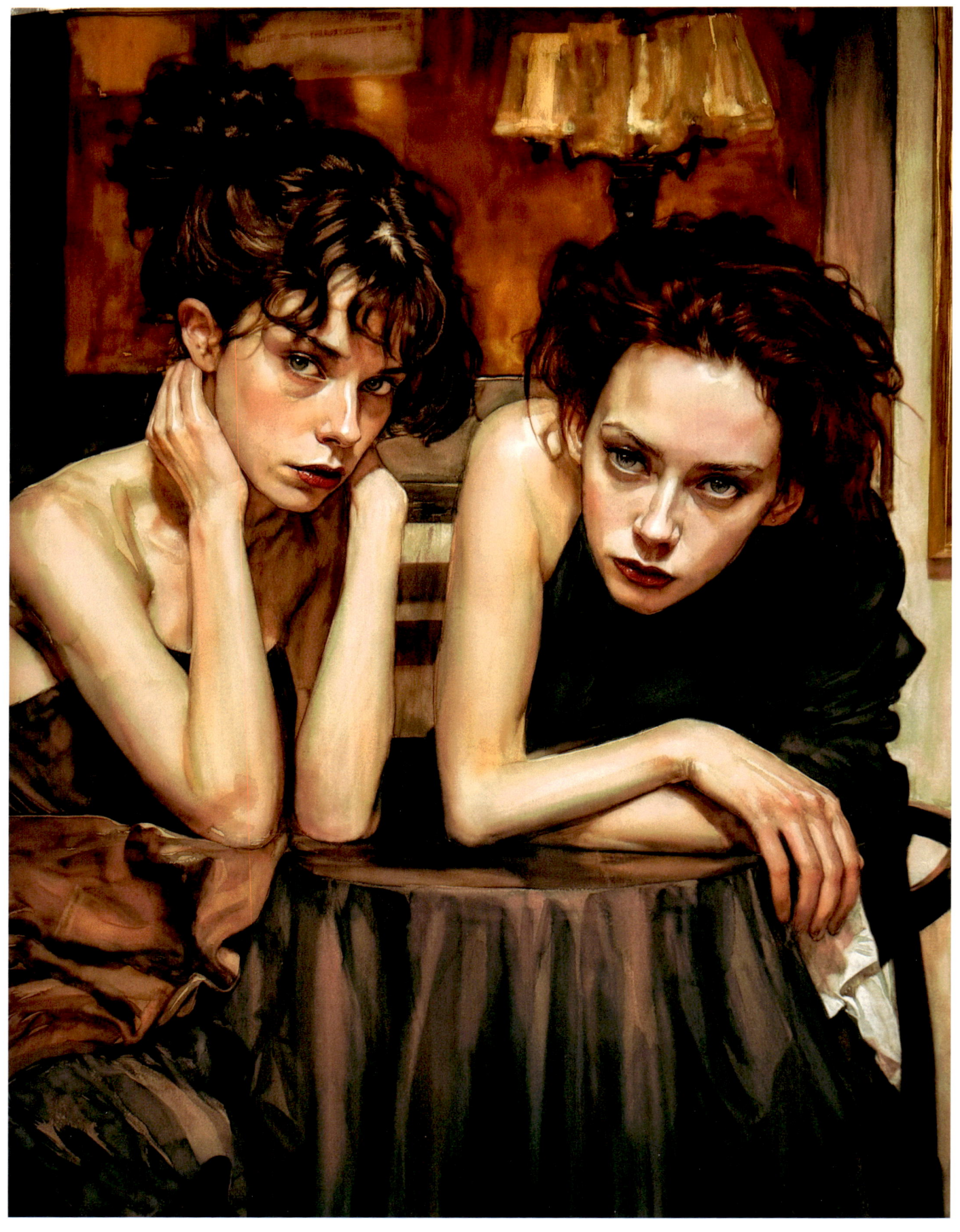

below: "Joy" | watercolor | 13" x 16" | Private Collection
opposite: "Poor Service" | watercolor | 26" x 20" | Private Collection
previous spread: "Summer" | oil on canvas | 27" x 38" | Private Collection

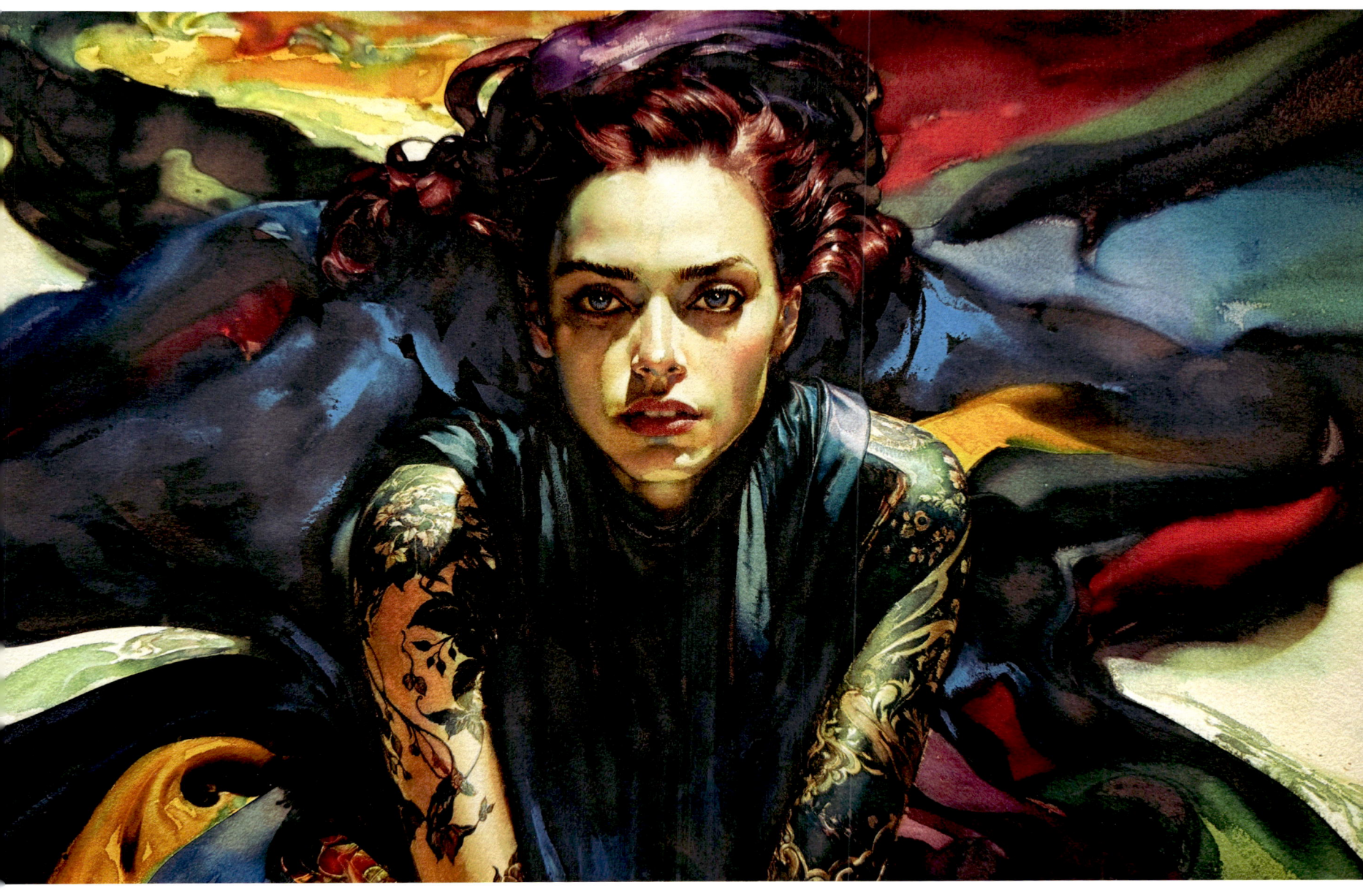

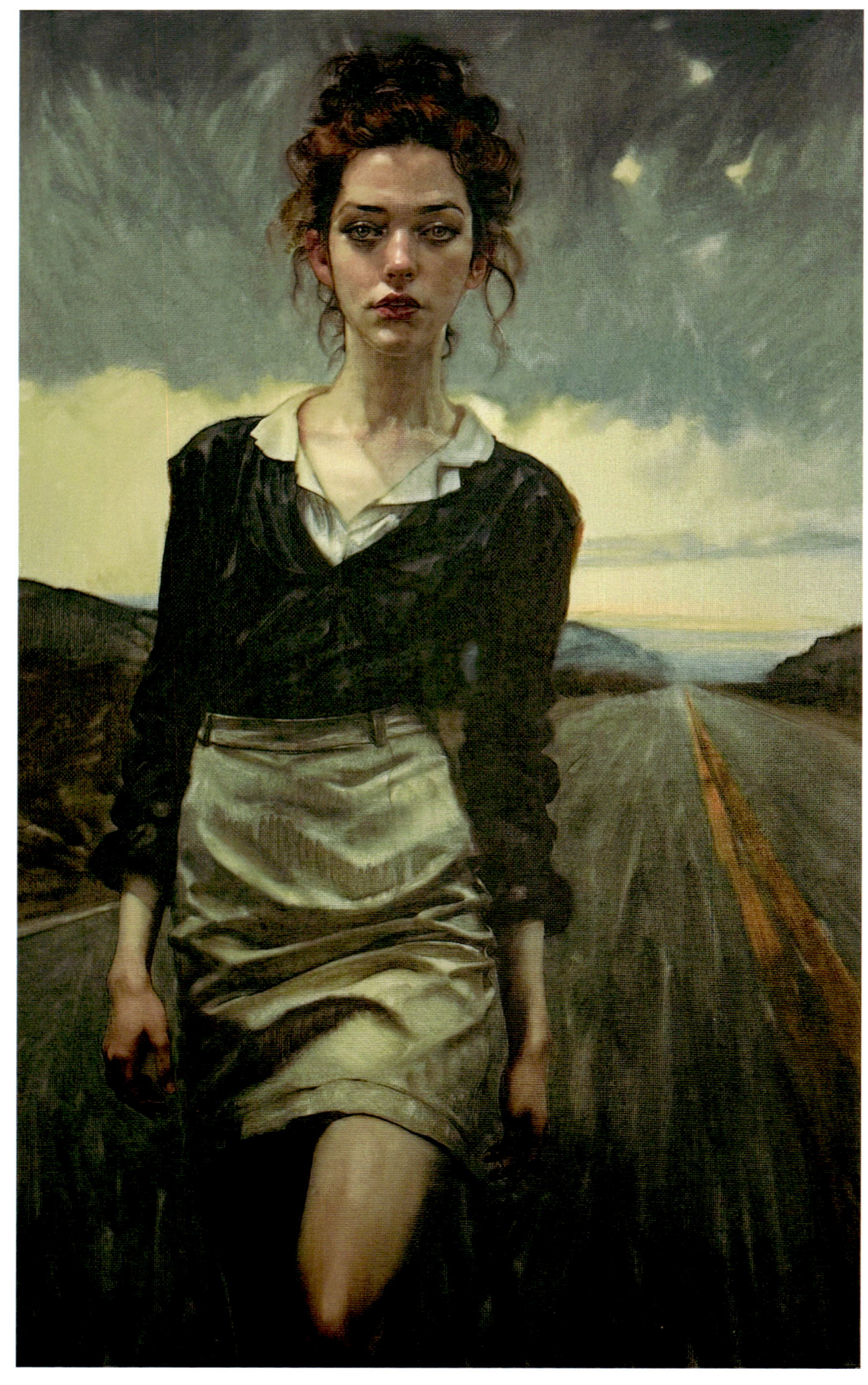

"The Long Road" | oil on canvas | 20" x 13"

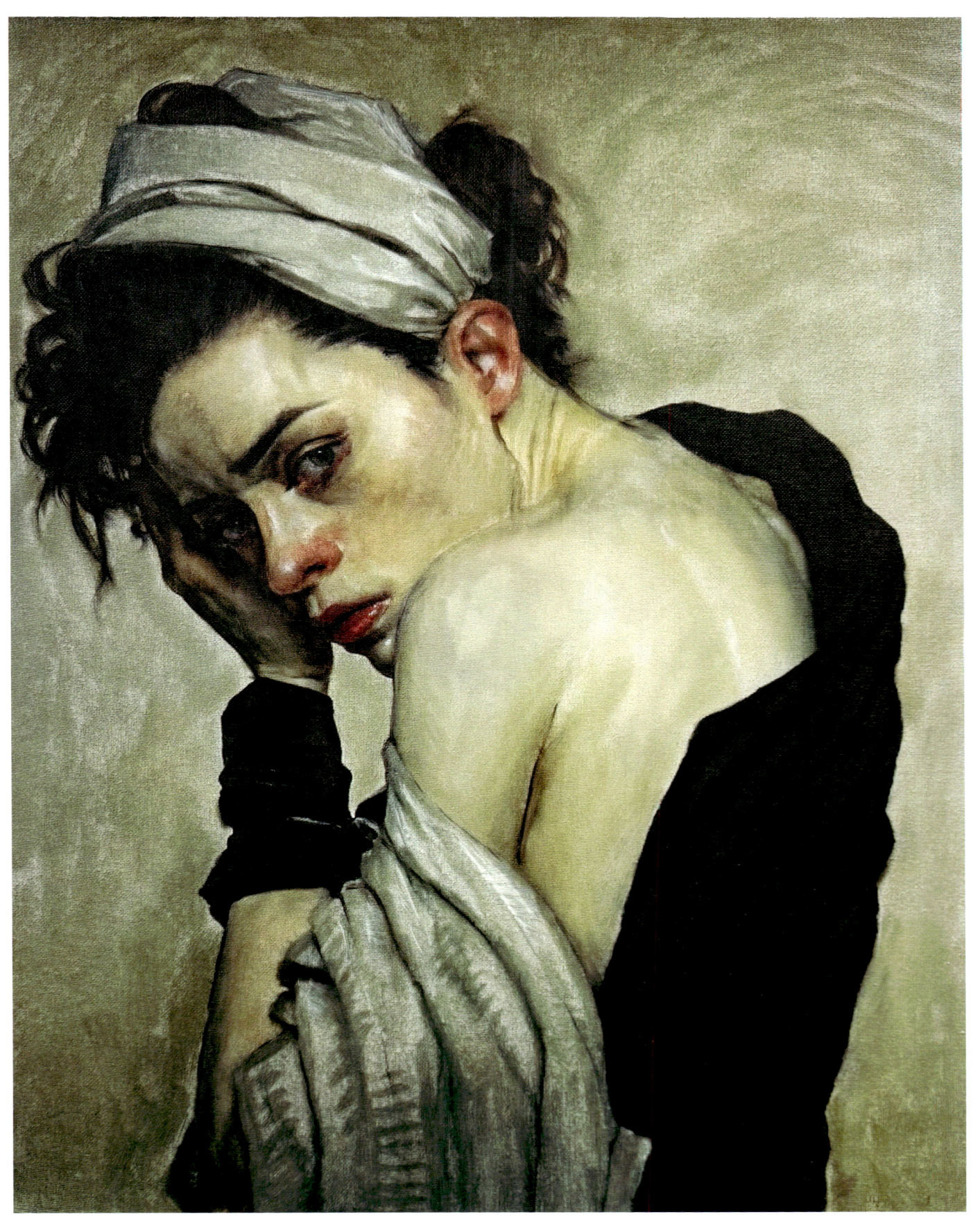

"Hymn" | oil on canvas | 24" x 18" | Private Collection

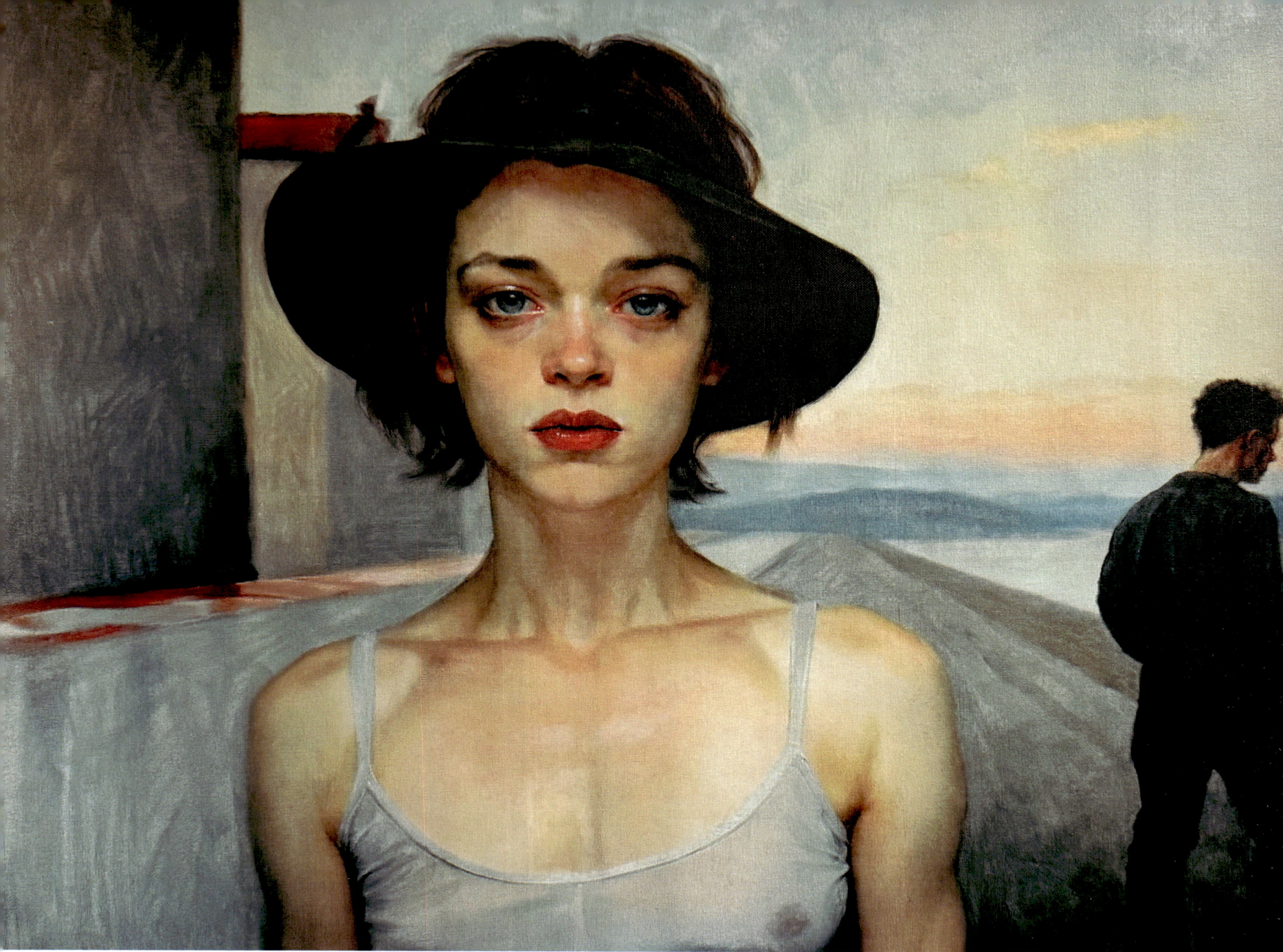

above: "Next Time" | oil on canvas | 25" x 35" | Private Collection
opposite: "A Day at the Races" | watercolor | 19" x 10"

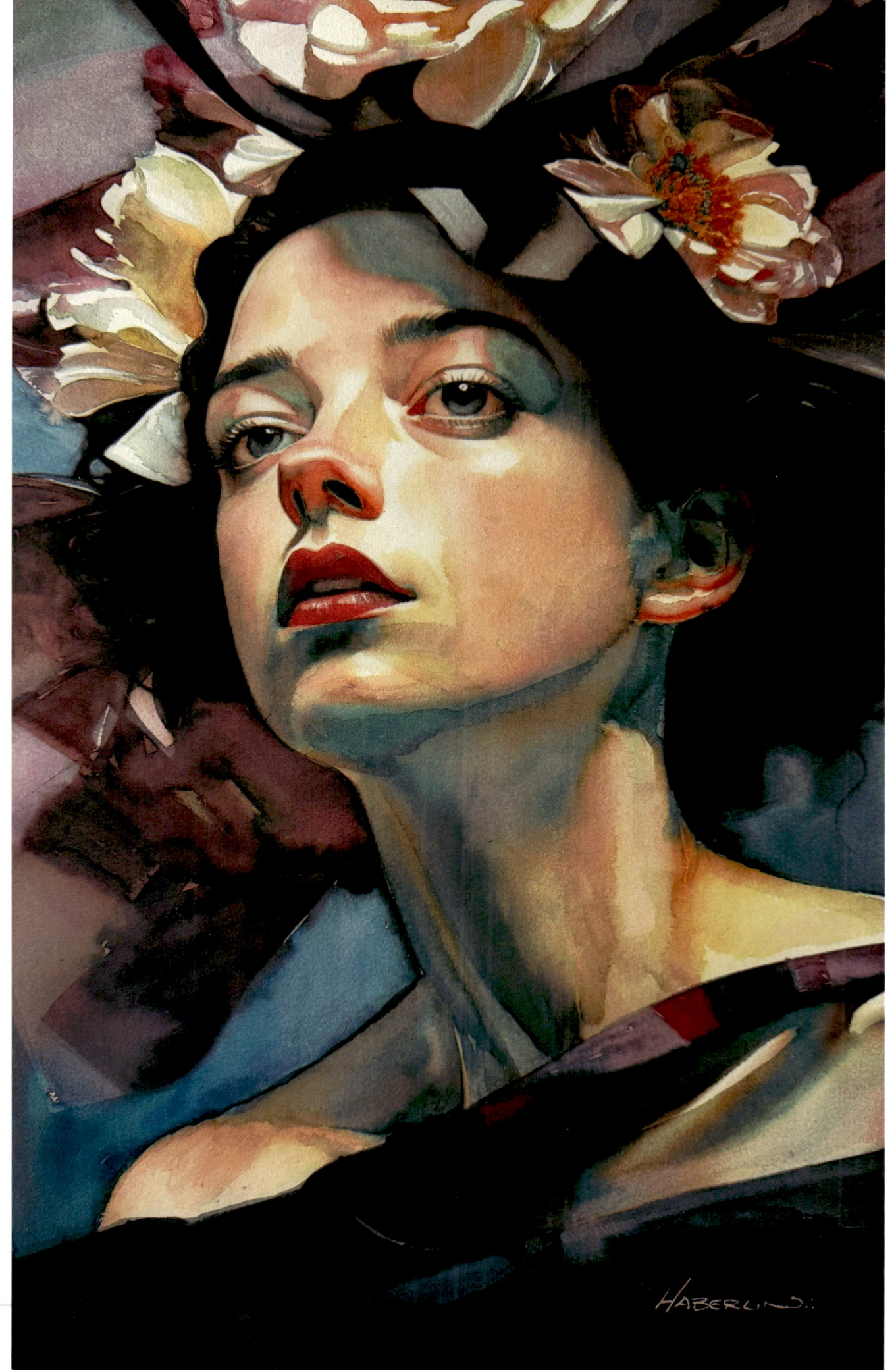

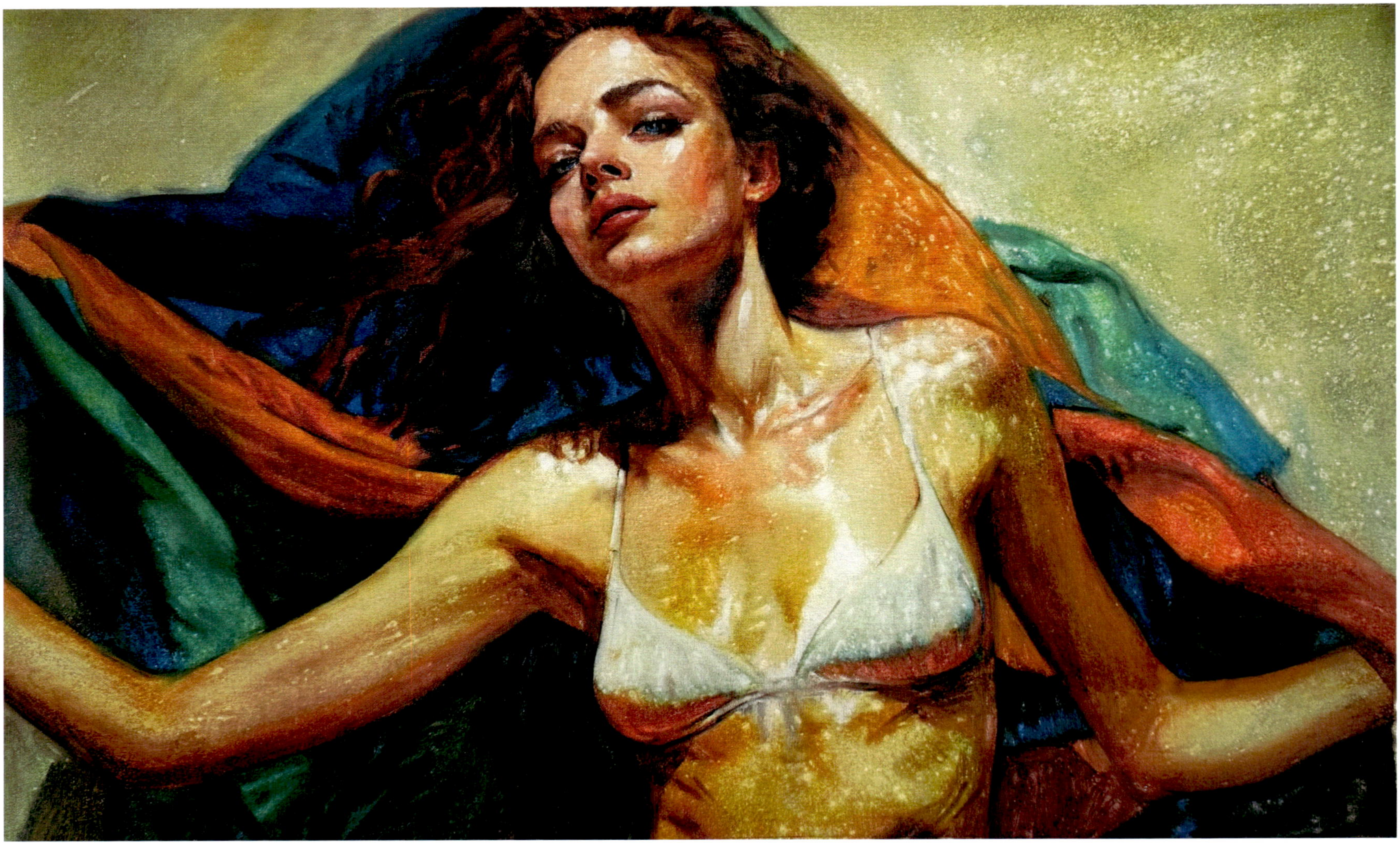

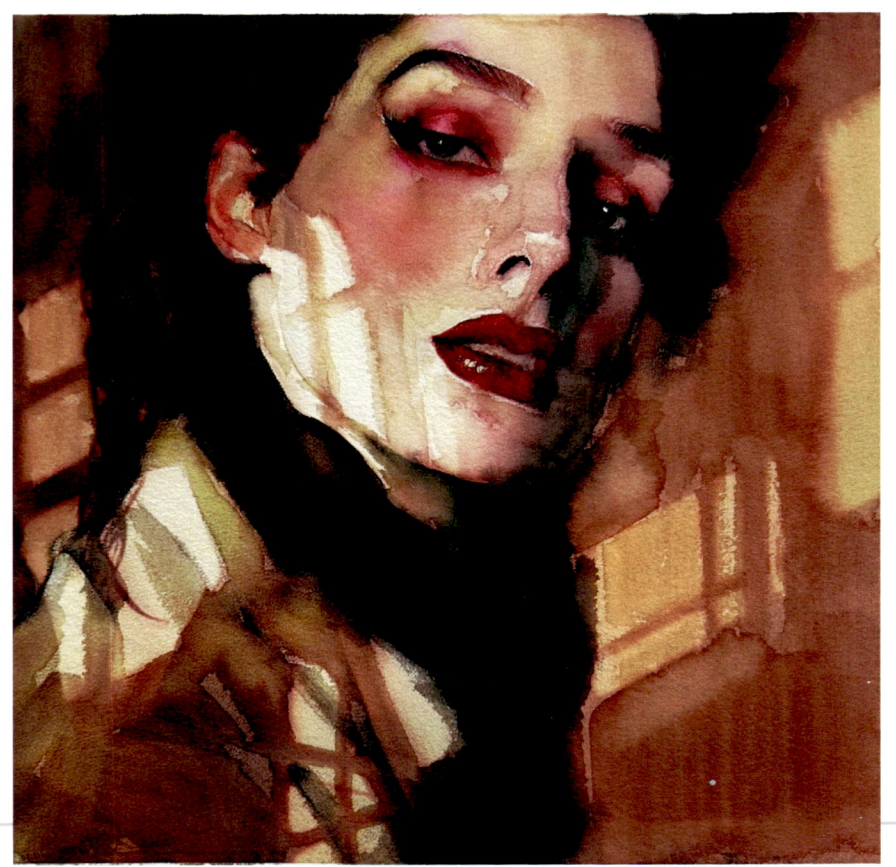

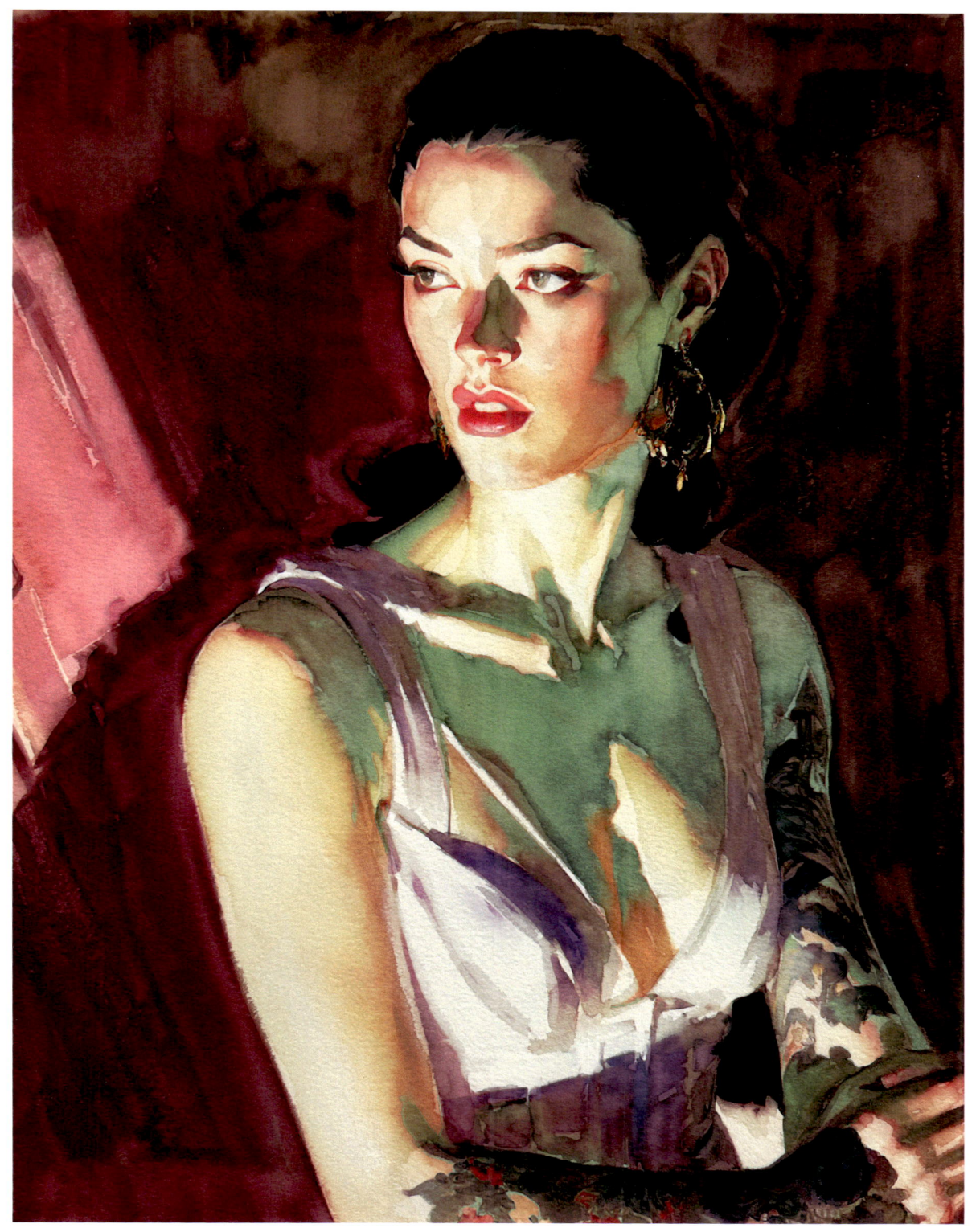

above: "Queen" | watercolor | 12" x 7" | Private Collection
opposite top: "Trip" | oil on canvas | 24" x 35"
opposite bottom: "Mist" | watercolor | 8" x 8"

opposite: "Rhonda" | watercolor | 14" x 8" | Private Collection
below: "Road Trip" | watercolor | 10" x 14" | Private Collection

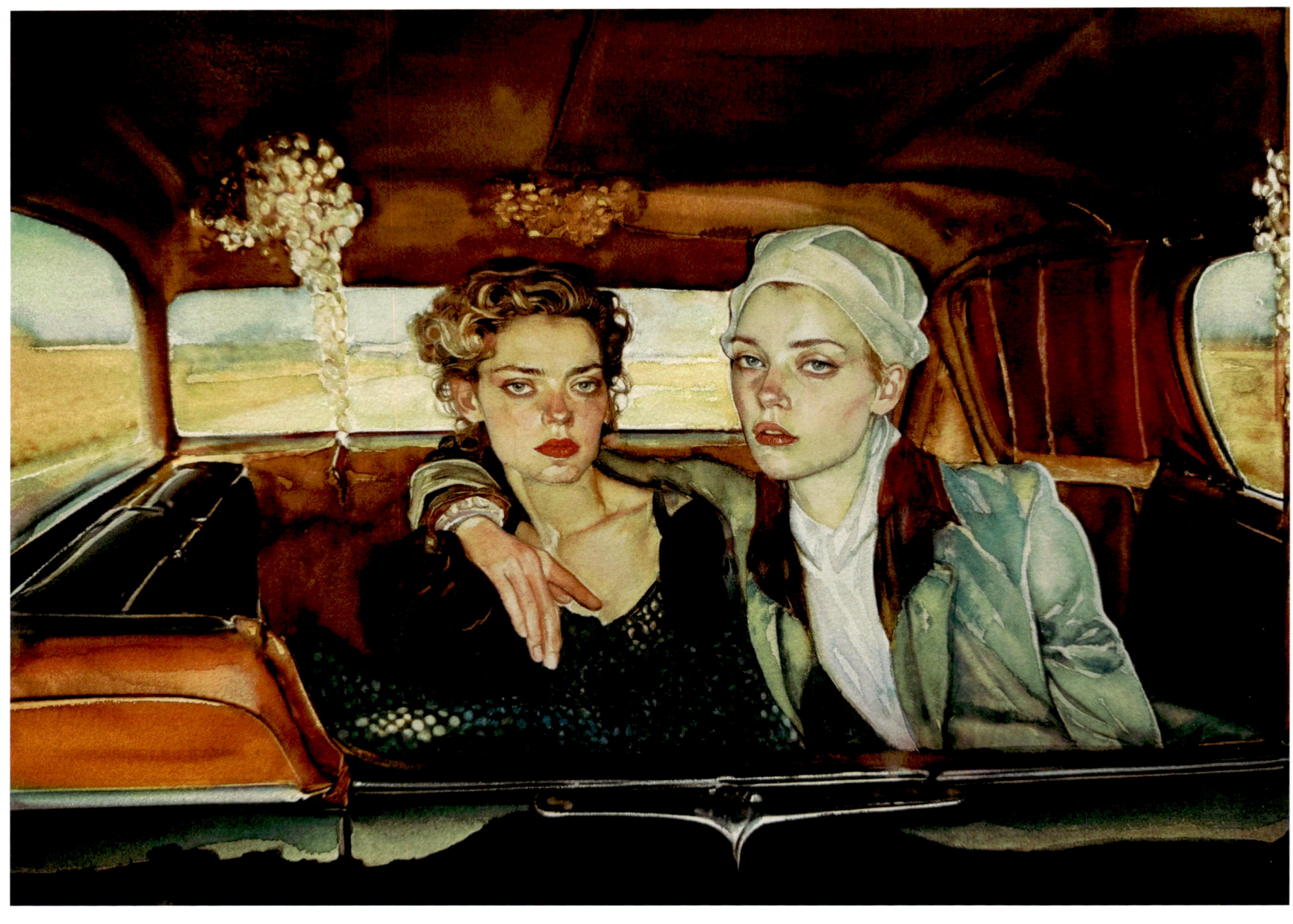

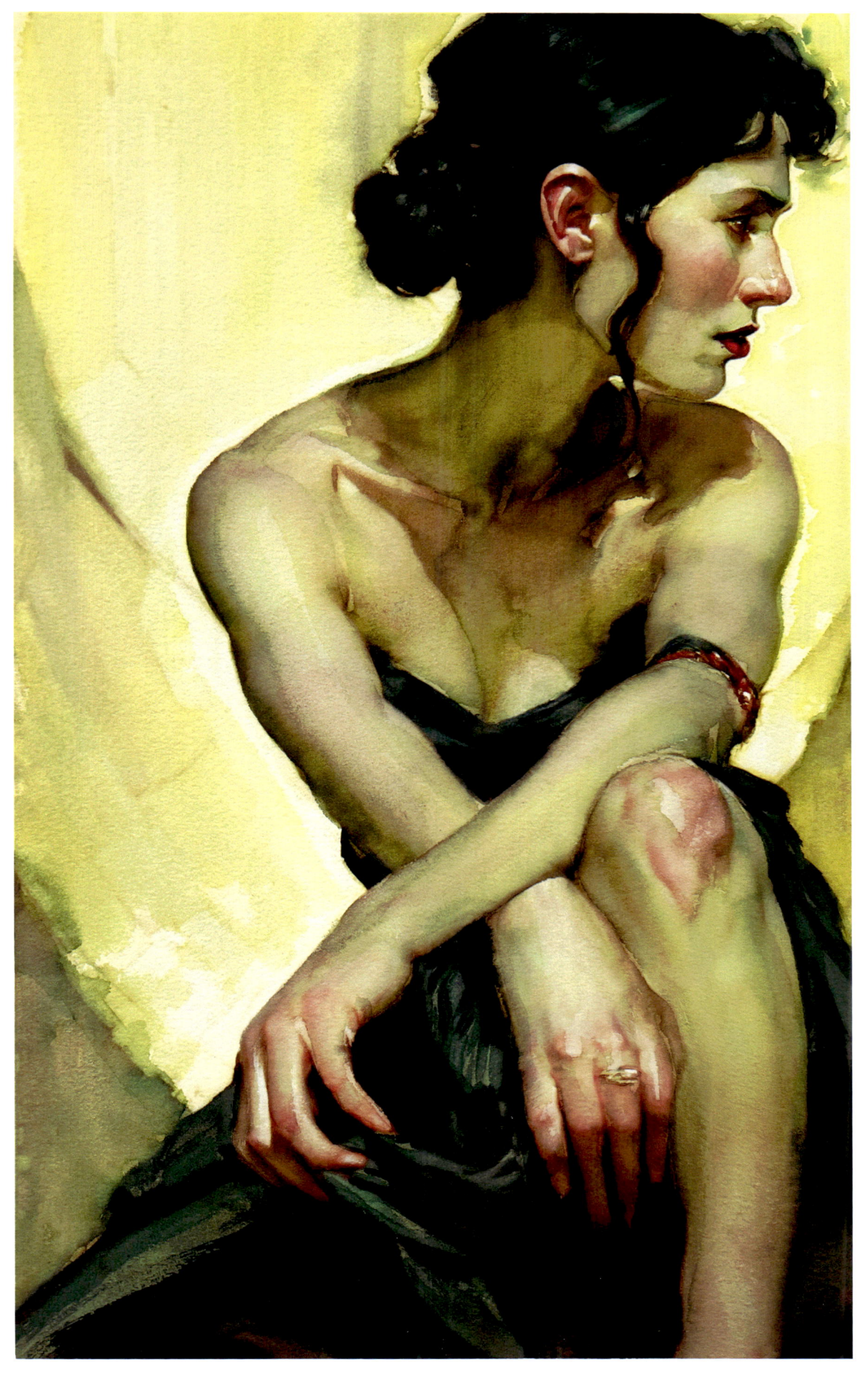

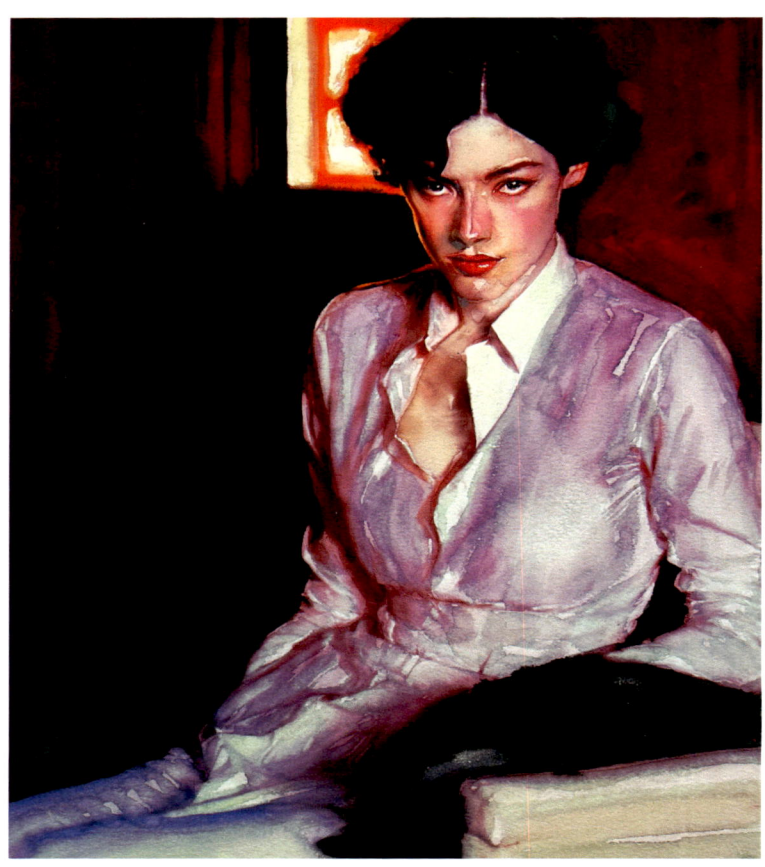

left: "I Know" | watercolor | 12" x 9"
below: "Emily" | watercolor | 8" x 14"
opposite: "Kenzie" | watercolor | 23" x 20" | Private Collection

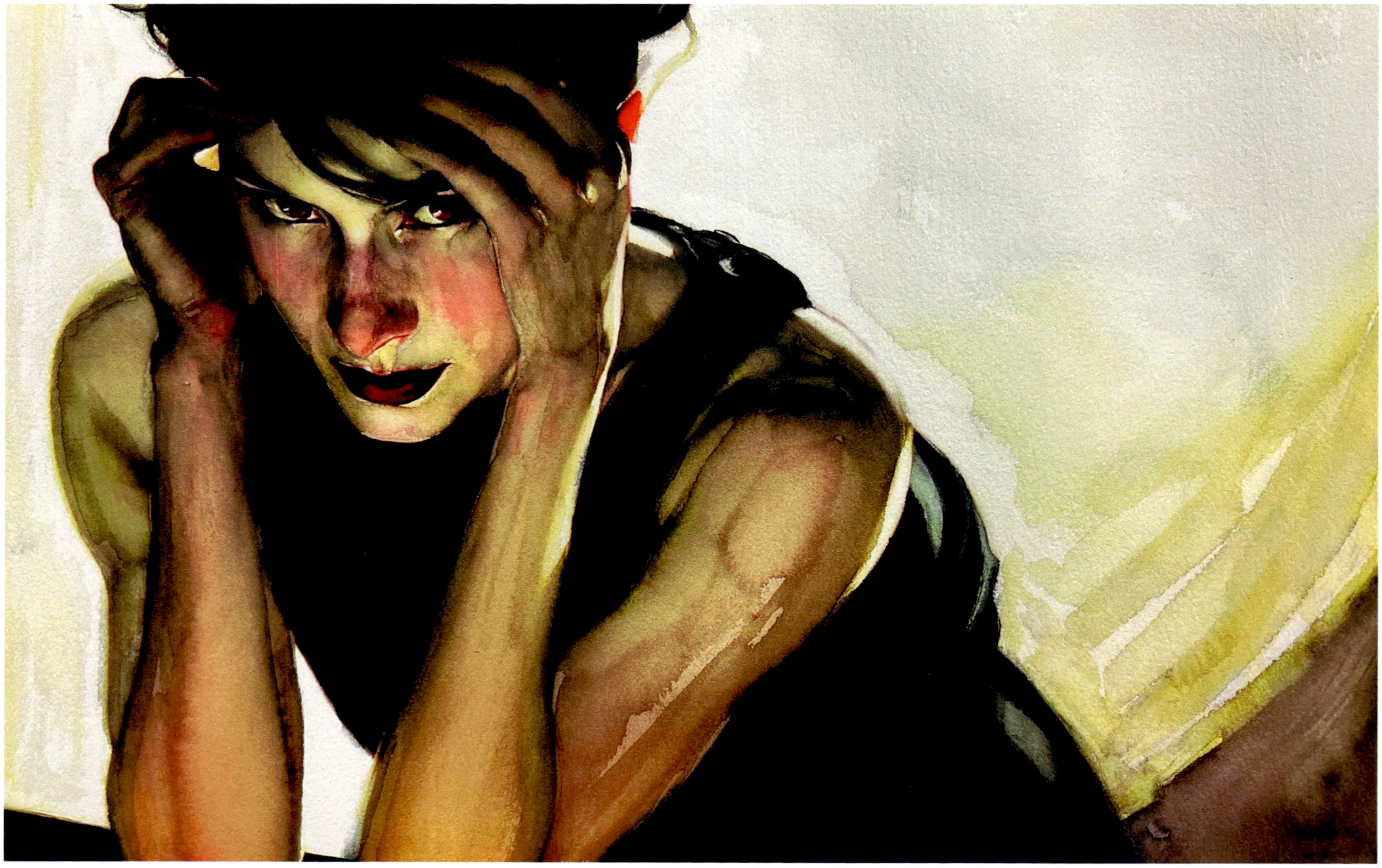

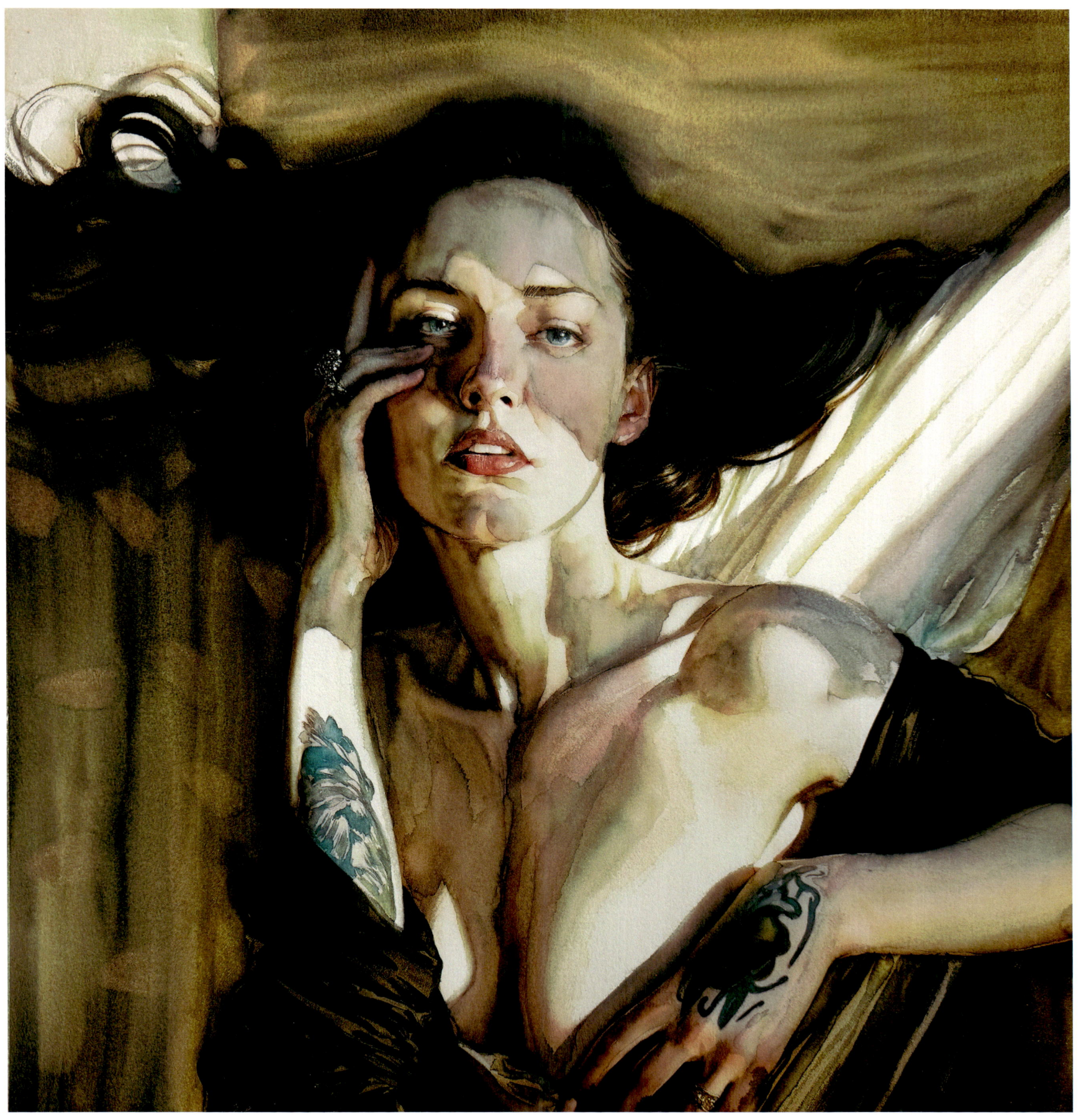

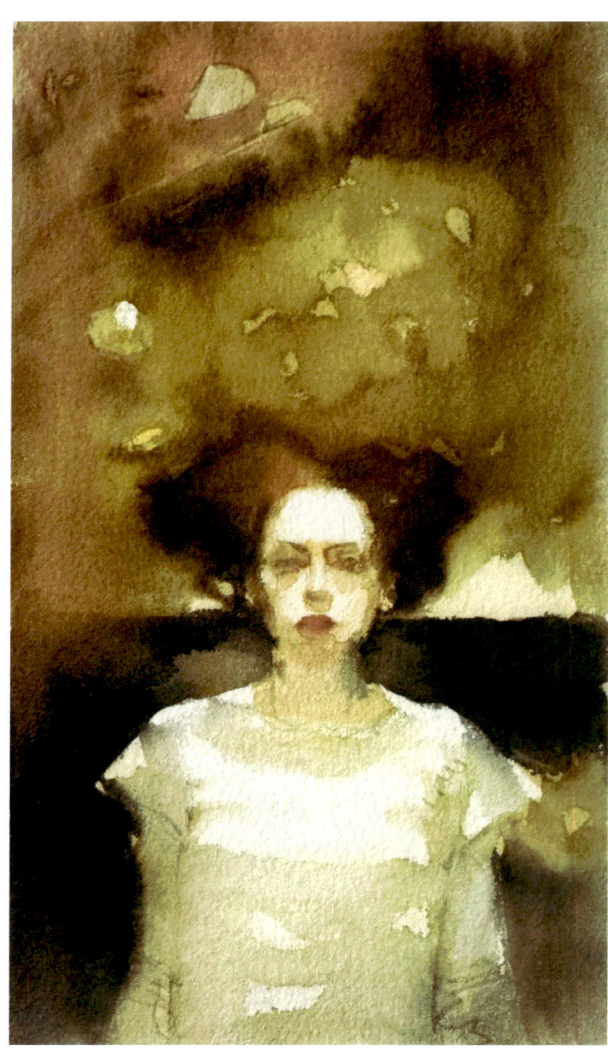

above: "Lillies" *Sketch*
right: "Lillies 1" | watercolor | 23" x 13"

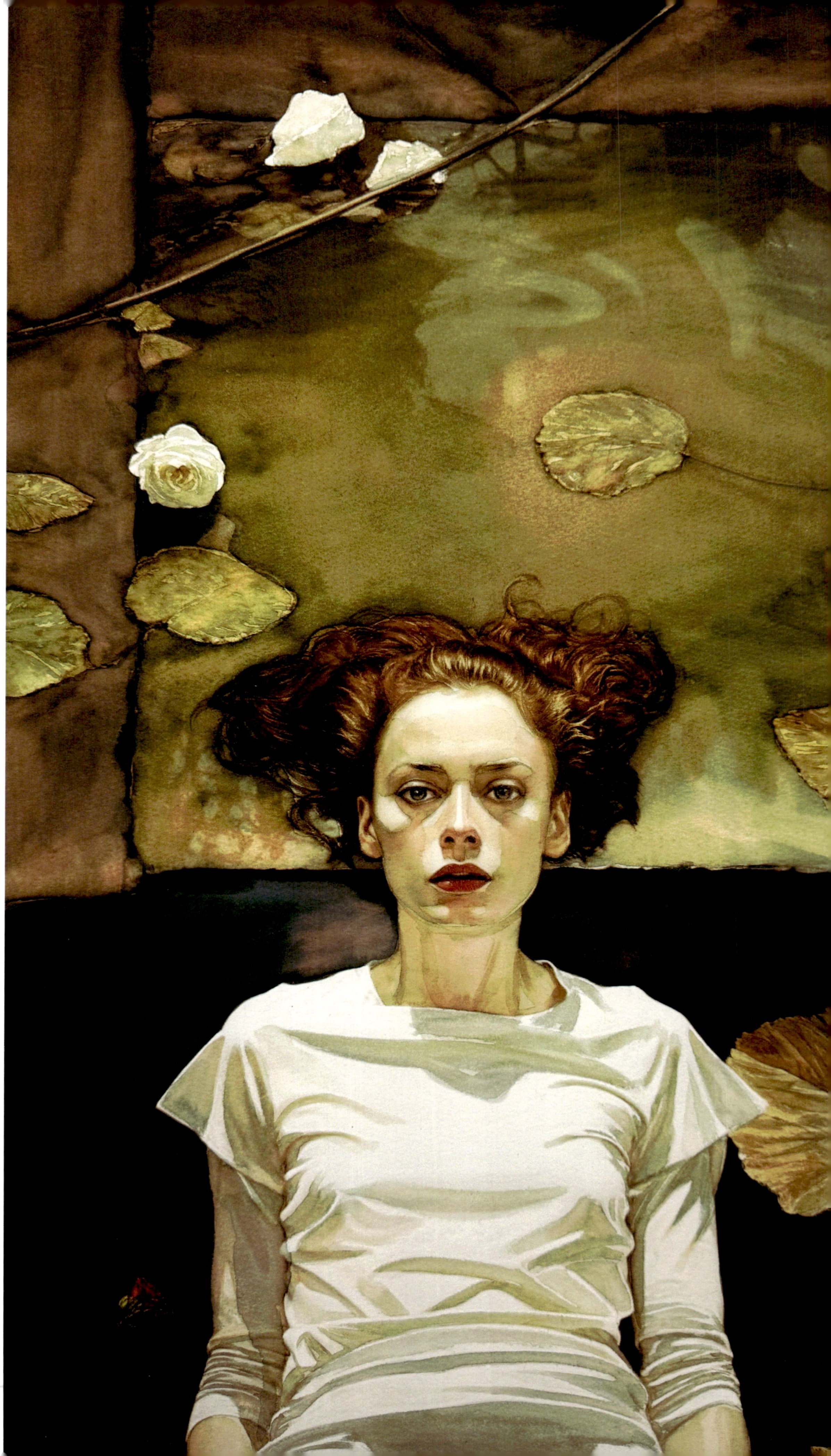

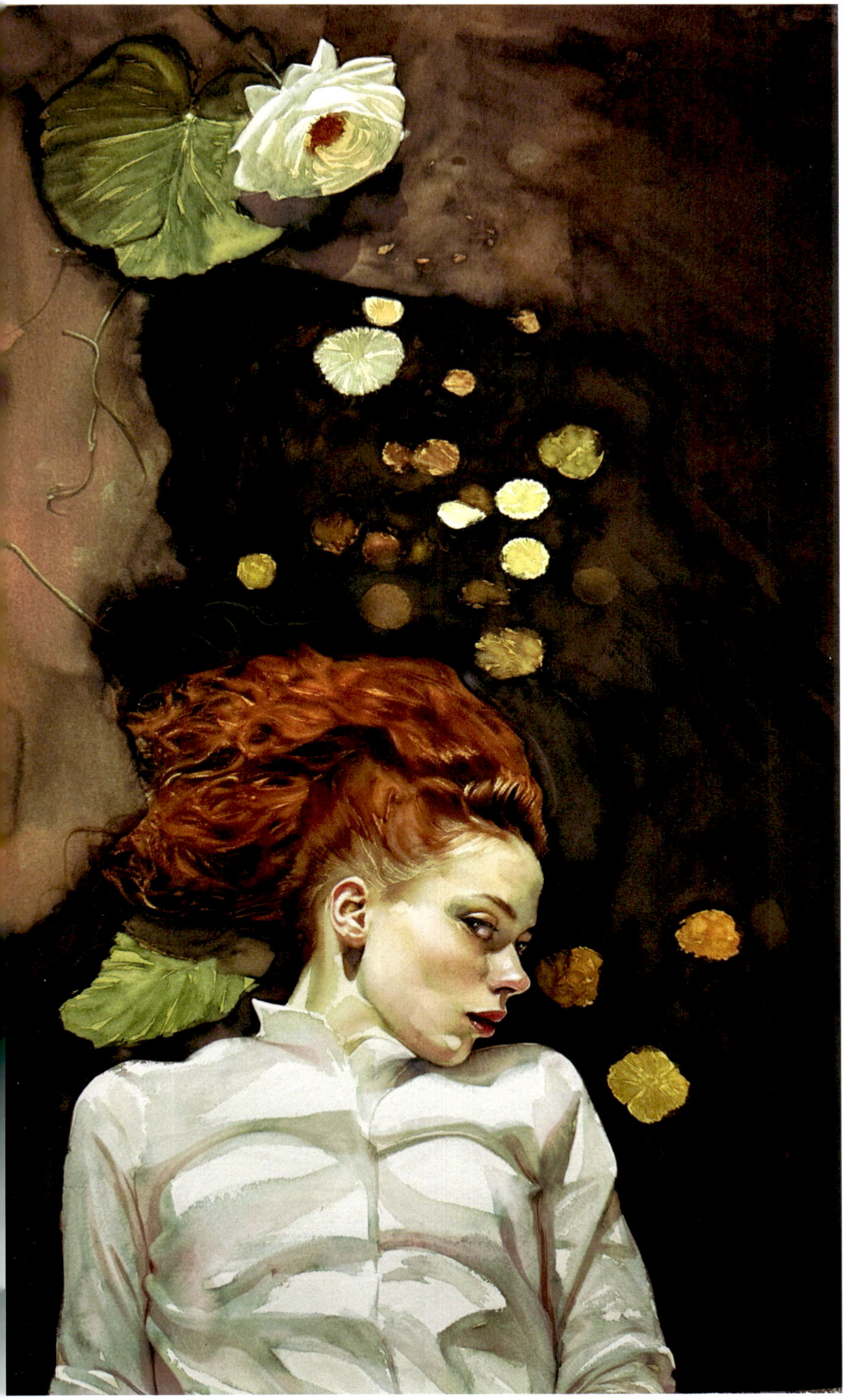

left: "Lillies 2" | watercolor | 20.5" x 12"
below: "Lillies 3" | watercolor | 23" x 13.5"

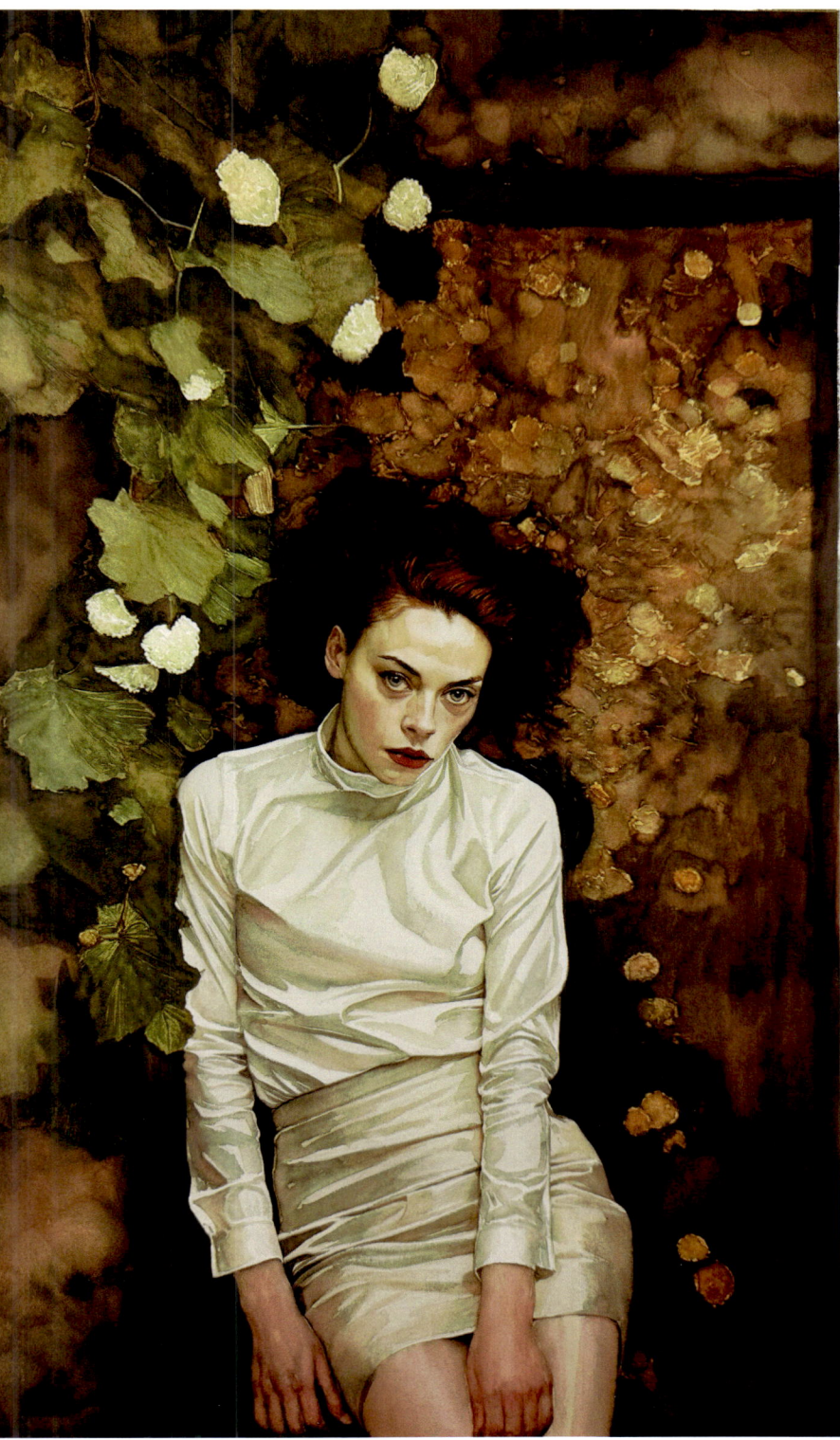

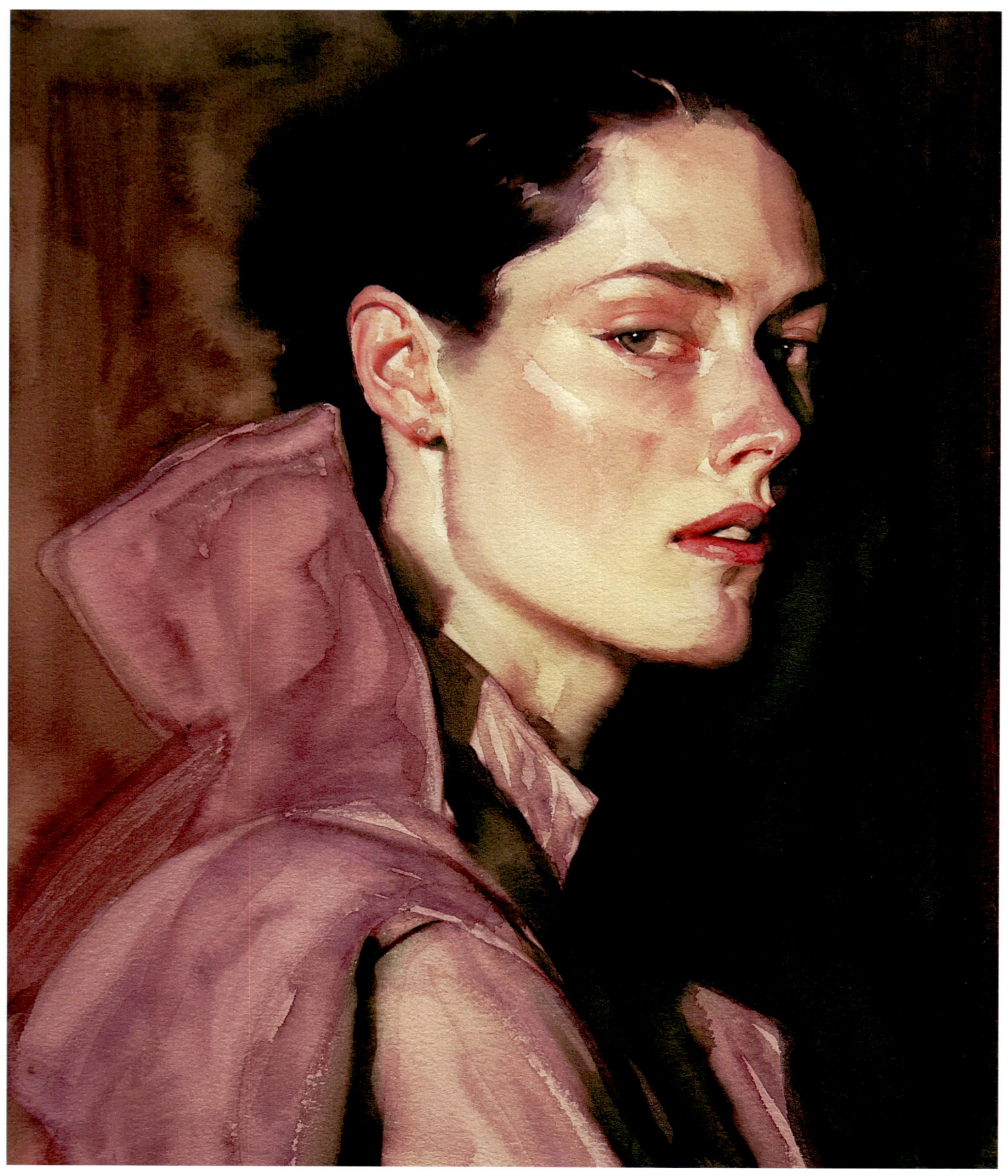

above: "Loomis" | watercolor | 12" x 9" | Private Collection
opposite: "Elisa" | watercolor | 12" x 8" | Private Collection

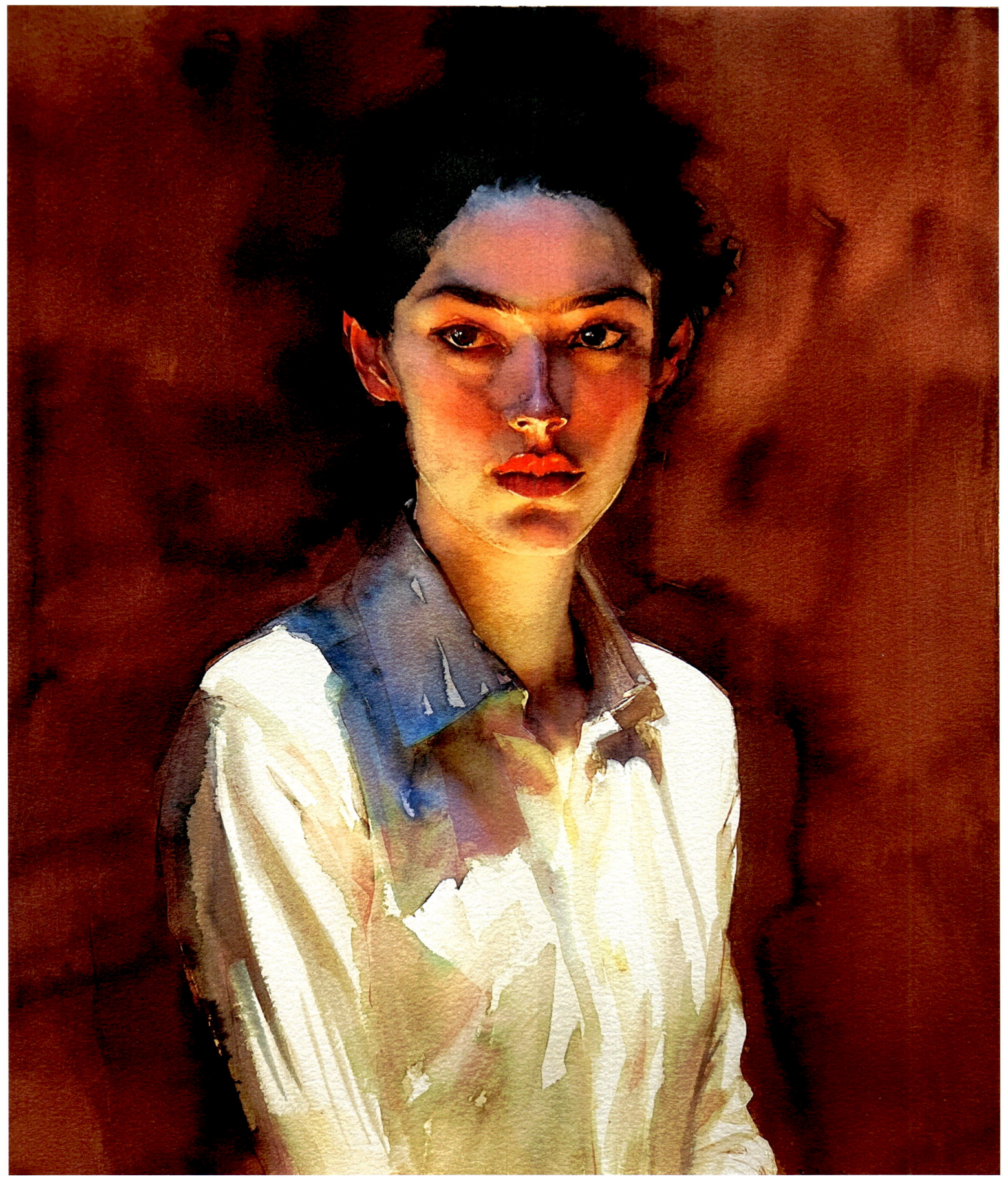

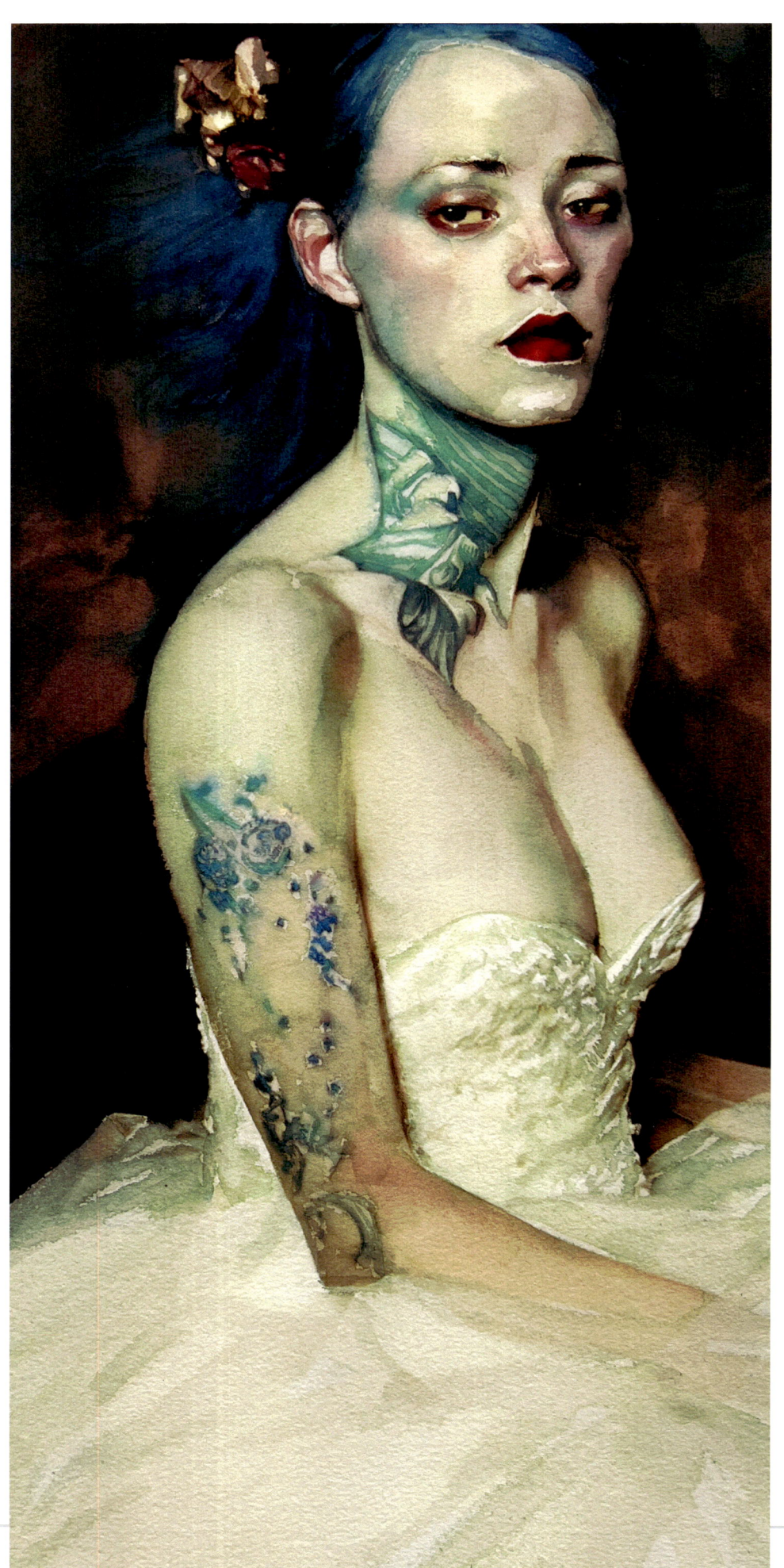

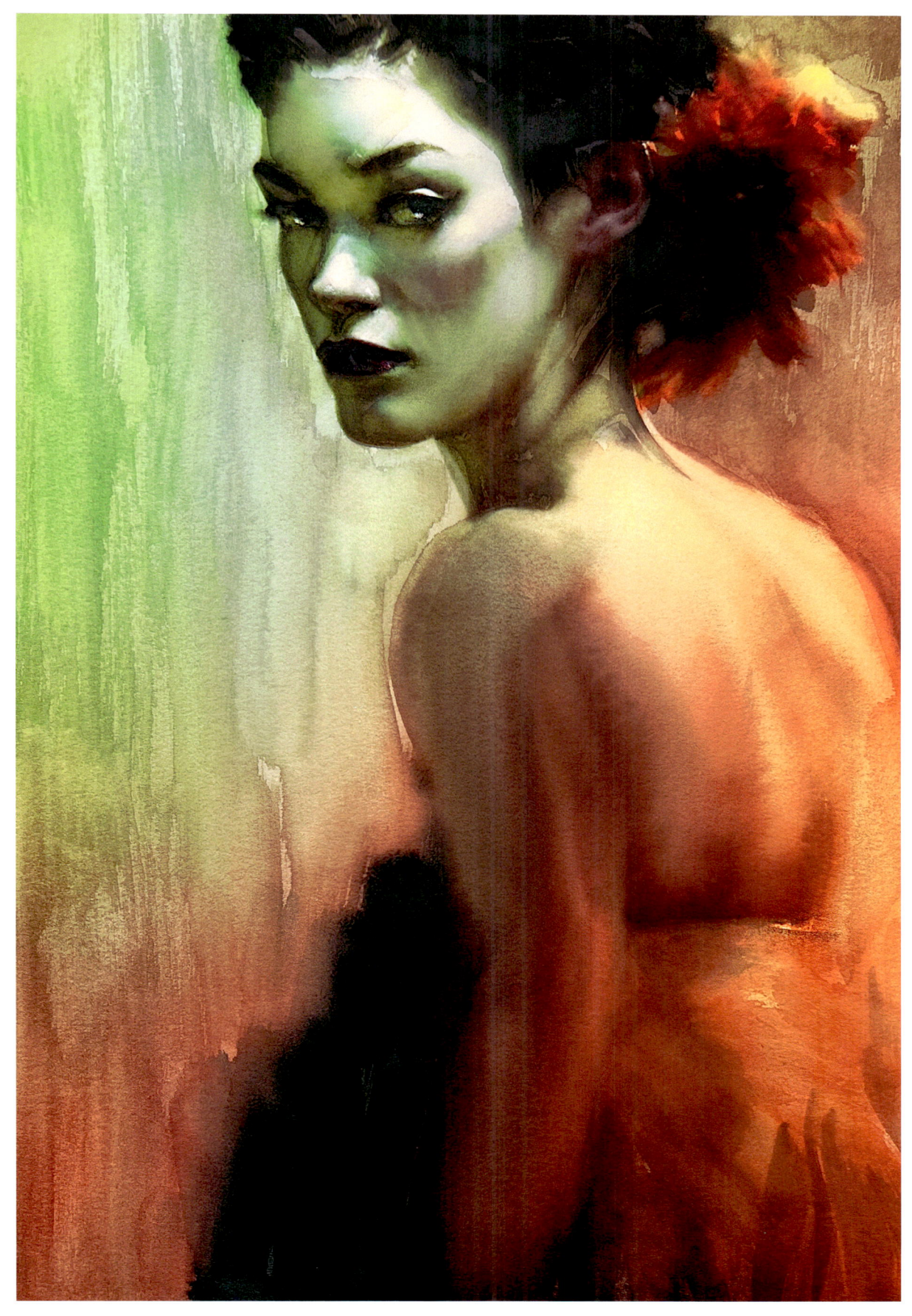

above: "The Road" | watercolor | 12" x 7" | Private Collection
opposite: "Ava" | watercolor | 14" x 7"

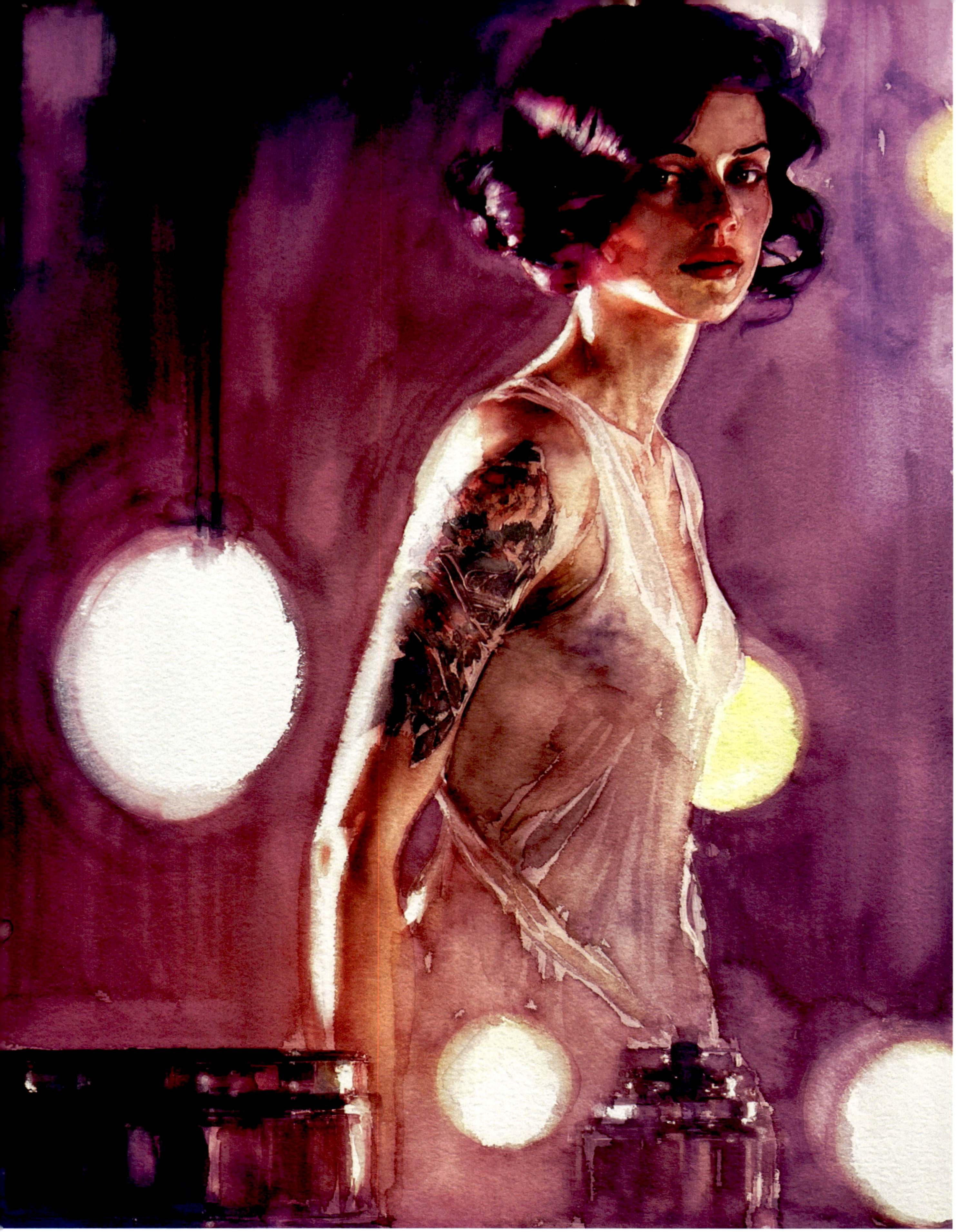

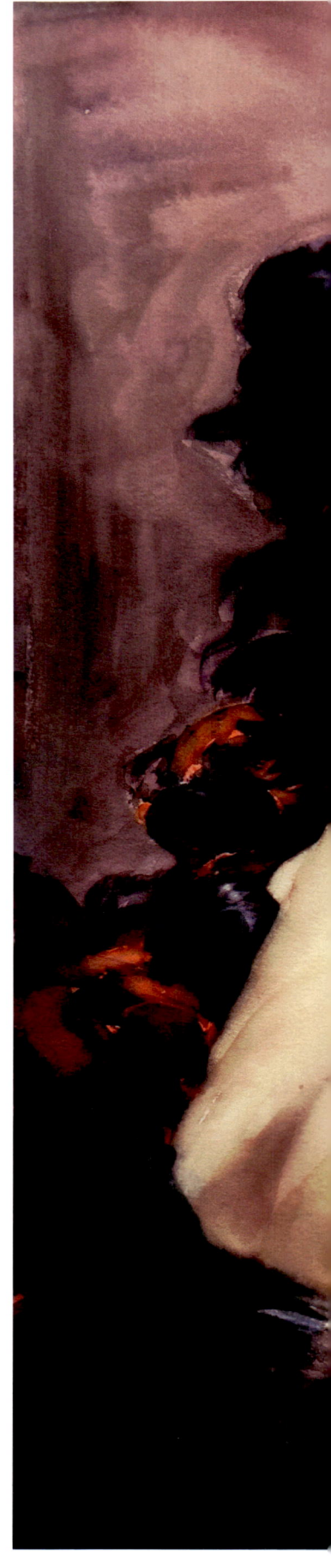

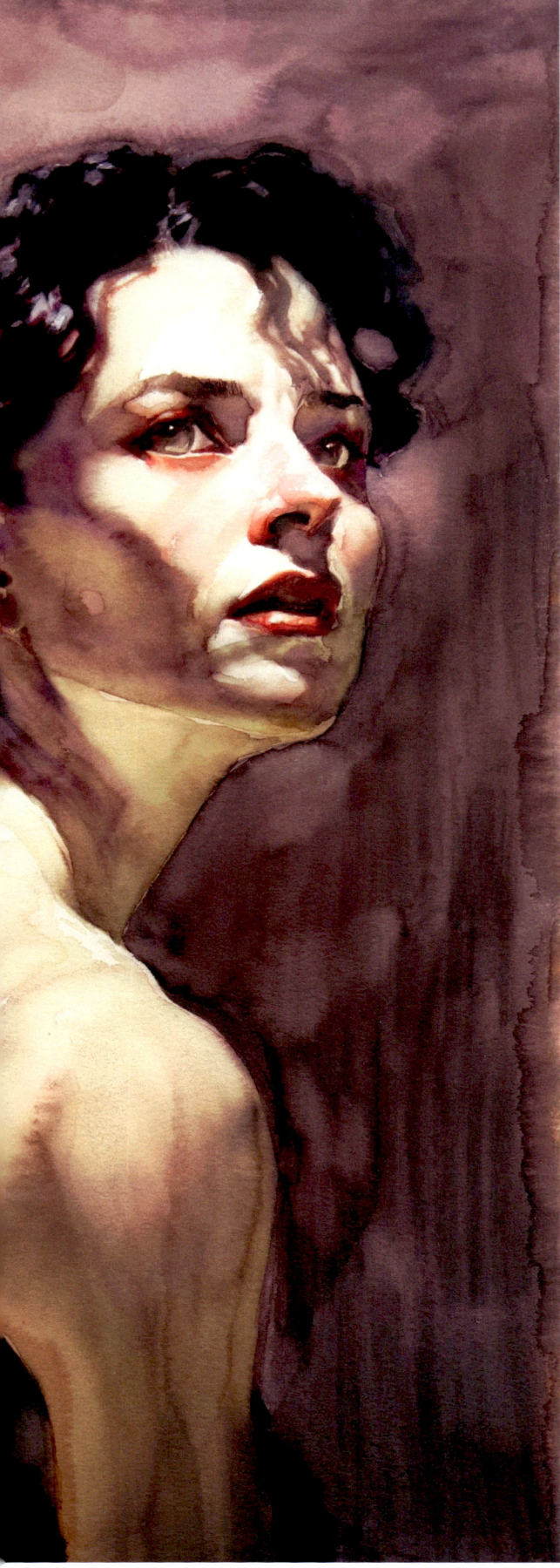

facing page: "Rose" | watercolor | 10" x 8" | Private Collection
middle: "Rush" | watercolor | 16" x 12" | Private Collection
below: "Stevie 2" | watercolor | 8.5" x 6.5" | Private Collection

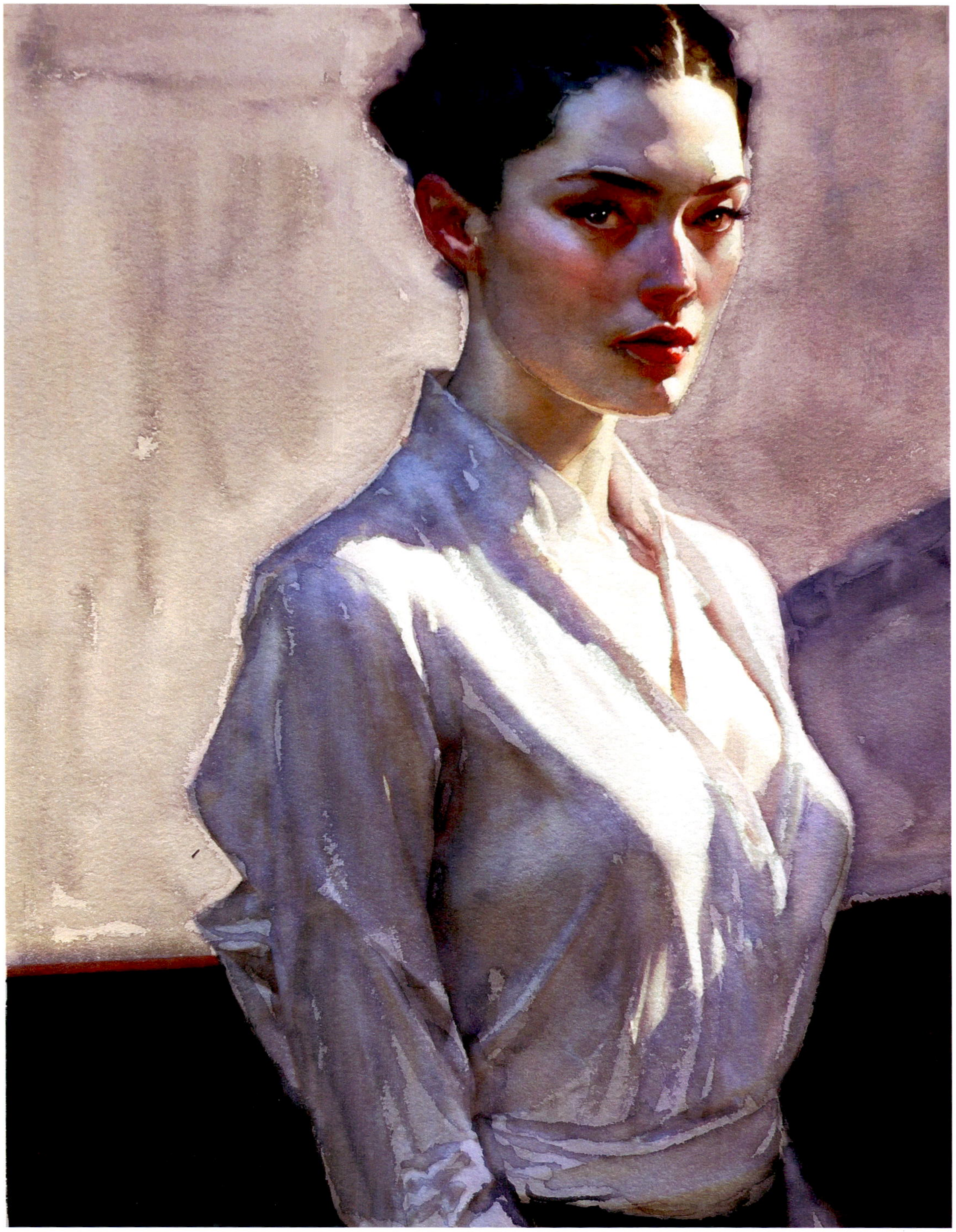

"Stevie 2" *Detail*

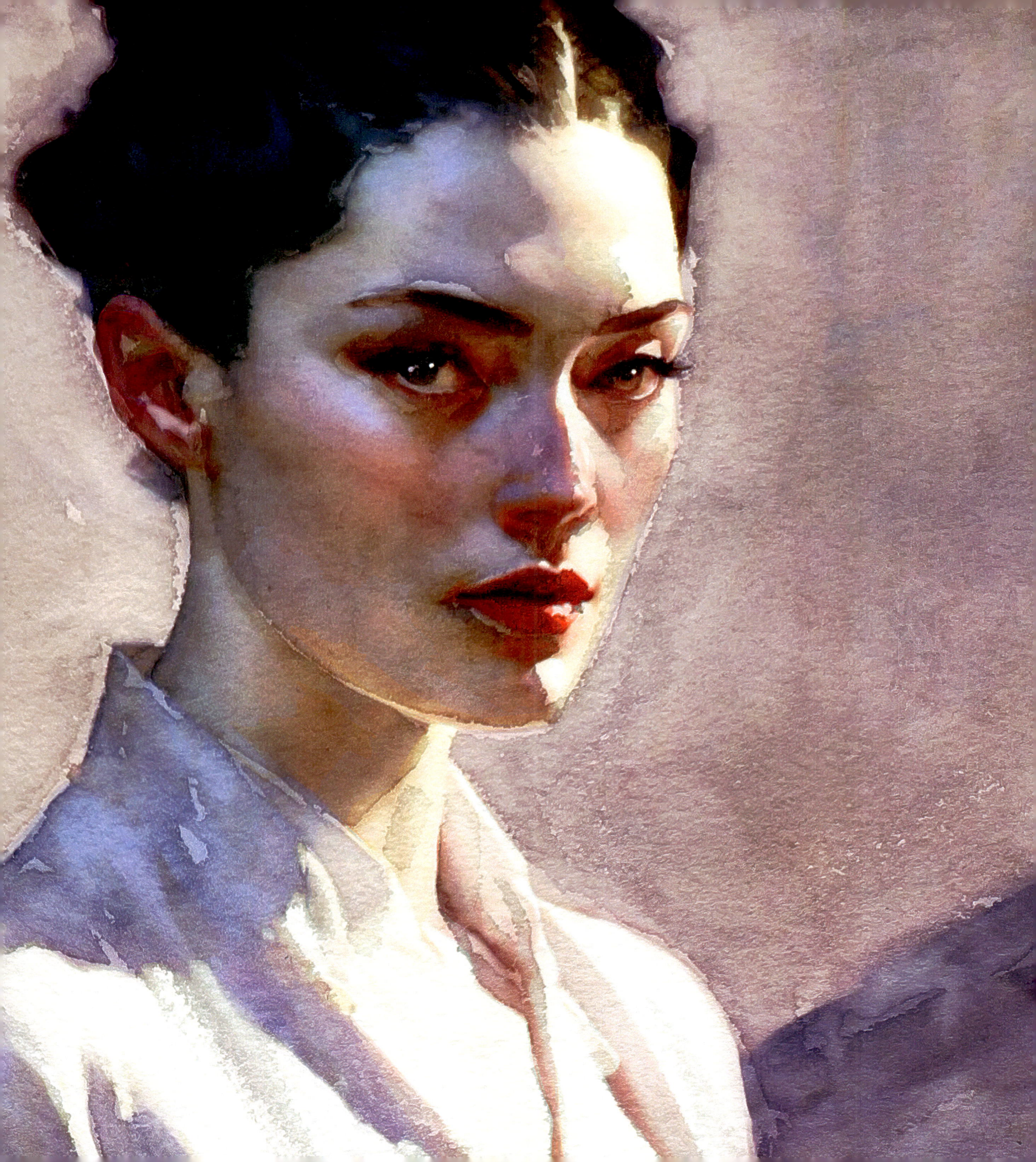

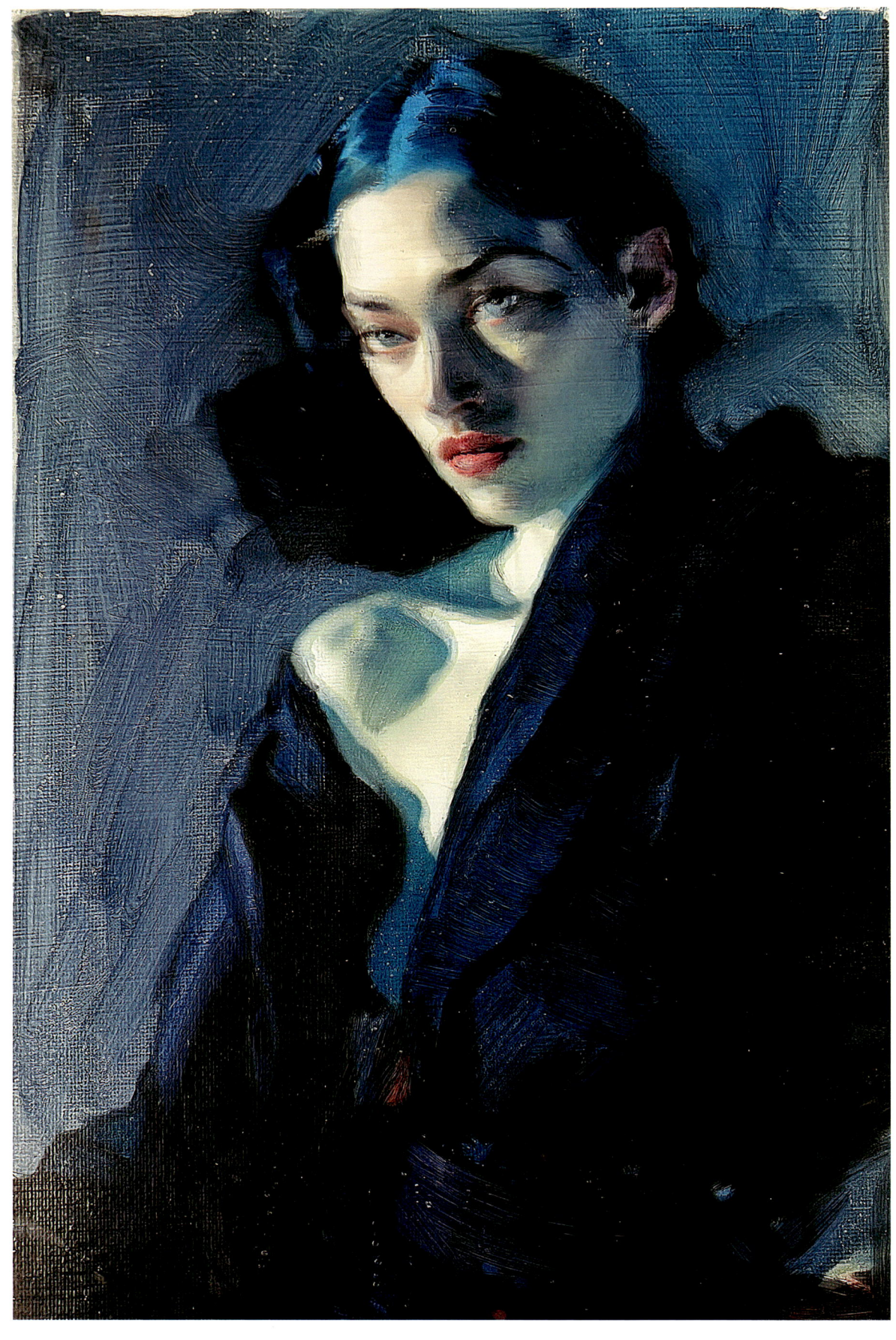

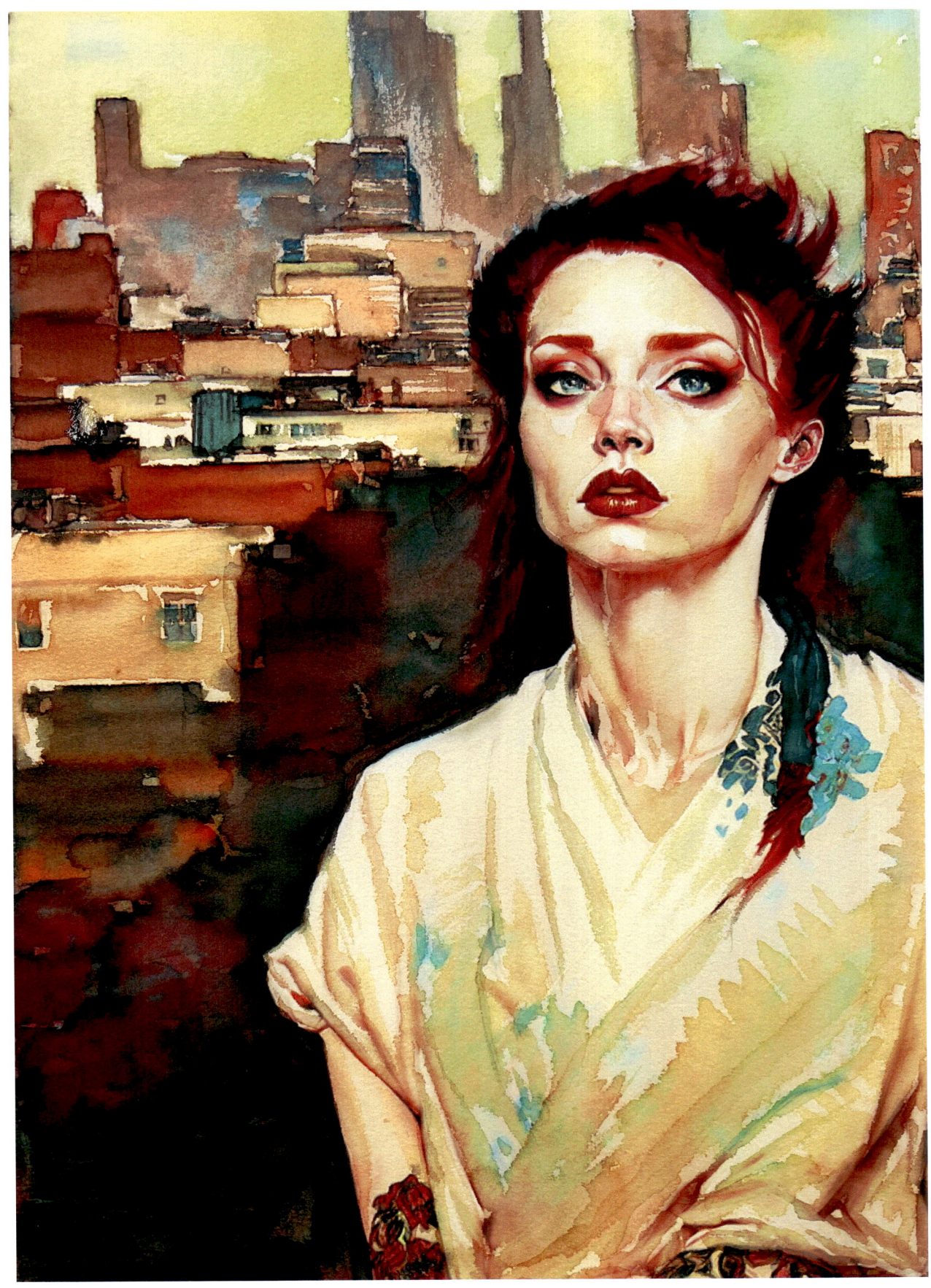

above: "Ronni" | watercolor | 13" x 9"
opposite: "Lexi" | oil on canvas | 12" x 9"

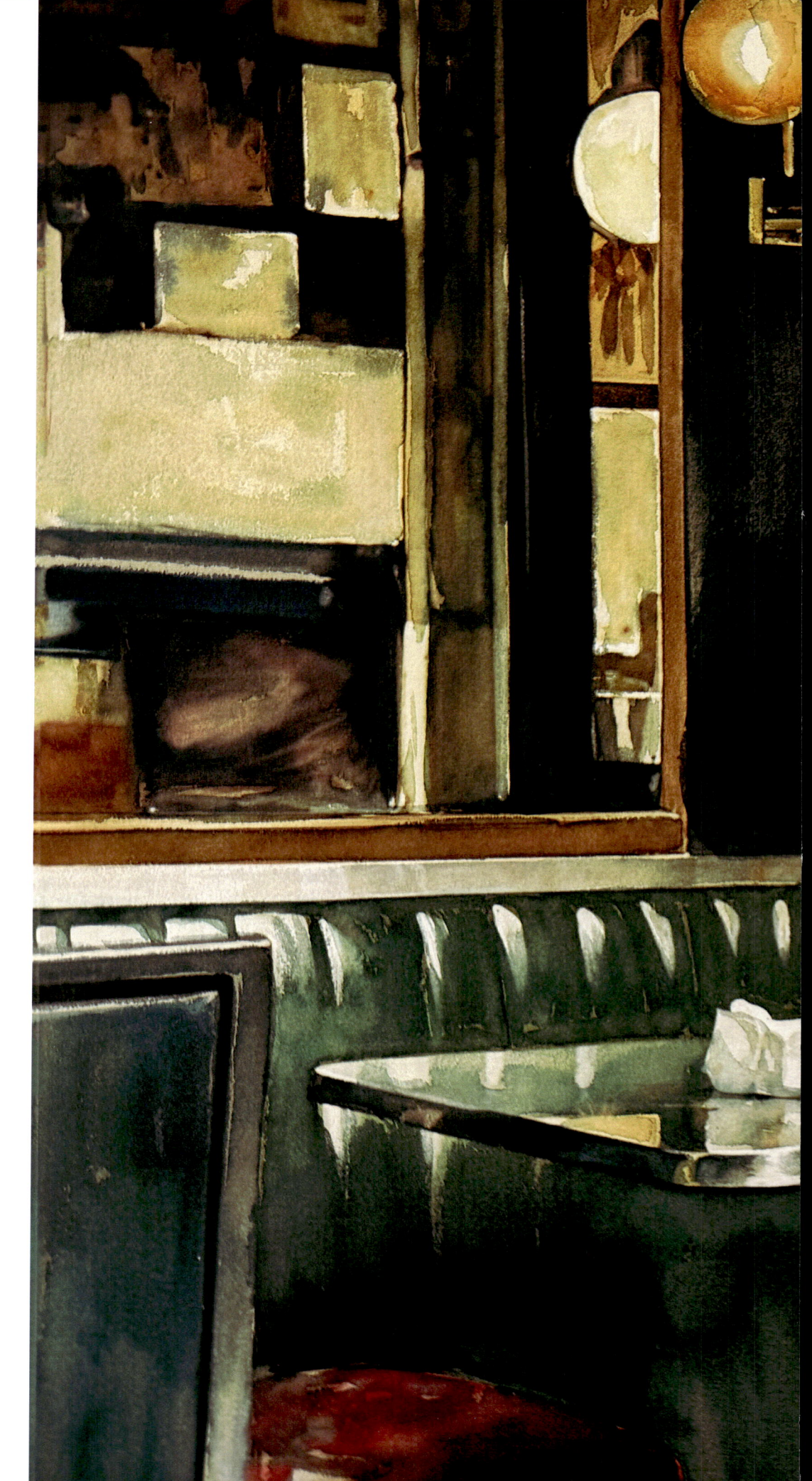

CAFES

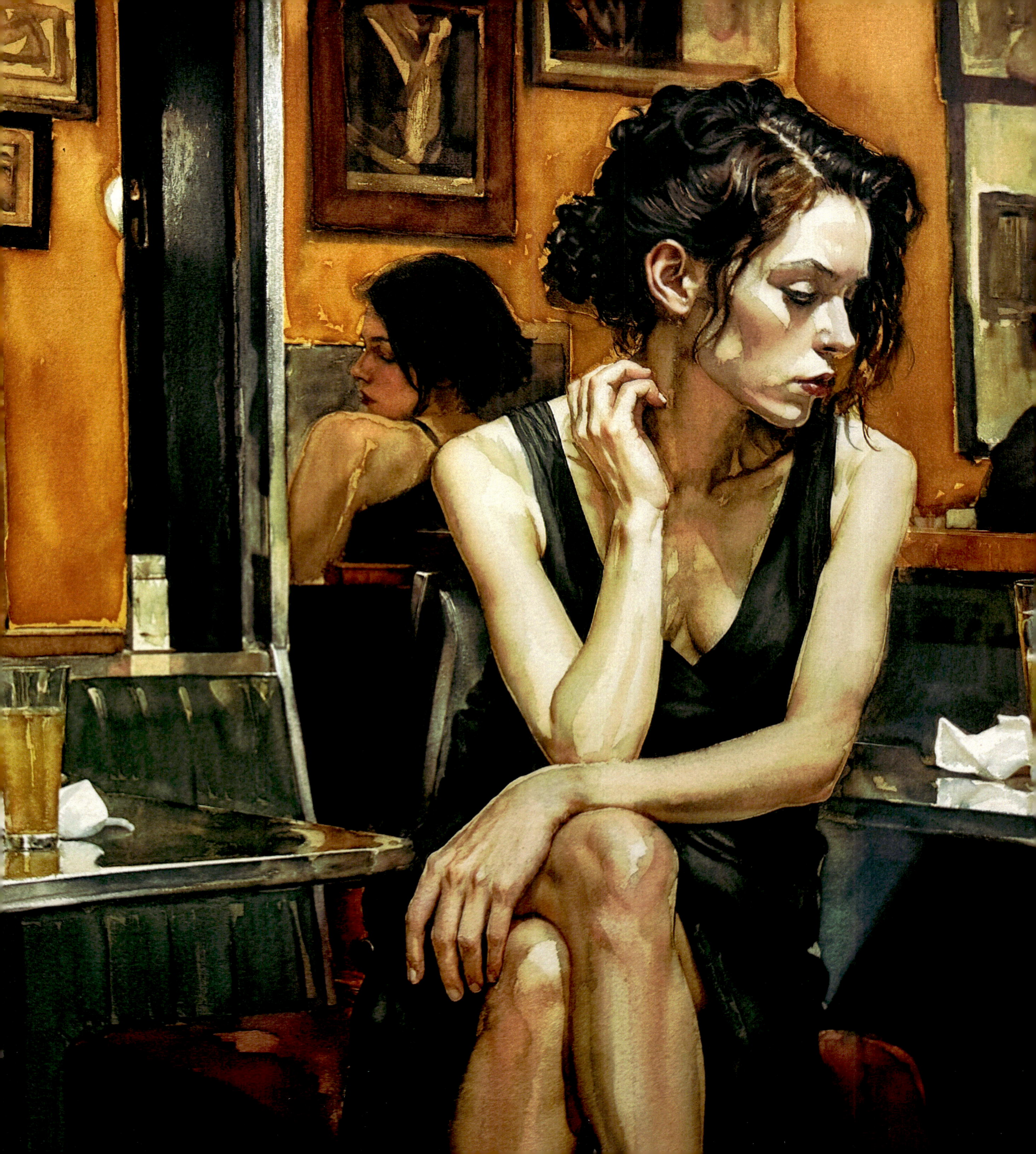

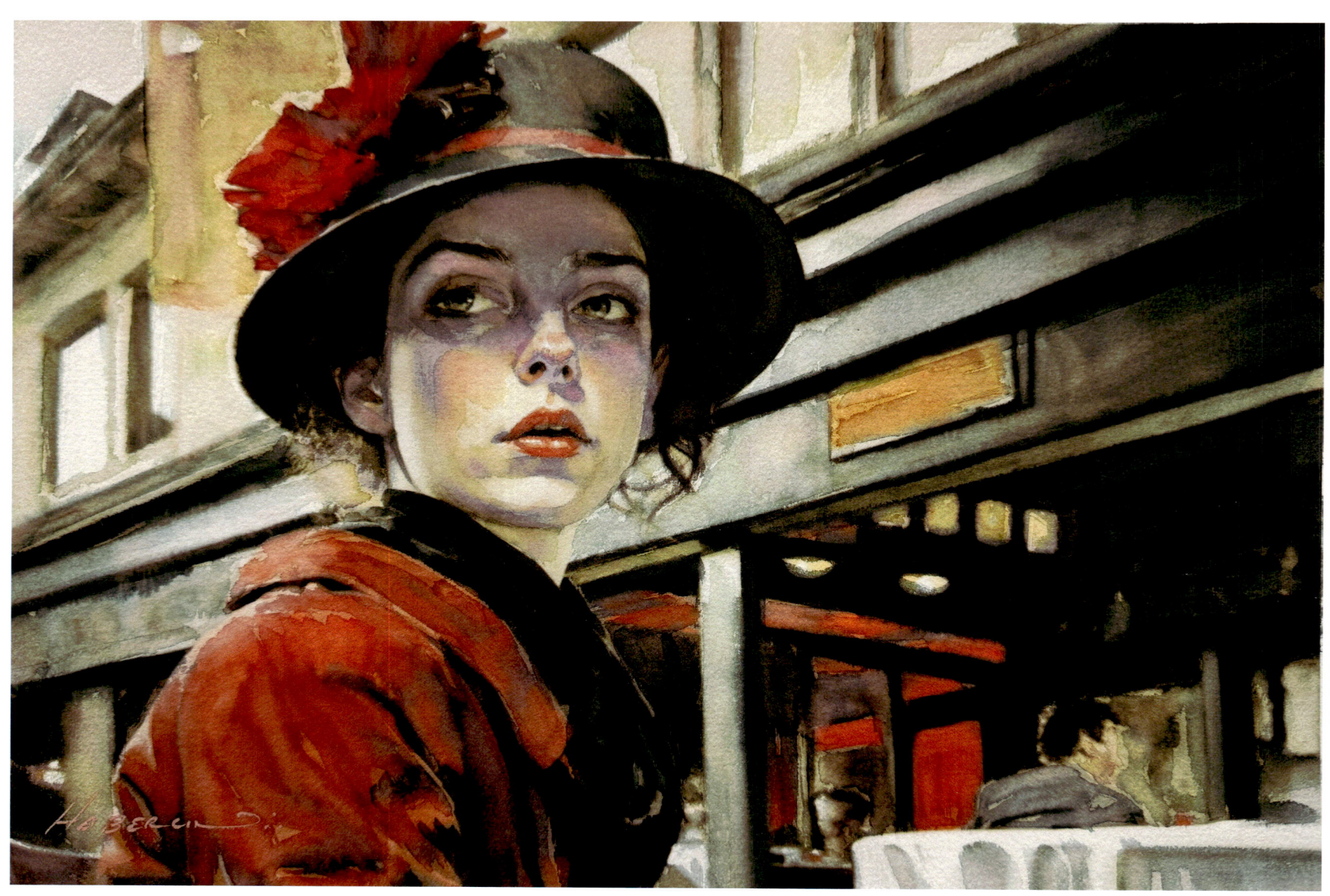

above: "Lyla" | watercolor | 8" x 12" | Private Collection
opposite: "About Time" | watercolor | 18" x 13" | Private Collection
previous spread: "Don't Tell Me" | watercolor | 11" x 15" | Private Collection

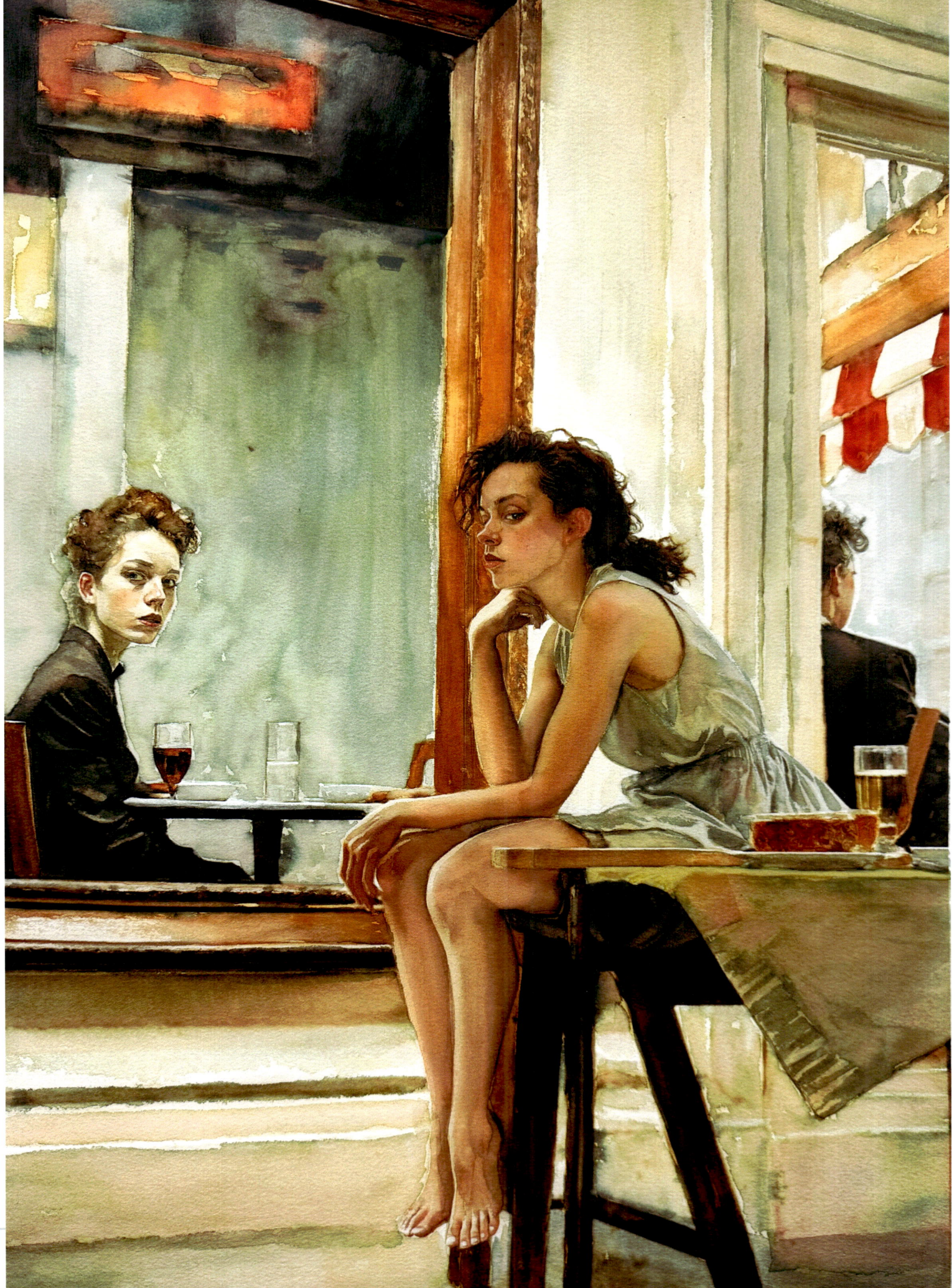

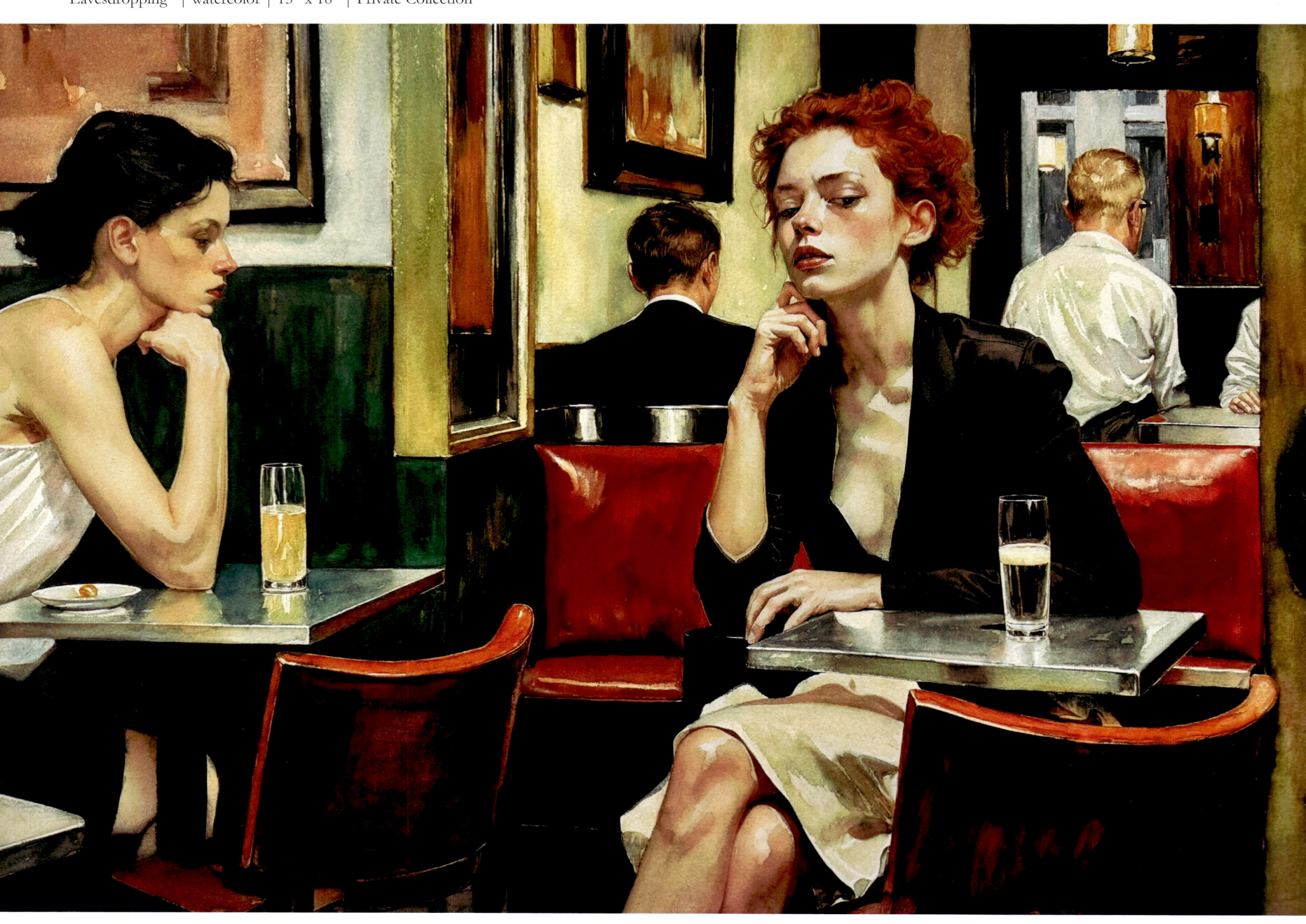

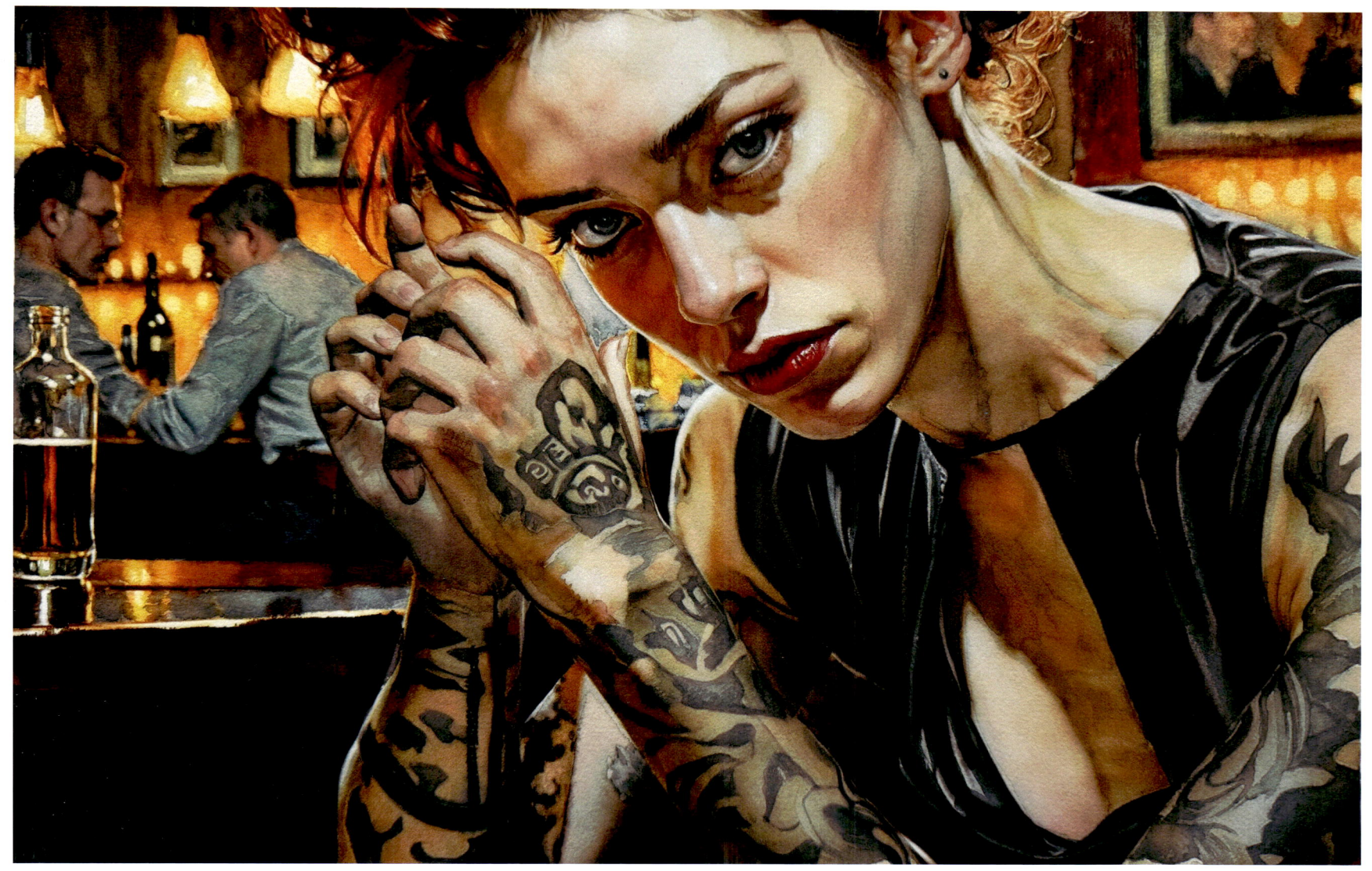

"One More" | watercolor | 10" x 16" | Private Collection

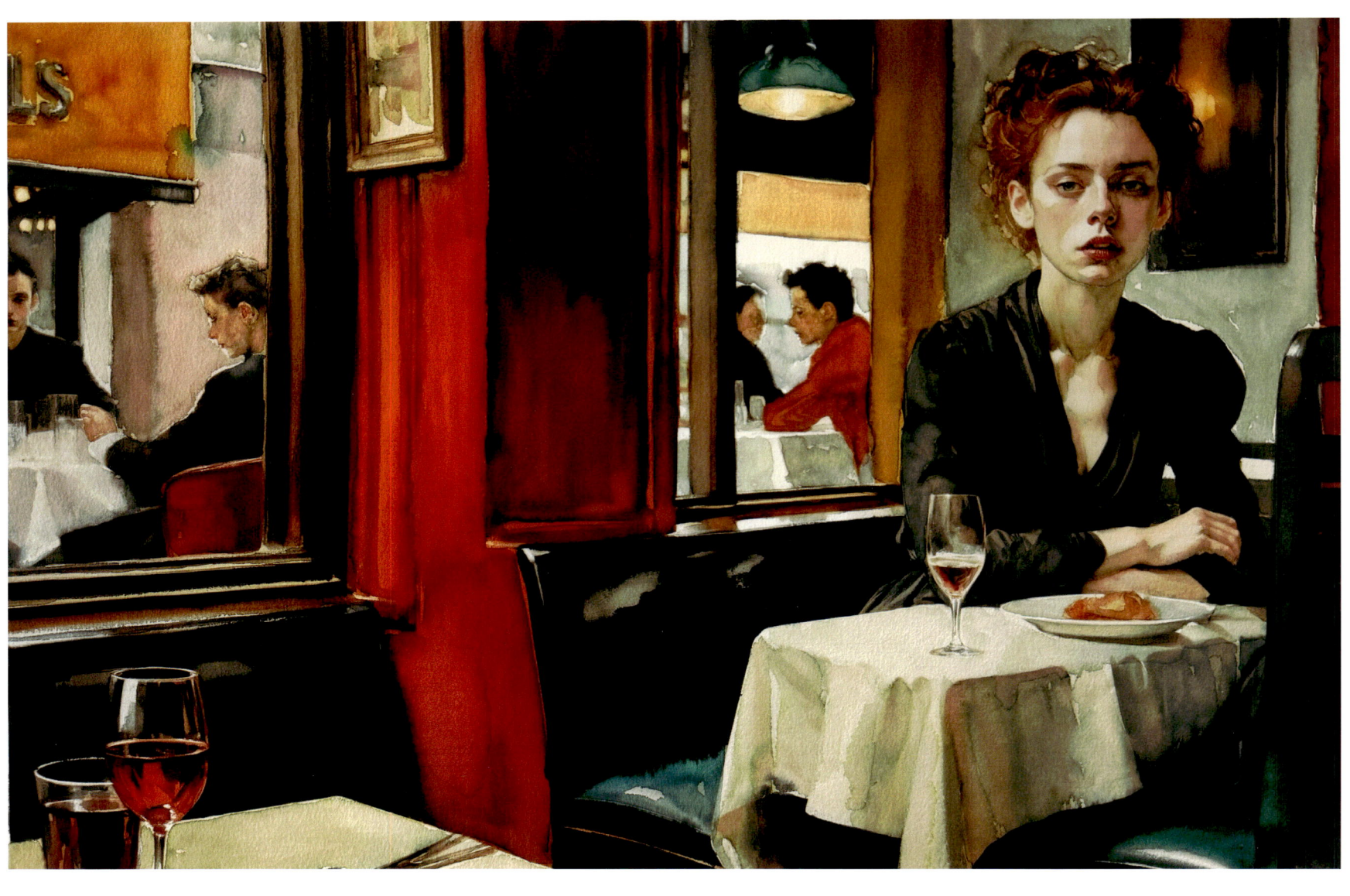

below: "Well?" | watercolor | 11" x 18" | Private Collection
opposite: "Have a Drink" | watercolor | 13" x 20" | Private Collection
next spread: "Blue Rapunzel" | watercolor | 14.5" x 22.5"

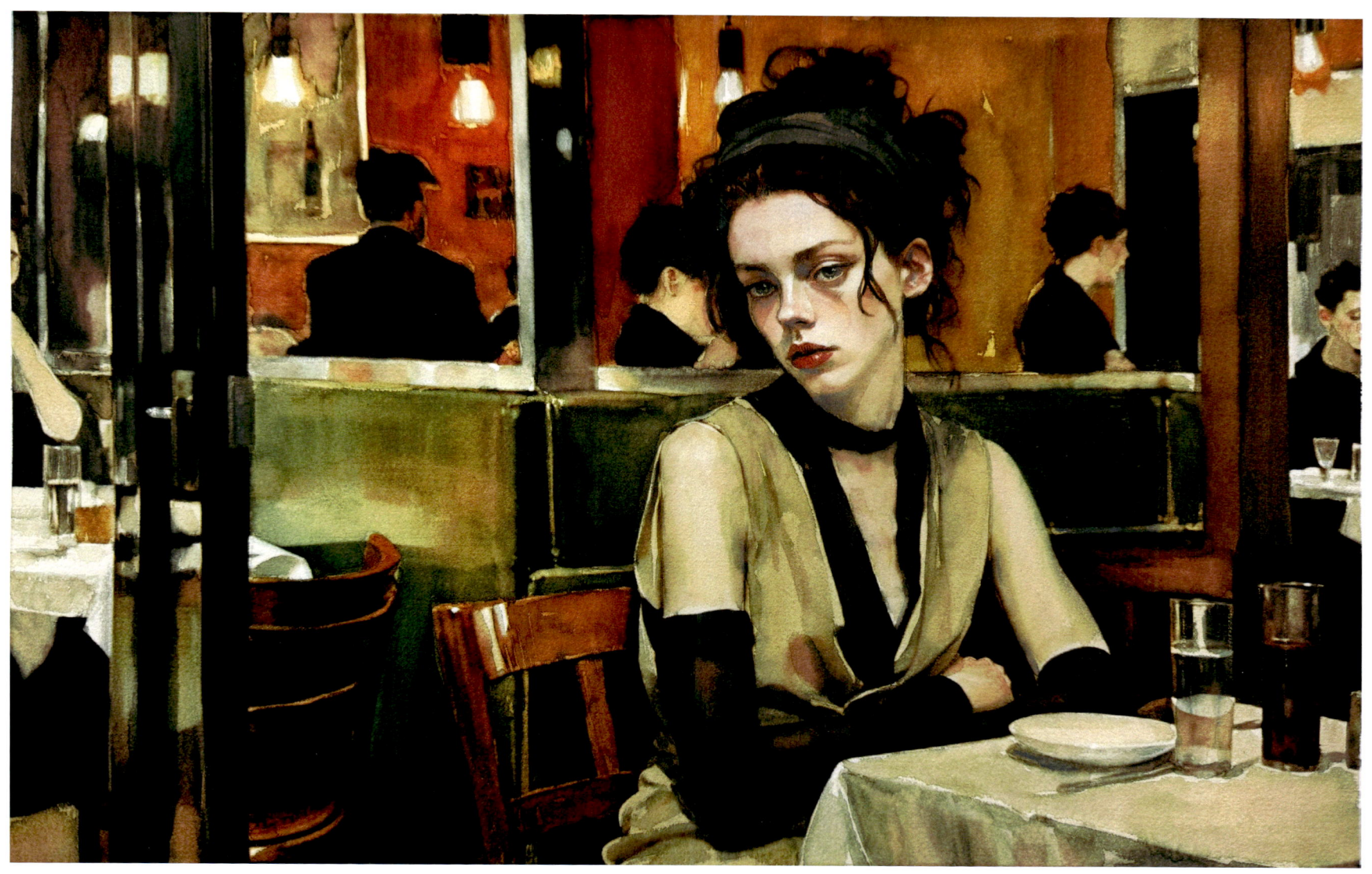

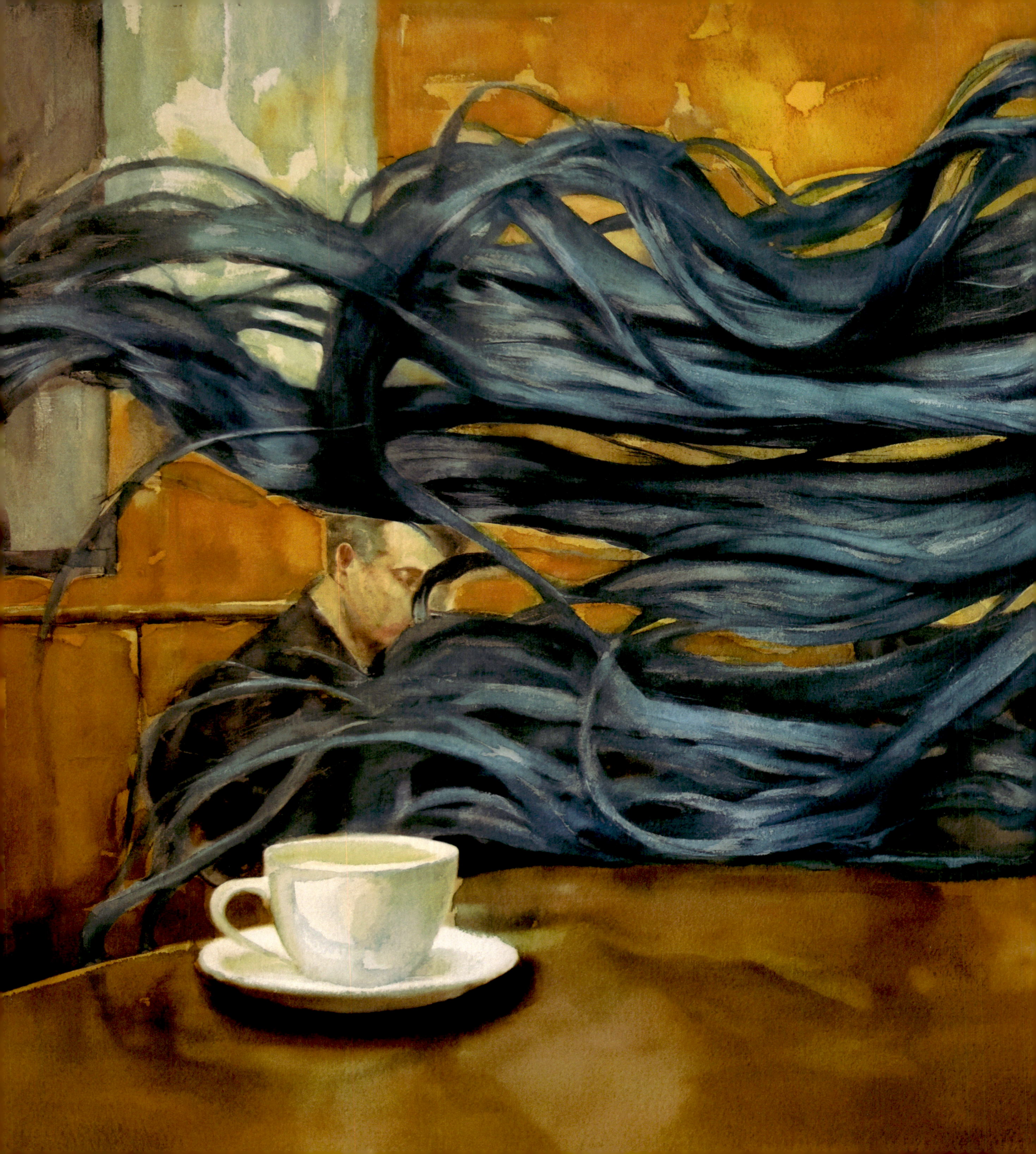

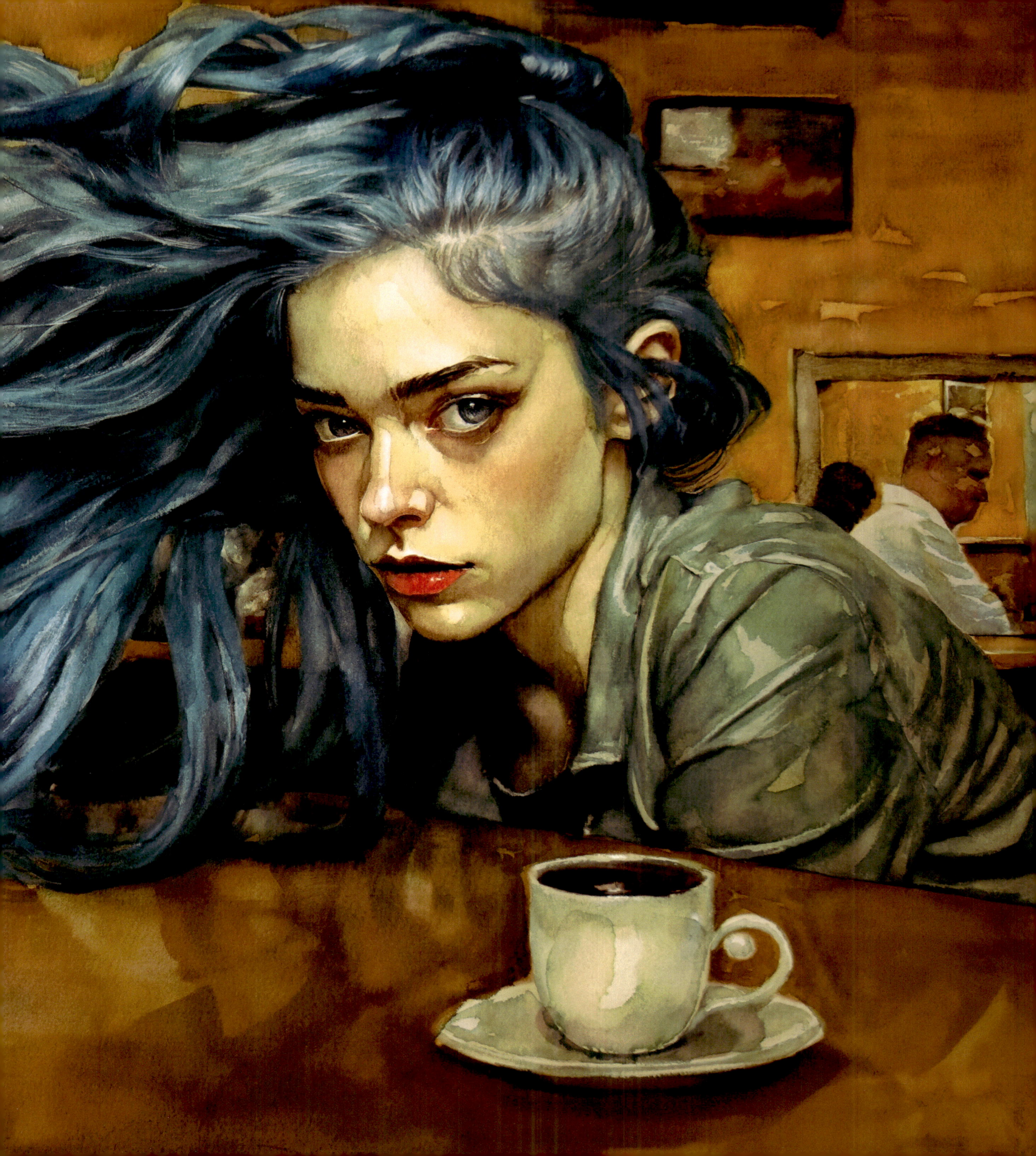

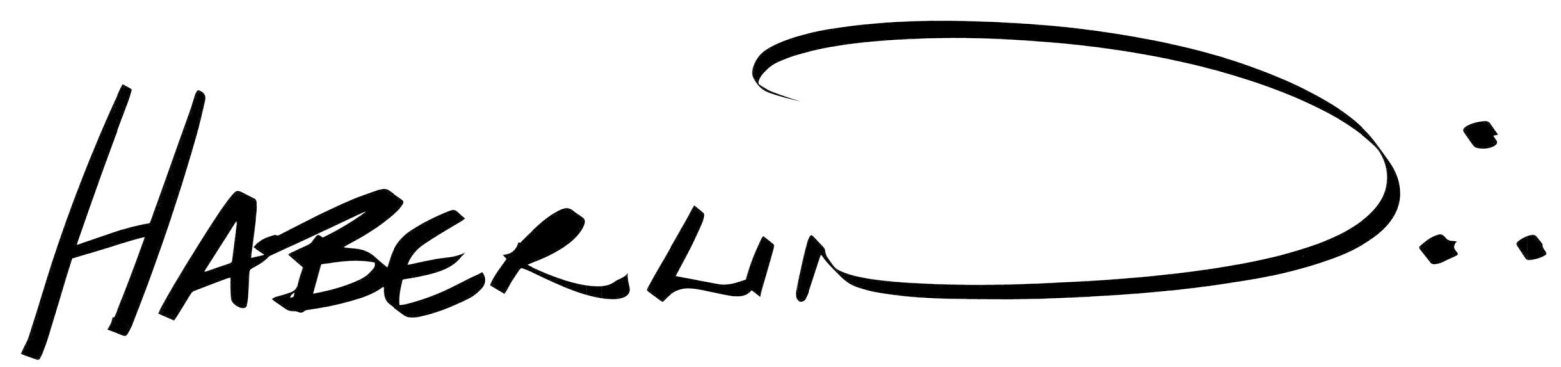

For the latest updates on Brian's work,
please visit Haberlin.com